French Politics, Society and Culture

Series Editor
Jocelyn Evans
School of Politics & International Studies
University of Leeds
Leeds, UK

This series examines all aspects of French politics, society and culture. In so doing it focuses on the changing nature of the French system as well as the established patterns of political, social and cultural life. Contributors to the series are encouraged to present new and innovative arguments so that the informed reader can learn and understand more about one of the most beguiling and compelling of European countries.

Jan Windebank

Domestic and Care Work in Modern France

Gender, Family and the State

palgrave
macmillan

Jan Windebank
University of Sheffield
Sheffield, UK

ISSN 2946-3750 ISSN 2946-3769 (electronic)
French Politics, Society and Culture
ISBN 978-3-031-33563-1 ISBN 978-3-031-33564-8 (eBook)
https://doi.org/10.1007/978-3-031-33564-8

This Palgrave Macmillan imprint is published by the registered company Springer Nature Switzerland AG.
The registered company address is: Gewerbestrasse 11, 6330 Cham, Switzerland

Contents

Abbreviations

ACPT	*Allocation compensatrice pour tierce personne*
ADL	*Activities of daily living*
AFEAMA	*Allocation des frais de l'emploi d'une aide maternelle agréée*
AGED	*Allocation de garde : employé à domicile*
AJPA	*Allocation Journalière du Proche Aidant*
ALMP	*Active labour market policy*
AMF	*Allocation de la mère au foyer*
ANLPF	*Alliance Nationale pour l'Accroissement de la Population Française*
ANSP	*Agence Nationale pour les Services à la Personne*
APA	*Allocation personnalisée pour l'autonomie*
APE	*Allocation d'éducation parentale*
ASU	*Allocation de salaire unique*
ASV	*Adaptation de la société au vieillissement*
CAP	*Certificat d'aptitude professionnelle*
CARE	*Capacités, aides et ressources des seniors*
CES	*Chèque emploi service*
CESU	*Chèque emploi service universel*
CF	*Complément familial*
CGP	*Commissariat General du Plan*
CGT	*Confédération Générale du Travail*
CLCA	*Complément de libre choix d'activité*
CLCMG	*Complément de libre choix de mode de garde*
CME	*Coordinated market economy*
CNAF	*Caisse Nationale d'Allocations Familiales*
CNPF	*Conseil National du Patronat Français*
CNSA	*Caisse Nationale de Solidarité pour l'Autonomie*
COLCA	*Complément optionnel de libre choix d'activité*

CPE	*Congé parental d'éducation*
CREDOC	*Centre de Recherche pour l'Etude et l'Observation des Conditions de Vie*
CSN	*Conseil Supérieur de la Natalité*
DARES	*Direction de l'Animation de la Recherche, des Etudes et des Statistiques*
DDL	*Domestic labour index*
DRESS	*Direction de la Recherche, des Etudes et de l'Evaluation des Statistiques*
EAJE	*Etablissements d'accueil du jeune enfant*
EHPA	*Etablissements d'hébergement pour personnes âgées*
EHPAD	*Etablissements d'hébergement pour personnes âgées dépendantes*
ESS	*European Social Survey*
EU	*European Union*
FEPEM	*Fédération des Particuliers Employeurs de France*
GALI	*Global activity limitation indicator*
GDP	*Gross domestic product*
GGS	*Generation and gender Survey*
GIR	*Groupe iso-ressources*
HSM	*Handicap-Santé Ménages*
IAD	*Intervenants à domicile*
IADL	*Instrumental activities of daily living*
ICLS	*International Conference of Labour Statisticians*
ILO	*International Labour Organization*
INED	*Institut National d'Etudes Démographiques*
INSEE	*Institut National des Statistiques et des Etudes Economiques*
ISCO	*International standard classification of occupations*
ISSP	*International Social Survey Programme*
LFS	*Labour Force Survey*
LME	*Liberal-market economy*
LTC	*Long-term care*
MEDEF	*Mouvement des Entreprises de France*
MLF	*Mouvement pour la libération des femmes*
NACE	*Nomenclature statistique des activités économiques dans la Communauté Européenne*
NSR	*New social risks*
OECD	*Organisation of Economic Co-operation and Development*
ONaPE	*Observatoire National de la Petite Enfance*
OPEC	*Organization of Petroleum Exporting Countries*
PACS	*Pacte civil de solidarité*
PAJE	*Prestation d'accueil du jeune enfant*
PCH	*Prestation de compensation du handicap*

PDS	*Prestation spécifique dependence*
PHS	*Personal and household services*
PMI	*Protection maternelle et infantile*
PreParE	*Prestation partagée d'éducation de l'enfant*
RPR	*Rassemblement pour la République*
RTT	*Reduction du temps de travail*
SDG	*Sustainable development goal*
SESP	*Syndicat des Entreprises de Services à la Personne*
SHARE	*Survey of health and ageing in retirement in Europe*
SRCV	*Statistiques sur les ressources et conditions de vie*
TCN	*Third-country national*
TEPA	*Travail, emploi et pouvoir d'achat*
TES	*Titre emploi-service*
TSOL	*Total social organisation of labour*
UN	*United Nations*
UNAF	*Union Nationale des Associations Familiales*
WFH	*Work from home*
WHO	*World Health Organization*

CHAPTER 1

Introduction

In this book, we explore the organisation and divisions of labour of domestic and care work in France, and through an analysis of these most routine of activities, we seek to shed light on some of the drivers of and obstacles to change in the relationship between gender, the family and the state in the country in the twentieth and twenty-first centuries. Domestic and care work is a vital component in assuring daily wellbeing and social reproduction across the generations. It is understood here as the paid and unpaid activities that produce the goods and services that fulfil the everyday needs of individuals, such as for food and clothing, respond to the specific needs of children and adults requiring long-term care and maintain the material space of the home. These activities occupy a very significant amount of time in the lives of many people and in society as a whole. According to the last nationally representative study conducted in 2010, more time was devoted to unpaid domestic and care work in France than to all professional activities. In addition, the domestic and care sector is a major employer. Care services, particularly for children, developed earlier in France than in many comparable countries, and the French state was the first in Europe to encourage households to hire domestic employees through tax subsidies. Whether paid or unpaid, domestic and care work tends to be delegated to those in a subordinated position in any given context. As such, the ways in which these quotidian activities are

J. Windebank, *Domestic and Care Work in Modern France*, French Politics, Society and Culture,
https://doi.org/10.1007/978-3-031-33564-8_1

organised, and the divisions of labour that this organisation entails, are important in understanding inequalities of gender, class, race and citizenship across the globe and are an integral aspect of the political economy of France (Devetter & Rousseau, 2009).

A significant proportion of domestic and care work has always been undertaken unpaid in the home by women. Consequently, through much of the twentieth century the contribution of domestic and care activities to standards of living and wellbeing, their status as work and place in the economy were ignored or at best underestimated by academics and policymakers due to the domination of the monetised economy, employment as the primary mode of work and the marginalisation of women (Laville, 2008). However, starting in the 1970s, two strands of academic thought and political activism began to re-evaluate the status of domestic and care activities, developments that would lead to a more holistic view of what constitutes work and the economy. French intellectuals and academics were at the forefront of these developments. On the one hand, second-wave feminists fought for the recognition of and liberation from the role of homemaker and carer for women. Simone de Beauvoir (1989) in her seminal work *The Second Sex* was an early critic of the confinement of women in marriage and domesticity and her work contributed significantly to the domestic labour debates of the 1970s. The domestic labour debates sought either to reappraise unpaid domestic and care work as a form of production rather than reproduction within Marxist theory, or to conceptualise women's domestic and care work within the marriage contract as the material basis of patriarchy.[1] The French materialist feminist Christine Delphy (2003) was at the forefront of these international discussions. On a practical level, a more equal gender division of unpaid domestic and care work in the home and state support for the outsourcing of a proportion of this work to paid providers was demanded (United Nations [UN] Commission on the Status of Women, 1977). On the other hand, academics and activists within the development and ecological movements sought to extend notions of productive activity beyond the confines of the formal economy and employment and in so doing lauded the possibilities for meaningful activity that was present in the private and non-monetised sphere.[2] For example, in the 1970s the UN Commission for Social Development sought to expand definitions of productive work to include

[1] For a full discussion of the domestic labour debates in France, see Windebank (1991).

[2] For a full discussion of the work of these movements in France, see Windebank (1991).

unpaid activities such as volunteering (Swiebel, 1999). Underpinning this endeavour was the idea that much formal economic activity damaged people and the planet but nonetheless was included in Gross Domestic Product (GDP) while other forms of activity that increased the wellbeing of individuals and the natural world, whether unpaid or undeclared paid work, were excluded. Again, French intellectuals and politicians, such as those belonging to the *autogestionnaire* (self-management) movement, were central in moving these debates forward. Andre Gorz wrote a number of books with international impact, such as *Paths to Paradise: On the Liberation from Work* (Gorz, 1985), that called for a reduction in employment time to free individuals to pursue more meaningful activity in the private sphere, including caring and domestic production. Meanwhile, the French Socialist politician and President of the European Commission from 1985 to 1995, Jacques Delors argued that society should be based on the self-regulation of time and that it was necessary to reduce employment time to allow the population the freedom to engage in informal economic and leisure activities in the private sphere (Delors & Foucauld, 1980).

The importance of domestic and care work is now better recognised by academics and in national and international policymaking. Understanding domestic and care work in all its manifestations has become a very significant research topic in the social sciences. In the political realm, international bodies such as the European Union (EU), UN, Organisation for Economic Cooperation and Development (OECD) and the International Labour Organisation (ILO) have all embraced the importance of studying domestic and care work and included unpaid work in analyses of wellbeing and economic development. Domestic and care work has been described as being "[...] at the heart of humanity" (ILO, 2018, p. 6). Following a resolution passed at its 19th Congress, the International Conference of Labour Statisticians (ICLS) expanded its definition of work to include activities that produce goods or services for own use as well as for use by others (ILO, 2018, p. 10). Internationally comparable time-use studies track unpaid domestic and care work trends across the world.[3] France has carried out time-use studies since the 1940s, with the first studies in 1947 and 1958 focused on women's time use. Since 1974 four time-use studies

[3] The Social and Gender Statistics section of the UN Statistics Division has taken a leading role in designing and implementing time-use surveys which are the principal method of generating measurable data on unpaid work (United Nations, 2020).

representative of the adult population have been carried out at 10- to 12-year intervals. A further study is underway at the time of writing. The UN has included the Triple R framework for Recognising, Reducing and Redistributing unpaid domestic and care work "through the provision of public services, infrastructure and social protection policies and the promotion of shared responsibility within the household and the family as nationally appropriate"[4] in its Sustainable Development Goals (SDG 5.4).[5] Many national governments and international bodies pay significant attention to paid domestic and care work due to the employment opportunities for the low skilled that it offers. The French state was an early adopter of policies to frame domestic and care work based on a recognition not only of its contribution to wellbeing but of its economic value and employment-creation potential (see Chap. 5). Interest in paid domestic and care work also stems from its place in the international migration of women from low and medium-income to higher income countries in "global care chains" (Lutz & Palenga-Möllenbeck, 2011, p. 350). The 2011 ILO Convention 189 on domestic workers recognises "the significant contribution of domestic workers to the global economy which includes increasing paid job opportunities [....], greater scope for caring for ageing populations, children and persons with a disability, and substantial income transfers between countries".[6] The challenges of the recent COVID-19 pandemic further illuminated the importance of these essential service workers.

These more holistic re-imaginings of work and the economic that developed in the late twentieth century not only allowed the importance of unpaid domestic and care work to be recognised, but also made it possible to differentiate types of work by the nature of the social relations in which they are embedded by questioning the supremacy of the employment relationship in defining what is and is not work. Applying this perspective, we can see that domestic and care work can be performed in a variety of social relations. It can be undertaken as paid work on an own-account basis, or within a range of employment relationships. This paid work may or may not be declared to the state. Alternatively, domestic and care work can be conducted on an unpaid basis for own consumption, or

[4] https://indicators.report/targets/5-4/

[5] https://indicators.report/goals/goal-5/

[6] https://www.ilo.org/dyn/normlex/en/f?p=NORMLEXPUB:12100:0::NO::P12100_ILO_CODE:C189

for other household members, individuals outside the household or on a volunteer basis within an organisation. Furthermore, identifying these different types of work based on the social relations in which they take place has made it possible to see how most end-consumption goods and services require input from a variety of different types of work to be made ready for use, including the unpaid work of the consumer. A range of academic concepts describe this process: for example, Warde and Martens' (2000, p. 10) "systems of provision", Gershuny's (2000, p. 18) "chains of provision" or Glucksmann's (2005, p. 21) "Total social organisation of labour" (TSOL). Additionally, it has been possible to see that over time the sites of production of specific goods and services shift "across the boundaries between different sectors of employment [...] and forms of unpaid work [...]" (Lyon & Glucksmann, 2008, p. 101). Although many of the social, economic and cultural drivers shaping the organisation and divisions of labour of domestic and care work are common across countries, and particularly across high-income countries, nationally specific policy frameworks, political and bureaucratic structures, economic conditions and cultural norms function as a prism to shape these trends in nationally specific ways (Lyon & Glucksmann, 2008). Consequently, it is not only important for the study of French society to discuss domestic and care work; it is also important for the understanding of domestic and care work to study it within a single national context, in this instance France.

Aims of the Book

The book has two related overarching aims. First, it seeks to establish how a nationally specific organisation of domestic and care work is constructed through the single-nation case study of France. This approach allows exploration of the complexity of the interrelationships between the diverse influences that come to bear on the construction of domestic and care work (Allwood & Wadia, 2009). Second, the book endeavours to assess the importance of the very particular approach to gender, the family and the state to be found in France for the social and economic life of the country which derives from its revolutionary and Republican legacies, using the case study of domestic and care work.

The first objective of this book is to identify how domestic and care work has been organised across different social relations of production in

France and to analyse the divisions of labour based on gender, class and citizenship status[7] that this organisation entails. The relative roles of the family, the state and the market in delivering these goods and services are explored. The book draws on multi-country studies on domestic and care work to position France in relation to other high-income countries, primarily but not exclusively within Europe. This chapter therefore sets out in detail the definition of domestic and care work as the term is used in the book and relates this definition to the wide variety of terms used in the academic and policy literature on the subject. Additionally, it explains more precisely the social relations within which domestic and care work can take place as well as the principal divisions of labour that are to be found in domestic and care work.

The second objective of the book is to explain why domestic and care work is organised and divided in this way in France. In order to do this, the book draws on resource-based and gender-based theories of individual behaviours concerning domestic and care work and relates these to welfare, family and care, labour-market and worktime, and migration policies and to cultural norms concerning work, gender, the family and the state operating at the national level. This chapter therefore reviews the theoretical work that the book draws on for these explanations. First, it discusses the resource-based and gender-based theories that have sought to understand why individuals and couples organise their domestic and care work in particular ways at the micro-level of the household. Second, it reviews the macro-level policy literature on welfare, labour market and migration regimes and relates this to domestic and care work.

Third, the book seeks to understand the material and ideational historical legacies that have influenced the policy frameworks and cultural norms in France that impact domestic and care work. This chapter therefore explores the mechanisms by which both policies and norms develop, and their interaction. The chapter concludes with a discussion of the structure of the book in relation to its aims.

[7] Divisions of domestic and care work in terms of race are difficult to analyse in the French context because of the paucity of data. Data are not gathered as asking questions in surveys about race is banned by the French constitution with only the occasional exception being granted for scientific purposes.

The Organisation and Divisions of Labour of Domestic and Care Work

Domestic work and care work are defined for the purposes of this book on the basis of the nature of the goods and services they produce, as opposed to the social relations in which they are conducted. This is because the book aims to discover how these activities are positioned across different social relations of production in France, how this organisation has evolved over time and how it compares with the situation in other countries. Domestic work covers the activities that produce the end-use goods and services necessary to ensure, first, the everyday maintenance of the health, wellbeing and social integration of individuals (food preparation/cooking, washing up, laundry/clothes maintenance, associated shopping and administration) and, second, the routine maintenance of the material space of the home (cleaning, tidying, gardening, small maintenance/repairs/DIY/decoration and related shopping and administration). Domestic work as defined for the purposes of this book is akin to what others describe as "indirect" or "non-relational" care (ILO, 2018, p. xxvii) or Instrumental Activities for Daily Life (IADL).

Care work describes activities that cater to the specific needs of children and adults who require supervision, personal and basic healthcare[8] and/or provision of developmental activities (Roy, 2011). These activities are also characterised as direct care or as Activities for daily life (ADL). In providing (direct) care, a carer often needs to undertake a number of domestic work activities for the person being cared for. Conversely, some, for example older children or adults with only limited needs, may require no or little direct care, and but still need assistance with some aspects of domestic work. For unpaid care within the family, (direct) care and domestic (indirect care) work are often difficult to tease apart. For paid carers, such as home helps or child carers, the extent of the domestic work/indirect care required of them is normally included in the employment contract, but they may be expected to go beyond their contracted duties by the care recipient or employer. Domestic and care work may involve not only practical tasks but also cognitive labour, such as anticipating needs, making plans and decisions or monitoring progress (Daminger, 2019). Cognitive labour is associated with multitasking (Sullivan & Gershuny, 2013) and

[8] The work of primary and secondary teachers and allied educational professionals and healthcare professionals will not be included in the discussions in this book

the "*charge mentale*" (mental burden) that multitasking entails (Haicault, 1984, p. 273). There is no coherent and unified use of the terms domestic and care work in the literature in this area. Some studies use the term domestic to cover all three sets of activities outlined above, as in the case of the French time-use studies, while others use care as the overarching terminology, as in the case of the ILO (2018).

The social relations in which any work activities, and in this instance, domestic and care work, can take place are defined primarily by the nature of the relationship between the person doing the work, and the person benefiting from it and the nature of the transaction that takes place between them. The primary distinction to be made is between work that is carried out for monetary reward and remuneration—paid work—and work that is not—unpaid work. Unpaid domestic and care work may be conducted for oneself, that is, for own consumption, or for others. These others may be those with whom one lives—the partner in a couple, members of the immediate family, such as children, or other kin or non-kin household members. Outside the household, work may be undertaken for kin, neighbours, friends, colleagues or members of a wider community. Providing services for those outside the household or extended family on a one-to-one basis is sometimes labelled informal volunteering (Davis Smith, 1998; Prouteau & Wolff, 2002). Unpaid work may also be undertaken as formal volunteering through an organisation. The expectations of the parties involved in transactions of unpaid work are framed by the nature of the relationships between them. These may be based on obligations determined legally or by social norms, or on short- or long-term reciprocity and exchange. Furthermore, the terms domestic and care are sometimes used to signify that activities are unpaid or carried out within the household. This is the case in time-use studies in France where *temps domestique* (domestic time) or *activités domestiques* (domestic activities) refer to unpaid domestic and care work and are one of four top-level categories[9] of potential time-use (Brousse, 2015).

Paid work can be carried out on an own-account basis or within a number of different types of employment relationship. The precise terms used for different types of employment are defined by national legislation, and

[9] The other three categories are *temps physiologique* (self-care and maintenance time), *temps professionnel et d'etudes* (professional and study/training time) and *temps de loisirs* (leisure time).

in the case of France, by the *Code du Travail* (Labour Code). Workers can be engaged in direct employment, that is, employed and paid directly by the person for whom they perform a service. In France, Article 7221-1 of the 2016 Labour Code defines the *particulier employeur* (direct employer) as a citizen who "employs one or more employees in their private home [...] or close to it, without pursuing a profit-making purpose and in order to satisfy needs related to their personal life, especially their family life, excluding those related to their professional life". Direct employment creates a bipartite structure between worker and client. Individual employers may use an agency to assist them in the recruitment process and in the administration of their employer obligations. This is known as the agency mode. The agency may be a non-profit organisation, state body or private company. Workers can also be employed by non-profit, for-profit or state organisations to whom consumers pay fees in order to benefit from their services or receive services as part of their citizenship rights or in respect of payment of social security contributions. This is labelled the service-provider mode and leads to a tripartite structure of client, service-providing organisation/employer, and employee. Some argue that a tripartite employment structure affords better conditions to the worker than a bipartite structure (Bouffartigue & Bouteiller, 2003). Paid work should normally be declared to state authorities for tax, social security and labour law purposes. When it is, it is deemed declared work, and when it fails to be declared in any or all of these ways it is classed as undeclared work. Undeclared work is more common in direct employment relationships even though it may also exist in the service-provider mode.

Domestic outsourcing is a term that refers to the use of goods or services to replace part or the totality of the domestic and care work that individuals may otherwise undertake on an unpaid basis for themselves or others according to social norms and accepted practices (Bittman et al., 1998). There are three principal forms of domestic outsourcing. First individuals may purchase goods that reduce or replace completely their own labour input into an end product or service or reduce its maintenance requirements (e.g., buying a ready meal, a robot vacuum cleaner or self-cleaning oven). Second, individuals may pay for out-of-home services to replace unpaid labour (e.g., a restaurant meal, laundry service or childminder). Third, individuals may pay for home-based services whereby a paid worker comes into the home to undertake domestic and care tasks. This is the form of domestic outsourcing that has attracted the most academic and policy attention in recent decades. Home-based domestic and care workers can be employed in any of the ways described above.

Over the last 20 years, a new sector has been constructed with policies developed to support the use of home-based services for the general public, these being in the majority housekeeping and gardening services, alongside childcare and LTC provision (Farvaque, 2013). France has been a pioneer country in this regard, with other countries and the EU following suit. In English, this sector is usually termed the Personal and Household Services (PHS) sector, but there are varying nomenclatures and definitions operating in different countries according to the policy regimes in force. The EU adopted the term PHS in 2012 as part of its Employment Package to cover "a broad range of activities that contribute to wellbeing at home of families and individuals: childcare, long-term care for the elderly and for persons with disabilities, cleaning, remedial classes, home repairs, gardening, [and] ICT support" (European Commission, 2012, p. 4). France groups all home-based domestic and care services including childminding together under the term *les services à la personne* (services to individuals) which was set into the Labour Code in 2005 by the *Plan de Cohesion Sociale (*Social Cohesion Plan*)*, more commonly known as the *Plan Borloo* (Borloo Plan) after the then-Minister for Labour and Social Cohesion. The Labour Code (articles L7231-1 et D7231-1) sets out the list[10] of activities included under this rubric that attract the social and tax advantages offered by the policy. This list is reviewed periodically. Services are included on the basis of their place of production—they must be undertaken in or near the home—and their end product of responding to the needs of individuals. They are divided into three categories of activity: *services à la famille* (services to the family), principally childcare and tutoring; *services de la vie quotidienne* (services for everyday life), principally housekeeping services such as cleaning and ironing, gardening and pet care services and *services aux personnes dependantes* (LTC services).

The variation in national definitions of PHS makes it difficult to produce comparative statistics on the size and shape of the sector across countries. In order to do this within the EU, researchers have relied on

[10] See https://www.service-public.fr/particuliers/vosdroits/F13244 for the official list of activities of services to individuals

two NACE[11] categories. Workers directly employed by individuals have their own statistical category, NACE 97 (activities of households as employers of domestic personnel),[12] which includes domestic and care work (Farvaque, 2013). NACE 97 is similar to the definition of the ILO Convention 189 on domestic workers that views a domestic worker as "a person engaged in domestic work within an employment relationship" with domestic work taken to mean "work performed in or for a household or households".[13] The second is NACE 88 (social work without accommodation for the disabled and elderly)[14] and includes social, counselling, welfare, referral and similar services that are aimed at the elderly and disabled in their homes or elsewhere and carried out by government offices or by private organisations, or national or local self-help organisations. Similarly, two categories of the International Standard Classification of Occupations (ISCO) can be used to measure employment in PHS. These are occupational categories and as such do not differentiate between direct employment, agency mode and service-provider mode. Category 9111 "Domestic cleaners and helpers" are those who perform tasks in private households in order to keep the interiors and fixtures clean. Category 5322 covers home-based personal care workers. However, neither the NACE nor ISCO categories are a perfect fit to the realities of home-based paid domestic and care services due to the complexities and variations of constructions of domestic and care work in different countries (Manoudi et al., 2018).

The principal reason why the question of who does domestic and care work for whom and under what conditions is so important is that whatever the social relations in which domestic and care work is undertaken, it is an activity that is constructed as lowly valued socially, culturally and economically. Consequently, these activities in most social relations are undertaken by individuals suffering from disadvantage based on combinations of gender, class, race and citizenship status (Charles & Galerand, 2017). The division of domestic and care labour is therefore central to questions of power and equality in a given society (Estevez-Abe & Hobson,

[11] NACE is the Statistical classification of economic activities in the European Union, derived from the French term *Nomenclature statistique des activités économiques dans la Communauté européenne*

[12] https://inspire.ec.europa.eu/codelist/EconomicActivityNACEValue/T.97.00

[13] https://www.ilo.org/wcmsp5/groups/public/@ed_protect/@protrav/@travail/documents/publication/wcms_168266.pdf

[14] https://inspire.ec.europa.eu/codelist/EconomicActivityNACEValue/Q.88.10

2015). The principal form of inequality in domestic and care work has been that of gender. It should be noted that at the micro-level, the majority of research has focused on different-sex couples and how and why the men and women in these couples specialise in particular types of work. However, a gender division of domestic and care labour also exists at the societal level. Resource allocations and gender norms concerning the rightful roles of men and women in relation to domestic and care work influence the behaviours and actions of those who live alone, as single parents, in non-kin households or in same-sex couples. Furthermore, commentators worry that attempts to address the gender inequalities of unpaid domestic and care work in high-income countries by encouraging the use of paid services are creating new and exacerbating existing inequalities based on class, race and citizenship status, leading to increased social polarisation within and between countries (Glenn, 2010).

There is discussion as to why domestic and care work is lowly valued. Some suggest that the low status of domestic and care work derives indirectly from the mechanisms that determine the social status of women who have traditionally carried out this work (Cox, 2006; Delphy, 2003; Hatton, 2017; Seiller & Silvera, 2020). Others argue that all domestic and care work is lowly valued because the majority of it is undertaken unpaid (Dussuet, 2016). Practically, this means that the pricing of paid services has to compete with self-provisioning. Symbolically this leads to a cultural script that tells us that it is work that anyone can do (Carbonnier & Morel, 2015). However, there are a number of explanations put forward that focus on the nature of the work itself and its inherent or socially ascribed characteristics. For example, a number of aspects of both domestic and care work can be construed as dirty work, that is, an activity judged as degrading, disgusting or humiliating (Seiller & Silvera, 2020). The work can be invisible for reasons of the spatiality of the work when it is conducted paid or unpaid in the home, or because unpaid work is ignored by the state other than in its absence, for example, in the case of neglect of minor children (Poster et al., 2016). Furthermore, paid domestic and care work is an occupation with one of the highest rates of undeclared work in the labour market (Hatton, 2017). Even declared paid domestic and care work may not be seen by the state to the same extent as other kinds of employment in that it is not equally protected by labour laws or inspections (Pendo, 2016).

The labour aspects of domestic and care work activities may also be lost to sight because they are so closely intertwined with emotional and intimate relationships and personal obligations (Lutz & Palenga-Möllenbeck, 2011; Lyon, 2010). Domestic and care work often involves emotional labour in supporting members of the household, kin or other groups psychologically (Daminger, 2019; ILO, 2018). The question of how care as work and care as a relationship or emotional attachment are related has been addressed by feminist researchers within the perspective of the feminist ethics of care. Those who subscribe to this perspective argue that care is an essential activity because vulnerability is an integral part of the human condition that only mutual support can allow us to navigate. However, those in power do not recognise or sufficiently value the central importance of care, which has repercussions for those undertaking caring duties (Jonsson et al., 2011). The feminist ethics of care are "rooted in a unique labour process directed to dependent populations" situated in emotional connection that constitutes a "feminine antithesis to the masculine values of individualism, competition, and rationality that pervade capitalist society" (Duffy et al., 2013, p. 148). As such, the feminist ethics of care must be contrasted to the ethics of work because the decisions individuals make about care are not subject purely to economic rationality (Williams, 2001). Those who promote a feminist ethics of care often call for the state to treat unpaid carers equally with employees as regards citizenship status and access to benefits.

The standpoint of the feminist ethics of care contrasts to an alternative feminist reading of the devaluation of domestic and care work which, rather than celebrate the importance of these activities, argues that a negative evaluation of this work is justified because it belongs to the realm of immanence. This is the crux of Simone de Beauvoir's existentialist and Hegelian critique of the mid-twentieth-century marriage contract. Activities in the sphere of immanence are limited to perpetuating life, and most must be repeatedly performed in order to do so, requiring much time and effort but producing nothing that is transformative or transcendent. As such, domestic and care work should not constitute the principal reason for anyone's existence (de Beauvoir, 1989, pp. 474–478). Existential justification can only be achieved by transcendent activity that extends beyond the routines of domesticity (Veltman, 2004).

Explaining the Organisation and Divisions of Labour of Domestic and Care Work

The book not only describes but also seeks to explain the organisation and divisions of labour of domestic and care work in France. A well-established comparative literature on care work (Jonsson et al., 2011; Sevenhuijsen, 2003; Williams, 2001), a body of comparative work on paid and unpaid domestic work (Baxter, 1997; Calasanti & Bailey, 1994; Craig & Mullan, 2010; Fuwa & Cohen, 2007; Noonan, 2013) and macro-economic explanations of the development of domestic outsourcing (Carbonnier & Morel, 2015; Farvaque, 2013) have shown how the preferences, beliefs, opportunities and constraints that inform the micro-level decisions and behaviours of individuals as concerns getting domestic and care work done are enacted within and shaped by social, economic, cultural, institutional and policy frameworks operational at the national level (Granovetter, 1985; Zimmerman, 2013). In this section, we first review the theoretical work that attempts to explain these micro-level behaviours, and then relate the mechanisms revealed in these theories to the macro-level factors of welfare, labour-market and migration regimes, gender orders and national cultural norms concerning gender, the family and the state in order to establish an analytical framework with which to explain why domestic and care work is organised and divided in the way that it is in France.

Explaining the Gender Division of Domestic and Care Work at the Micro-Level: Resource-Based and Gender-Based Theories

A vast literature on domestic and care work at the micro-level has debated resource-based and gender-based theories. These micro-level theories have focused principally on the gender division of unpaid domestic and parenting work in different-sex couples. For LTC, particularly for older people, the focus has extended to the gendered division of labour within the kinship group, primarily between adult siblings. Similar theoretical and conceptual constructs have been used to explain why individuals and households do or do not outsource particular domestic and care tasks to home-based service providers (Windebank & Martinez-Perez, 2018).

The resource-based theories argue that domestic and care work is allocated according to time, financial- and human-capital resources (Coverman, 1985). There are three variants of resource-based theory, namely, the time-availability thesis, the rational-allocation thesis and the resource-bargaining thesis. First, the time-availability thesis argues that unpaid domestic and care work is allocated to individuals according to the time they have available to do it (Stafford et al., 1977). The higher commitments an individual has to the labour market, the less capacity they have for unpaid domestic and care work. In other words, their "demand/response capability" (Coverman, 1985, p. 186), or capacity to respond to domestic and care requirements, is lesser. Characteristics such as age, household structure, relationship status, presence and number of children and levels of (dis)ability are important factors determining the demand/response capability of individuals (Cancedda, 2001). For those living in couples, the more partners have equal employment commitments, the more the division of unpaid domestic and care work is expected to be equal. In the same vein, for members of the extended family, responsibility for the care of parents or grandchildren may be explained by the relative time availability of different family members (Bertogg & Strauss, 2020). Similarly, if households or individuals have limited free time and therefore difficulty in responding to domestic and care responsibilities, and if they have the necessary financial resources, they may use outsourcing more often than those with more time and less money (Bittman et al., 1998).

Second, the rational-allocation thesis (Becker, 1981; Lemmenicier, 1988) proposes that individuals make economically rational decisions about how they divide their labour between domestic and care work and employment in order to maximise efficiency and output given their human capital. Many proponents of the thesis assume that couples share a common interest and specialise in particular activities for the common good according to their individual attributes. It is implied that in different-sex couples, women have a comparative advantage in unpaid domestic and care work due to their role in parenting, and the ensuing tendency for their human capital to be less valuable in the employment market than that of men. Men's comparative advantage in wage-earning results in their concentration on paid work (Lemmenicier, 1988). Those with the highest opportunity costs of engaging in unpaid domestic and care work will be those expected to engage in it the least. The most efficient strategy to get domestic and care work done for high-earning individuals or couples may be to outsource it to release more time for money earning (Halldén & Stenberg, 2018).

Lastly, the resource-bargaining thesis argues that couples or members of other groups such as siblings do not rationally allocate tasks for a common good. Rather, each individual has their own interest in avoiding domestic and care work, and therefore mobilises their relative resources, principally financial capital in the form of income or human capital in the form of educational level, to bargain their way out of it (Brines, 1994; Sofer, 1999). The allocation of domestic and care work within couples or other groups therefore reflects power relations among its members. These relative resources can be used to reduce one's share of unpaid work by obliging other members of the household to conduct these tasks, or to reduce the overall unpaid work burden by outsourcing them to paid providers (Cheung & Lui, 2017).

The outcome of research applying these micro-level resource theories is that they have some validity as concerns explaining the divisions of unpaid domestic and care work, and levels of outsourcing domestic work among working-age households but cannot explain the full extent of the gender division of this labour particularly in different-sex couples and mixed-gender sibling groups. Even when time availability and relative resources point to an outcome of equality of domestic and care work, whether this be in terms of relative shares within a couple or kin group, societal aggregates of men's and women's contribution to domestic and care work, or the beneficiaries of outsourcing strategies, gender differences remain.[15] Gender perspectives therefore contest the gender-neutrality of the economistic models, which are criticised for their assumption that individuals do or do not carry out domestic and care work due to factors that in principle can affect men and women equally. In contrast, they argue that gender is the overriding determinant of one's place in the division of domestic and care work.

Proponents of the gender perspective argue that it is social constructions of femininity and masculinity that determine individuals' expectations around, engagement with or avoidance of domestic and care work, and that resultant gender identities outweigh the influence of the resource context in which people find themselves. Children learn about gender roles, including participation or non-participation in domestic and care work activities, through socialisation in the family, observing and internalising the ways its members organise themselves and relate to one another according to their gender (Connell & Messerschmidt, 2005; Genest Dufault & Castelain Meunier, 2017; Greenstein, 1996). The enduring influence of this early socialisation is evoked to explain the "lagged adaptation" (Sullivan et al., 2018, p. 155) of the gender division of unpaid

[15] For a review of this research, see Bianchi et al. (2001) and Windebank and Martinez Perez (2018).

domestic and care work in the face of the changed resource landscape brought about by the increase in women's engagement in the labour force seen in the last 40 years in France as elsewhere. Furthermore, domestic and care work has been found to be a site of the practice of gender deviance neutralisation, that is, the engagement by men or women in more or less domestic and care work to compensate for other behaviours, such as in relation to their employment, that contradict accepted gender norms (Bittman et al., 1998; Brines, 1994; Greenstein, 2000; Kan, 2008). For example, unemployed men whose women partners are employed have been found to compensate the negative effect of joblessness on their masculine identity by refusing to increase the amount of domestic work they do in line with their increased time availability (Van der Lippe et al., 2018).

However, not all agree that gender identities are fixed in childhood. A dynamic reading of the gender perspective has emerged from Butler's (1990) theory of gender performativity. "Performativity" for Butler (1990, p. 32) is "the reiterative and citational practice through which discourse produces the effects that is names". It is argued that gender is not a stable characteristic of the subject that emanates from a biologically determined or culturally inscribed binary structure. Rather, gender identity is practised through the repetitive performance of certain acts. Gender must be continually re-enacted to secure its apparent stability. In this way, the performance or non-performance of certain domestic and care tasks by individuals, the division of unpaid domestic and care work between different-sex partners or siblings, as well as decisions regarding outsourcing domestic and care tasks to paid service providers, can be viewed as performances of gender roles. This is termed the "doing gender" theory (West & Zimmerman, 1987, p. 126). The doing gender theory proposes that "housework is a symbolic enactment of gender relations" and men and women "[...] display their 'proper' gender roles through the amount and type of housework they perform" (Bianchi et al., 2001, pp. 194–195). Within couples or kin groups, this performance is relative, that is, in direct relationship to what others do or not do. Within other contexts, for example, in single-person households, it is more related to societal expectations around what or how much domestic and care work one should do for oneself, and what it is acceptable to outsource, or simply not to do at all (Craig & Baxter, 2014). Although there are some core needs determined by human biology that domestic and care work must satisfy, much work is created by societal conventions that "[script], and [re-script] normality" (Jack, 2016, p. 77) as regards expectations around standards and quality of domestic life and care for others. If gender identities need to be constantly enacted, there exists the possibility for the disruption of traditional gender roles, or the undoing of gender (Deutsch, 2007) with change occurring because the gender order cannot completely and consistently reproduce itself. It has been found that more gender-egalitarian values favour more gender-equal divisions of domestic and care work, controlling for individual characteristics and resource indicators (Carriero, 2021; Cunningham, 2001). For example, women holding traditional attitudes have been found to spend longer on domestic work than women holding more progressive attitudes with similar social and economic characteristics (Greenstein, 2000; Kan, 2008). However, it should be noted that attitude surveys find more support for the equal sharing of domestic and care work between men and women than that exists in practice (Cunha & Atalaia, 2019).

Explaining the Organisation and Divisions of Labour of Domestic and Care Work at the National Level

National differences in the organisation and divisions of domestic and care work result from the differing characteristics of the national population as regards age profile and dependency ratios, household structures, rates of marriage and cohabitation, birth rates, and economic activity and employment rates. For example, characteristics such as the birth rate, age profiles and dependency ratios affect the volume of domestic and care work required in a country while economic activity rates determine the demand/response capability of the population to meet these needs with unpaid work (Cancedda, 2001). However, after controlling for such differences in population characteristics, variations in the organisation and divisions of domestic and care work between countries remain (Granovetter, 1985; Zimmerman, 2013). These are the result of the influence of policy frameworks concerning welfare, family and care, labour market and worktime, and migration, and nationally specific cultural norms concerning gender, the family, work and the state.

Policy frameworks in these areas have both material and ideational influences on the organisation and divisions of labour of domestic and care work. These policies materially affect the conditions in which individuals and households make decisions and negotiate domestic and care work strategies, setting a framework for how domestic and care work gets done (Dex, 2010; Fuwa & Cohen, 2007). Welfare and labour-market policies influence the economic resources and bargaining power of individuals in relation to their domestic and care work responsibilities, and the costs and benefits of particular divisions of unpaid labour. Together with migration policies, they also influence the availability and affordability of paid services to replace unpaid labour and in so doing, the costs and benefits of self-provisioning as compared with outsourcing. Furthermore, these policies structure the employment opportunities, pay and working conditions of domestic and care employees, and influence the supply and costs of labour in this area. At the ideational level, policy contributes to defining social and cultural norms and structuring world views in areas related to domestic and care work (Fuwa & Cohen, 2007; Sjoberg, 2004).

Welfare, family and care policies impact the ways domestic and care work is organised and divided in a country in a number of ways. Welfare policies influence the extent to which individuals, or particular categories of people, are obliged or have the opportunity to participate in the labour market, which in consequence influences their availability for unpaid domestic and care work. In his original welfare regime typology, Esping-Andersen (1990, p. 4) differentiated between welfare states according to the degree of decommodification that they afforded citizens, that is, the possibility to sustain a socially acceptable standard of living without reliance on commodified activity, usually employment, through the provision of unemployment benefits, family benefits, sickness benefits and pensions. On this basis, Esping-Andersen (1990) identified three types of welfare regimes: Liberal regimes characterised by low levels of decommodification, encouragement of market solutions to social problems and means-tested benefits providing only a minimum safety-net for social risks; Social Democratic regimes providing a high degree of decommodification on the basis of universalistic social security systems and generous welfare benefits and care services; and lastly Conservative regimes, the category in which France is included, providing relatively generous benefits deriving from a social insurance model of social security and emphasis on the role of the family in providing care.

Esping-Andersen's initial work on decommodification was quickly criticised for its lack of reflection on the differing meanings of decommodification for men and women, inadequate theorisation of gender and disregard for unpaid domestic work and care. Esping-Andersen had overlooked the fact that particularly in Conservative welfare states, such as in France from the 1930s to 1960s, decommodification for mothers, facilitated by generous family benefits, undermined their employment opportunities and financial independence. Although family benefits rendered women independent from the labour market, they remained dependent on a male breadwinner, all the more so since in many countries eligibility for family benefits for married women was derived from their husband's employment. Decommodification meant that women were available and responsible for unpaid domestic and care work in the family in these countries (Lewis, 1992).

These critiques of Esping-Andersen's work spawned a new line of institutionalist research in the 1990s that focused on the role of the welfare state in determining how and by whom care is delivered and funded and what this means for women's employment opportunities (see e.g., Daly, 1994; Gornick & Meyers, 2003; Lewis, 1992). Researchers were interested in how the welfare state gives opportunities for employment to those traditionally charged with undertaking unpaid work, namely women, by de-familialising care work, in particular, childcare. For example, Lewis (1992) focused on the degree to which welfare states encourage dual-earning in different-sex couples, identifying strong (single-earner), weak (dual-earner) or modified (one-and-a-half earner) male breadwinner regimes on the basis of their childcare provisions and work-family reconciliation policies. France was deemed a modified male breadwinner state in this model. Meanwhile, Leitner (2003) discussed the degree to which policy is based on the expectation that the family will provide child- and eldercare and categorised regimes by their degree and type of familialism. Referring to the situation in the country in the late 1990s, Leitner (2003) categorised France as an explicit familialist state as regards LTC, meaning that the state "explicitly enforce[d] the caring function of the family because of the lack of public and market-driven provision coupled with strong familialism" (p. 358) and as an optional familialist state as regards childcare, that is, one in which "the caring family is strengthened but it is also given the option of being (partly) relieved of its caring" (p. 359).

Fraser (1994) differentiated between three ideal-type welfare regimes on the basis of the parity between rights based on employment and those based on caring, identifying a universal breadwinner model that promotes women's employment and the commodification or collectivisation of care work; a caregiver parity model that provides allowances and entitlement to social rights for unpaid carers; and a universal caregiving model that supports equal contributions to unpaid caregiving and employment for men and women. Meanwhile, Saraceno and Keck (2010, p. 676) focus on degrees and types of familialism as regards LTC and differentiate between regimes characterised by "familialism by default", in which there is an absence of publicly provided alternatives or financial support for family care and sometimes legal obligations on the family to care; "supported familialism" in which financial transfers including taxation and paid leaves support family members to care, this being the category in which France is placed; and "de-familialisation" in which the individualisation of social rights to receive care significantly reduces but does not necessarily eradicate family responsibilities and dependencies.

Others have categorised welfare regimes according to the degree to which they attempt not only to de-familialise care but also to de-gender unpaid care responsibilities within the family by encouraging a more equal sharing of this work between men and women (Saxonberg, 2013). In Saxonberg's model, France was deemed to have a low degree of de-gendering. Similarly, varying fatherhood regimes have been identified on the basis of the ways in which policy expresses social norms around the obligations and expectations of fatherhood, and the degree of promotion of active parenthood for men (Doucet & Merla, 2007; Gregory & Milner, 2011). Geist (2005) discusses how Social Democratic states de-familialise a significant amount of care work by providing or subsidising child and elder care services and pursue de-gendering policies for the remaining unpaid care work that specifically target the behaviour of men. This sets in motion a cycle of social feedback that spreads more gender-equal behaviours through the population. In Liberal regimes, a high percentage of couples, particularly those with children, cannot attain a socially acceptable standard of living with one salary due to the lack of worker protections and family benefits. Limited work-family reconciliation support means that care and employment have to be managed within the family. These conditions can have a de-gendering effect on unpaid domestic and care work in different-sex couples as lack of state support puts pressure on men to change their behaviour (Windebank, 2001). Lastly, in Conservative regimes the state has traditionally provided significant support for the family through family allowances and benefits, which translated in some countries to low employment participation rates for women with parenting responsibilities, and little or no encouragement of men to participate in unpaid work in the home. As work-family reconciliation policy has developed in some of these countries, including France, it has often focused on the de-familialisation rather than the de-gendering of care work.

The modalities of policies for childcare and LTC, in particular welfare states affect the unpaid domestic and care workload of individuals, possibilities for its outsourcing, the distribution of unpaid work between men and women, and the work conditions and career prospects of paid domestic and care workers (Schmid et al., 2011). Childcare provision in conjunction with the education system frames how childrearing work is shared between parents and the wider kin group and community, on the one hand, and paid providers working for the state, commercial organisations, or as direct employees of parents/guardians on the other. The structure of state education (school times, school holidays, compulsory school age, pre-school provision) and the availability and affordability of care for pre-school children and before- and after-school and holiday care for older children, all or some of which may be provided in kind or subsidised in cash by the state, are of significance. The greater the provision and funding of childcare by the state, the more opportunities are afforded to parents (usually women) to combine parenting and employment, and publicly funded childcare challenges traditional attitudes about women's social roles (Hook, 2006).

Lack of childcare provision and long and low-paid parental leaves reduce women's ability to maintain continuous careers while parenting, receive training and develop their human capital, and reinforce a full-time caregiver expectation. However, childcare provision, if not accompanied by explicitly de-gendering policies or strategies, may help maintain attitudes and practices that limit men's role in parenting as state provision makes it possible for women to combine childrearing and employment with little contribution by men. Such provision may therefore facilitate men both symbolically and materially to adhere to traditional gender roles concerning the parental division of labour (Geist, 2005; Windebank, 2001). Furthermore, the funding of collective facilities such as creches, nursery and pre-schools and after-school clubs may be more beneficial to childcare workers in terms of their work conditions and career opportunities than support for individualised and direct employment childcare solutions such as childminders and nannies. This is because the former promotes a tripartite employment relationship, whereas the latter promotes bipartite employment relationships. It will be discussed in Chap. 3 how an early and well-developed framework for creche and nursery school provision and childcare benefits in France geared towards the de-familialisation rather than the de-gendering of parental work helped to reinforce a traditional gender division of unpaid domestic and care work in the country despite the significant integration of women, and particularly women with parenting responsibilities, into the labour market.

LTC is a more complex area of policy than childcare because adults with care needs are a very diverse group. The level of support required by adults varies significantly, ranging from occasional help with household tasks to daily help with bodily maintenance such as feeding, washing and dressing. Policy towards LTC includes care in institutions and care at home and may be compartmentalised on the criterion of age with specific policies for seniors (usually defined as over 60 or 65) as opposed to younger populations with care needs, as has been the case in France since the 1990s. Care at home may be provided in kind by state authorities (care in-kind) or supported by the payment of benefits to care recipients (cash-for-care). These benefits can be used to pay for services from commercial or non-profit organisations or from direct employees. Some schemes allow the employment of family members. Benefits may also be paid to informal carers to compensate their full or partial withdrawal from the labour market for care reasons (Bertogg & Strauss, 2020). Support may be means tested or universal; the threshold of dependency above which one is entitled to receive support may vary as may the proportion of how much of the overall cost is covered, and in the case of elder care, how much is recouped from a deceased person's estate. Whereas the legal obligation of parents to maintain and support their minor children is common across countries, the legal obligation to support wider kin financially or in kind varies more significantly. As will be discussed in more detail in Chap. 4, in France, adults have the legal obligation to care for their parents, and other ascendant relatives. In similarity to childcare, a lack of state support for LTC translates as a de facto obligation for the family to care, with or without an accompanying legal obligation.

In combination with welfare, family and care policies, labour-market and work-time policies are of importance to understand national patterns of the organisation and divisions of labour of domestic and care work. The responses of governments to the economic shocks and restructuring of the 1970s and 1980s have had implications for the employment opportunities, and therefore availability for domestic and care work, of particular groups within society. Conservative states, including France, responded to these economic conditions by using the welfare state to reduce labour supply (Bonoli, 2013). On the one hand, workers were removed from the labour force by a variety of means, for example, by reducing the statutory retirement and state pension age, offering early retirement schemes, extending further and higher education opportunities and supporting long parental leaves. On the other hand, work time was reduced, for example, by extending paid annual leave entitlements, shortening the working week and encouraging part-time work. Some labour-reduction policies, particularly the encouragement of part-time work and long parental leaves, are criticised for their gendered impacts: structural gender inequalities mean that women are more likely to accept both long parental leaves and part-time work than men, weakening their labour-market position further over the life course (Fagnani & Math, 2011). In contrast, policies such as the reduction of the working week as enacted in France by Socialist governments in the early 1980s and again in the early 2000s could be expected to give men the opportunity to take on a greater share of unpaid work (Gornick & Meyers, 2003), given that long work hours have been shown to encourage gender specialisation in different-sex couples by reducing the availability of the primary breadwinner, most usually the man, for these duties (Hook, 2006).

In response to these same economic conditions, Liberal countries turned to policies of labour-market deregulation and shrinkage of the welfare state to reduce wage costs (Bonoli, 2013). The resulting high degree of wage and numerical flexibility allowed wages to fall in low-skilled service occupations, which resulted in the lowering of prices and increasing demand for these services (Gershuny, 2000; Hall & Soskice, 2001; Lallement, 2013). This created job opportunities for workers displaced from manufacturing industry or newly entering the labour market (Carbonnier & Morel, 2015). In contrast, the Social Democratic Nordic countries, which were relatively sheltered from the economic restructuring of this period, embarked on what would come to be known as Active Labour Market Policies (ALPM). This approach seeks to include as high a percentage of those of working age as possible in employment and activate sectors of the population who may have previously remained marginal to the labour market. It intersects with welfare models that aim to develop universal breadwinners (Fraser, 1994), or what Manske (2005, p. 242) calls a society of "autonomous worker-citizens", where all employable adults enter the labour market. An ALMP approach prioritises human-capital investment and the removal of obstacles to labour-market participation. Unpaid care work is viewed as one such obstacle (Knijn & Ostner, 2002). ALMP has spread across Europe since the early 2000s, but France was a late adopter of this approach as will be discussed further in Chap. 5.

These differing labour-market policies also had implications for the development of PHS in different countries particularly for domestic, as opposed to care-related services (Gershuny, 2000). In many sectors, services can be rendered more affordable to consumers without reducing the income of producers by increasing productivity, that is, by reducing the amount of labour time required per unit of output. Increasing the productivity of PHS is difficult, however, because the time spent on the activity is often an essential part of the service and for those services delivered in the home, increasing productivity through systematised practices or technology is limited (Picchi, 2016). Affordability of PHS depends significantly on the opportunity cost to the consumer of undertaking the task themselves unpaid as compared with the price of the service. Consequently, either the wage gap between the consumer and the producer of the service needs to be wide enough to make the service affordable or the state needs to subsidise the service to the consumer through in-kind provision, benefits or by reducing employer tax and social security burdens (Carbonnier & Morel, 2015). Therefore, in Liberal countries PHS has been able to develop due to the significant wage gap that has been permitted to exist between producers and consumers. Better-off households with demanding jobs can use their earnings to employ lower paid workers for domestic and care services without the need for state subsidy. On the supply side, this model has had the effect of making dual-earning financially necessary for a high proportion of couples with children. Without extensive work-family reconciliation support, this has translated to a one-and-a-half earner model based on part-time work, particularly for lower skilled women, thereby creating a pool of flexible labour for the paid domestic and care services sector.

However, in more regulated labour markets where labour costs are high due to labour-market regulations, worker-protection legislation, employers' social security contributions and/or restrictive union practices such as France, state support for PHS has been key to its availability and affordability. In these countries, lower skilled workers have no incentive to accept very low-paid service-sector jobs because of high marginal tax rates and the loss of benefits that comes with low earnings. In the Social Democratic Nordic countries, populations have been willing to accept high levels of taxation in exchange for good quality public services, and the state was able to provide in-kind care services for children and adults funded by taxation (Gershuny, 2000). This situation equates to the ILO's (2018, p. 31) concept of the "high road" to care policy. Domestic tasks have been left for individuals to undertake on an unpaid basis.

Since the 1990s Conservative countries have used public policy to encourage growth of the PHS sector by subsidising the cost to the consumer of directly employing workers in their homes to produce a market for individualised care and domestic work services within bipartite employment arrangements (Carbonnier & Morel, 2015; Iversen & Wren, 1998). Such policies have been part of a shift away from labour reduction policies to ALMP since the early 2000s which necessitates de-familialising some aspects of care and domestic work and creating jobs, particularly for lower skilled or inexperienced workers. France has been at the forefront of the development of policy to encourage PHS in Europe, despite the resistance in the country to attempts to modify aspects of its labour-shedding policies such as the 35-hour week or relatively early retirement age. In more recent times, and in response to tightening budgets and increasing demands, Social Democratic countries have also started to stimulate demand for domestic and care services in the private sector through cash-for-care benefits, and tax breaks and social security subventions for direct employers under the umbrella of PHS. Such measures have been used in some instances to allow the state to withdraw from costly in-kind provision and in others to allow the expansion of support without attempting to dismantle existing in-kind care structures (Carbonnier & Morel, 2015).

Lastly, migration policies are important to the organisation and divisions of labour of domestic and care work because they influence the composition of the childcare, LTC and PHS labour force, its working conditions, and the affordability of paid domestic and care services. Global socio-economic transformations have given rise to a supply of domestic and care workers from lower- and middle-income countries and regions who migrate to higher income areas in what have been termed global care chains as discussed above. Countries differ in the extent to which the childcare, LTC and PHS sectors are reliant on global care chains. This depends on their migration regime, that is, the sum of rules governing who is allowed to work or settle in a country, under what conditions and for what purpose (Lutz, 2008). Illegality in the migrant labour market is constructed by state categories that divide people into documented migrants on the one hand, that is, those who have the right to reside and be employed in the country, and, on the one hand, those who do not have such rights, that is, undocumented migrants. This status determines whether an individual is available for declared or only undeclared work (Triandaifyllidou, 2013). Documented migrants may enter a country under specific arrangements for the recruitment of domestic or care employees. Points-based immigration systems may be more or less conducive to the entry of domestic and care workers. Domestic and/or care work may or may not feature on lists of occupations to which migrant labour can be recruited. Domestic and care work has not featured on such lists in France. Documented migrants may also enter a country under a general migration agreement and subsequently take on domestic and care work. Super-state institutions such as the EU offer free movement for citizens of member states or bilateral agreements between states may exist. Being undocumented and working on an undeclared basis increases the degree of imbalance in terms of power and status between the consumer and provider for paid domestic and care services.

Although policy regimes may create a framework that favours particular configurations of domestic and care work, it must be recognised that the relationship between policy and outcomes is not straightforward or guaranteed. Policy frameworks do not determine the reaction of individuals to them or dictate behaviours (Daly, 1994; Leira, 1992). Cultural norms can work with or against the successful implementation of a policy and the achievement of its objectives (Connell, 1987; Leira, 1992; Pfau-Effinger, 2012). Cultural norms are understood here as "shared beliefs, values, and norms within a group which may shape preferences and beliefs, make some goals more valuable than others (values), or render some behaviours more desirable or costly than others" (Hitlin & Piliavin, 2004, p. 360). National, local or group-specific cultures, rooted in path-dependent historical legacies, both inform and are informed by policy and institutions that reflect and feed back ideal types, whether these concern work, gender, family or the role of the state. Indeed, policy in a democratic country is shaped in part by the cultural assumptions of its citizens as political parties must put forward policies to the electorate which are acceptable within these norms (Pfau-Effinger, 2012). Moreover, policy feedback means that when policies are in place for sufficient time, they themselves become sources of social norms and cultural models shaping citizens' preferences and attitudes defining what is normal, acceptable or merit-worthy for the country or for specific populations within it (Edlund & Öun, 2016). Indeed, Treas and Widmer (2000, p. 1411) suggest that "one indicator of the success of state interventions is whether state ideology is internalized by citizens and manifest in public opinion".

Gender cultures are of central importance to the questions addressed in this book. The gendered behaviours of individuals around domestic and care work, informed by gender socialisation, performativity and attitudes, are framed within national or local gender cultures (Aboim, 2010; Carriero, 2021; Ruppanner & Maune, 2016). For example, Connell's

(1987 p. 20) "gender orders" represent ideals of masculinity and femininity that both shape and are shaped by policymaking, labour markets and individual practices. In Connell's framework, the gender order is composed of a series of "gender regimes," that is, specific institutions (e.g., the workplace or the family) which may be in tension with one another. Similar is Pfau-Effinger's (2004, 2012) theoretical framework of "gender regimes" which considers the interaction of norms, culture and social-economic factors with policies and their impact on gendered social practices. These gender regimes frame the values and models that people use as orientation for their behaviour "regarding the family and the societal integration of women and men" (Pfau-Effinger, 2004, p. 382). Chapter 2 will explore the path dependencies of policy, institutional and cultural legacies that have helped shape the modern organisation and divisions of domestic and care work in France.

The book will engage in a final explanatory stage and seek to understand why the policies and cultural norms that impact on the organisation of domestic and care work in France developed in the ways that they did. First, the material factors that have combined to produce new challenges and provide windows of opportunity for societal and political actors to turn policy opportunities into policy change will be considered. Second, the ideational factors such as social norms around work, gender, the family and the state that have facilitated or blocked the adoption or successful implementation of particular policies will be discussed. Ideas form a public discourse that, through framing processes, can help convince policymakers, interest groups and the general population that a particular approach is necessary (Schmidt, 2002). Furthermore, some policy ideas attain the status of culturally resonant keywords (Williams, 1976) that influence policy decisions and public opinion over a long term (Beland, 2009). Actors can promote policy change by reframing traditional or historical keywords in order to make a particular policy culturally resonant (Cox, 2004). Third, it is necessary to consider the role of different actors in promoting or resisting specific policies, whether these be political actors (political parties, interest groups, policy elites, supranational bodies) or social actors (the electorate; civil society). Interested parties compete to insert their definition of problems to be addressed into the policy debate, giving leverage to their proposed solution (Allwood & Wadia, 2009). The success of different actors depends on their place with the political opportunity structure (e.g., access to institutions or relationships with influential allies). Political actors must pay attention to the ideational factors discussed above in order to frame their goals in such a way that they are likely to be achieved. In these discussions, the book will consider both the path-dependent historical legacies and the international trends and pressures for policy convergence that have shaped the policies that impact on domestic and care work in France. Path dependency is understood as the process by which institutional, political or ideational historical precedent continues to shape policy and its outcomes while policy convergence is understood as countries adopting a common policy paradigm, resulting in the implementation of similar policy tools and instruments, even if at differing rates (Pierson, 2000).

Structure of the Book

The book is structured chronologically and thematically. The main focus of the book is on domestic and care work in modern France, taken to mean France in the twenty-first century. However, the discussion will begin in Chap. 2 with an analysis of how and why the organisation of domestic and care work evolved in France over the course of the twentieth century. This discussion has two objectives. First, it illustrates how the organisation of domestic and care work, its sites of production and divisions of labour have shifted over time and that the current configuration of this work in France is a snapshot in a continuously developing process. Second, in discussing why these shifts took place, it is possible to identify the historical legacies and path dependencies in French politics, bureaucratic institutions and cultural norms that help explain contemporary configurations of domestic and care work. Chapters 3–5 analyse domestic and care work in France in the twenty-first century, each chapter focusing on a specific set of activities. Chapter 3 discusses parenting and childcare work; Chap. 4 discusses paid and unpaid LTC work; and Chap. 5 discusses domestic work and PHS. Each chapter will explore the organisation of the work across varying combinations of social relations, its divisions of labour and the policy frameworks and cultural norms that explain its organisation in the national context of France. Chapters 3 and 4 focus on the direct care aspects of looking after children and adults with care needs. The intersections between domestic and care work, or direct and indirect care, feature in Chaps. 3–5 as appropriate. Chapter 6 brings the discussion up to date with a consideration of the immediate and possible longer-term impacts of the COVID pandemic on configurations of domestic and care work in France. Chapter 7 concludes with an evaluation of the main drivers that explain the configuration of domestic and care work in France today.

References

Aboim, S. (2010). Gender cultures and the division of labour in contemporary Europe: A cross-national perspective. *The Sociological Review, 58*(2), 171–196. https://doi.org/10.1111/j.1467-954X.2010.01899.x

Allwood, G., & Wadia, K. (2009). *Women and policy in France*. Palgrave Macmillan.

Baxter, J. (1997). Gender equality and participation in housework: A cross-national perspective. *Journal of Comparative Family Studies, 28*, 220–247.

Becker, G. (1981). *A treatise on the family*. Harvard University Press.

Beland, D. (2009). Back to bourgeois? French social policy and the idea of solidarity. *International Journal of Sociology and Social Policy, 29*(9/10), 445–456. https://doi.org/10.1108/01443330910986243

Bertogg, A., & Strauss, S. (2020). Spousal care-giving arrangements in Europe. The role of gender, socio-economic status and the welfare state. *Ageing and Society, 40*(4), 735–758. https://doi.org/10.1017/S0144686X18001320

Bianchi, S. M., Milkie, M. A., Sayer, L., & Robinson, J. (2001). Is anyone doing the housework? Trends in the gender division of household labor. *Social Forces, 79*(1), 191–228. https://doi.org/10.1093/sf/79.1.191

Bittman, M., Matheson, G., & Meagher, G. (1998). The changing boundary between home and market: Australian trends in outsourcing domestic labour. *Work, Employment and Society, 13*(2), 249–273. https://doi.org/10.1177/09500179922117935

Bonoli, G. (2013). *Origins of active social policy: Labour market and childcare policies*. Oxford University Press.

Bouffartigue, P., & Bouteiller, J. (2003). À propos des normes du temps de travail. De l'érosion de la norme fordienne aux normes émergentes. *Revue de l'IRES, 2*, 137–160.

Brines, J. (1994). Economic dependency, gender and the division of labor at home. *American Journal of Sociology, 100*, 652–688. https://doi.org/10.1086/230577

Brousse, C. (2015). La vie quotidienne en France depuis 1974. Les enseignements de l'enquête Emploi du temps. *Economie et Statistique, 478-479-480*, 79–117.

Butler, J. (1990). *Gender trouble: Feminism and the subversion of identity*. Routledge.

Calasanti, T., & Bailey, C. (1994). Gender inequality and the division of household labor in the United States and Sweden: A socialist-feminist approach. *Social Problems, 38*(1), 35–53. https://doi.org/10.1525/sp.1991.38.1.03a00030

Cancedda, A. (2001). *Employment in household services*. European Foundation for the Improvement of Living and Working Conditions. Retrieved March 25, 2005, from http://publications.europa.eu/resource/cellar/b5cc9365-e89f-4710-8c27-d685dd5bed75.0003.02/DOC_1

Carbonnier, C., & Morel, N. (Eds.). (2015). *The political economy of household services in Europe*. Palgrave Macmillan.

Carriero, R. (2021). The role of culture in the gendered division of domestic labor: Evidence from migrant populations in Europe. *Acta Sociologica, 64*(1), 24–47. https://doi.org/10.1177/0001699320930073

Charles, A., & Galerand, E. (2017). Du travail ménager au service domestique, de l'emploi féminin au travail militant : critiques féministes en évolution. *Recherches féministes, 30*(2), 1–16. https://doi.org/10.7202/1043919ar

Cheung, A. K., & Lui, L. (2017). Hiring domestic help in Hong Kong: The role of gender attitude and wives' income. *Journal of Family Issues, 38*(1), 73–99. https://doi.org/10.1177/0192513X14565700

Connell, R. W. (1987). *Gender and power*. Polity Press.

Connell, R. W., & Messerschmidt, J. W. (2005). Hegemonic masculinity. Rethinking the concept. *Gender and Society, 19*(6), 829–859. https://doi.org/10.1177/0891243205278639

Coverman, S. (1985). Explaining husbands' participation in domestic labor. *Sociological Quarterly, 26*, 181–197. https://doi.org/10.1111/j.1533-8525.1985.tb00217.x

Cox, R. (2004). The path dependence of an idea: Why Scandinavian welfare states remain distinct. *Social Policy and Administration, 38*(2), 204–219. https://doi.org/10.1111/j.1467-9515.2004.00386.x

Cox, R. (2006). *The servant problem: Paid domestic work in a global economy*. I.B. Tauris.

Craig, L., & Baxter, J. (2014). Domestic outsourcing, housework shares and subjective time pressure: Gender differences in the correlates of hiring help. *Social Indicators Research, 125*(1), 271–288. https://doi.org/10.1007/s11205-014-0833-1

Craig, L., & Mullan, K. (2010). Parenthood, gender and work-family time in the United States, Australia, Italy, France and Denmark. *Journal of Marriage and the Family, 72*(5), 1344–1361. https://doi.org/10.1111/j.1741-3737.2010.00769.x

Cunha, V., & Atalaia, S. (2019). The gender(ed) division of labour in Europe: Patterns of practices in 18 EU countries. *Sociologia, 90*, 113–137. https://doi.org/10.7458/SPP20199015526

Cunningham, M. (2001). Parental influences on the gendered division of housework. *American Sociological Review, 66*(2), 184–203. https://doi.org/10.2307/2657414

Daly, M. (1994). A matter of dependency: Gender in British income maintenance provision. *Sociology, 28*(3), 779–797. https://doi.org/10.1177/0038038594028003008

Daminger, A. (2019). The cognitive dimension of household labor. *American Sociological Review, 84*(4), 609–633. https://doi.org/10.1177/0003122419859007

Davis Smith, J. (1998). *The 1997 national survey of volunteering.* Institute for Volunteering Research.
de Beauvoir, S. (1989). *The second sex* (H. M. Parshley, Trans.). Vintage Classics (Original work published 1952).
Delors, J., & Foucauld, M. (1980). *La Révolution du temps choisi.* Albin Michel.
Delphy, C. (2003). Par où attaquer le partage inégal du travail ménager? *Nouvelles questions féministes, 22*(3), 47–71. https://doi.org/10.3917/nqf.223.0047
Deutsch, F. M. (2007). Undoing gender. *Gender and Society, 21*(1), 106–127. https://doi.org/10.1177/0891243206293577
Devetter, F.-X., & Rousseau, S. (2009). *Du balai : essai sur le ménage à domicile et le retour de la domesticité.* Editions Raisons d'Agir.
Dex, S. (2010). Can state policies produce equality in housework. In J. Treas & S. Drobnič (Eds.), *Dividing the domestic: Men, women & household work in cross-national perspective* (pp. 79–104). Stanford University Press.
Doucet, A., & Merla, L. (2007). Stay at home fathering: A strategy for balancing and home in Canadian and Belgian families. *Community, Work & Family, 10*(4), 455–473. https://doi.org/10.1080/13668800701575101
Duffy, M., Albelda, R., & Hammonds, C. (2013). Counting care work: The empirical and policy applications of care theory. *Social Problems, 60*(2), 145–167. https://doi.org/10.1525/sp.2013.60.2.145
Dussuet, A. (2016). Genre, frontières du travail domestique et marges du salariat. Le cas des aides à domicile. *Revue française de Socio-Economie, 17*(2), 123–141. https://doi.org/10.3917/rfse.017.0123
Edlund, J., & Öun, I. (2016). Who should work and who should care? Attitudes towards the desirable division of labour between mothers and fathers in five European countries. *Acta Sociologica, 59*(2), 151–169. https://doi.org/10.1177/0001699316631024
Esping-Andersen, G. (1990). *The three worlds of welfare capitalism.* Princeton University Press.
Estevez-Abe, M., & Hobson, B. (2015). Outsourcing domestic (care) work: The politics, policies, and political economy. *Social Politics, 22*(2), 133–146. https://doi.org/10.1093/sp/jxv011
European Commission. (2012). *Commission staff working document on exploiting the employment potential of the personal and household services sector.*
Fagnani, J., & Math, A. (2011). The predicament of childcare policy in France: What is at stake? *Journal of Contemporary European Studies, 19*, 547–561. https://doi.org/10.1080/14782804.2011.639990
Farvaque, N. (2013). *Developing personal and household services in the EUA focus on housework activities.* Report for DG Employment, Social Affairs and Social Inclusion. Retrieved March 8, 2022, from https://www.employment-studies.co.uk/resource/developing-personal-and-household-services-eu-focus-housework-activities

Fraser, N. (1994). After the family wage: Gender equity and the welfare state. *Political Theory, 22*(4), 591–618. https://doi.org/10.1177/0090591794022004003

Fuwa, M., & Cohen, P. N. (2007). Housework and social policy. *Social Science Research, 36*, 512–530. https://doi.org/10.1016/j.ssresearch.2006.04.005

Geist, C. (2005). The welfare state and the home: Regime differences in the domestic division of labour. *European Sociological Review, 21*(1), 23–41. https://doi.org/10.1093/esr/jci002

Genest Dufault, S., & Castelain Meunier, C. (2017). Masculinités et familles en transformation. *Enfance, Familles, Générations : revue interdisciplinaire sur la famille contemporaine, 26*, 1–17. https://doi.org/10.7202/1041057ar

Gershuny, J. (2000). *Changing times. Work and leisure in post-industrial society.* Oxford University Press.

Glenn, E. (2010). *Forced to care: Coercion and caregiving in America.* Harvard University Press.

Glucksmann, M. (2005). Shifting boundaries and interconnections: Extending the 'total social organisation of labour'. *The Sociological Review, 53*, 19–36. https://doi.org/10.1111/j.1467-954X.2005.00570.x

Gornick, J. C., & Meyers, M. K. (2003). *Families that work: Policies for reconciling parenthood and employment.* Russell Sage Foundation.

Gorz, A. (1985). *Paths to paradise: On the liberation from work.* Pluto Press.

Granovetter, M. (1985). Economic action and social structure: The problem of embeddedness. *American Journal of Sociology, 91*, 481–493. https://doi.org/10.1086/228311

Greenstein, T. N. (1996). Husbands' participation in domestic labor: Interactive effects of wives' and husbands' gender ideologies. *Journal of Marriage and the Family*, 585–595. https://doi.org/10.2307/353719

Greenstein, T. N. (2000). Economic dependence, gender, and the division of labor in the home: A replication and extension. *Journal of Marriage and Family, 62*(2), 322–335. https://doi.org/10.1111/j.1741-3737.2000.00322.x

Gregory, A., & Milner, S. (2011). What is 'new' about fatherhood: The social construction of fatherhood in France and the UK. *Men and Masculinities, 14*(5), 588–606. https://doi.org/10.1177/1097184X11412940

Haicault, M. (1984). La gestion ordinaire de la vie en deux. *Sociologie du travail, 26*(3), 268–277. https://doi.org/10.3406/sotra.1984.2072

Hall, P., & Soskice, D. (2001). An introduction to varieties of capitalism. In P. Hall & D. Soskice (Eds.), *Varieties of capitalism* (pp. 1–70). Oxford University Press.

Halldén, S., & Stenberg, A. (2018). The relationship between hours of outsourced domestic services and female earnings: Evidence from a Swedish tax reform. *Research in Social Stratification and Mobility, 55*, 120–133. https://doi.org/10.1016/j.rssm.2018.04.003

Hatton, E. (2017). Mechanisms of invisibility: Rethinking the concept of invisible work. *Work, Employment and Society, 31*(2), 336–351. https://doi.org/10.1177/0950017016674894

Hitlin, S., & Piliavin, J. A. (2004). Values: reviving a dormant concept. *Annual Review of Sociology, 30*, 359–393. https://doi.org/10.1146/annurev.soc.30.012703.110640

Hook, J. L. (2006). Care in context: Men's unpaid work in 20 countries, 1965–2003. *American Sociological Review, 71*(4), 639–660. https://doi.org/10.1177/000312240607100406

International Labour Office (ILO). (2018). *Care work and care jobs for the future of decent work*. Retrieved March 8, 2022, from https://www.ilo.org/wcmsp5/groups/public/%2D%2D-dgreports/%2D%2D-dcomm/%2D%2D-publ/documents/publication/wcms_633135.pdf

Iversen, T., & Wren, A. (1998). Equality, employment and budgetary restraint: The trilemma of the service economy. *World Politics, 50*, 507–546. https://doi.org/10.1017/S0043887100007358

Jack, T. (2016). Cleanliness and consumption: Exploring material and social structuring of domestic cleaning practices. *International Journal of Consumer Studies, 41*, 70–78. https://doi.org/10.1111/ijcs.12315

Jonsson, I., Daune-Richard, A.-M., Odena, S., & Ring, M. (2011). The implementation of elder care in France and Sweden: A macro and micro perspective. *Ageing and Society, 31*, 625–644. https://doi.org/10.1017/S0144686X10001327

Kan, M. Y. (2008). Does gender trump money? Housework hours of husbands and wives in Britain. *Work, Employment and Society, 22*(1), 45–66. https://doi.org/10.1177/0950017007087416

Knijn, T., & Ostner, I. (2002). Commodification and de-commodification. In B. Hobson, J. Lewis, & B. Siim (Eds.), *Contested concepts in gender and social politics* (pp. 141–169). Edward Elgar.

Lallement, M. (2013). Economic crises and new modes of social regulation in Europe (2008–2012). *Employee Rights and Employment Policy, 17*(2), 257–290.

Laville, J.-L. (2008). Services aux personnes et sociologie économique pluraliste. *Revue Française de Socio-Économie, 2*(2), 43–58. https://doi.org/10.3917/rfse.002.0043

Leira, A. (1992). *Welfare states and working mothers: The Scandinavian experience*. Cambridge University Press.

Leitner, S. (2003). Varieties of familialism: The caring function of the family in comparative perspective. *European Societies, 5*, 353–375. https://doi.org/10.1080/1461669032000127642

Lemmenicier, B. (1988). *Le marché du mariage et de la famille*. Presses Universitaires de France.

Lewis, J. (1992). Gender and the development of welfare regimes. *Journal of European Social Policy, 2*, 159–173. https://doi.org/10.1177/095892879200200301

Lutz, H. (2008). When home becomes a workplace: Domestic work as an ordinary job in Germany. In H. Lutz (Ed.), *Migration and domestic work: A European perspective on a global theme* (pp. 43–60). Ashgate.

Lutz, H., & Palenga-Möllenbeck, E. (2011). Care, gender and migration: Towards a theory of transnational domestic work migration in Europe. *Journal of Contemporary European Studies, 19*(3), 349–364. https://doi.org/10.1080/14782804.2011.610605

Lyon, D. (2010). Intersections and boundaries of work and non-work. *European Societies, 12*(2), 163–185. https://doi.org/10.1080/14616690903100456

Lyon, D., & Glucksmann, M. (2008). Comparative configurations of care work across Europe. *Sociology, 42*(1), 101–118. https://doi.org/10.1177/0038038507084827

Manoudi, A., Weber, T., Scott, D., & Hawley Woodall, J. (2018). *An analysis of PHS to support work-life balance for working parents and carers.* Synthesis report ECE thematic review. Retrieved March 8, 2022, from https://ec.europa.eu/social/BlobServlet?docId=20330&langId=en

Manske, A. (2005). Eigenverantwortung statt Wohlfahrtstaatlicherabsicherung. Anmerkungen zum Gestaltwandel sozialer Absicherung. *Berliner Journal für Soziologie, 2*, 241–245. https://doi.org/10.1007/s11609-006-0120-3

Noonan, M. (2013). The impact of social policy on the gendered division of housework. *Journal of Family Theory & Review, 5*, 124–134. https://doi.org/10.1111/jftr.12008

Pendo, E. (2016). Hidden from view: Disability, segregation, and work. In M. Crain, W. Poster, & M. A. Cherry (Eds.), *Invisible labor: Hidden work in the contemporary world* (pp. 115–129). University of California Press.

Pfau-Effinger, B. (2004). Socio-historical paths of the male-breadwinner model – An explanation of cross-national differences. *British Journal of Sociology, 55*, 377–399. https://doi.org/10.1111/j.1468-4446.2004.00025.x

Pfau-Effinger, B. (2012). Women's employment in the institutional and cultural context. *International Journal of Sociology and Social Policy, 32*(9/10), 530–543. https://doi.org/10.1108/01443331211257634

Picchi, S. (2016). The elderly care and domestic services sector during the recent economic crisis. The case of Italy, Spain and France. *Investigaciones Feministas, 7*(1), 169–190. https://doi.org/10.5209/rev_INFE.2016.v7.n1.52067

Pierson, P. (2000). Three worlds of welfare state research. *Comparative Political Studies, 33*(6–7), 791–821. https://doi.org/10.1177/001041400003300605

Poster, W. R., Crain, M., & Cherry, M. A. (2016). Introduction: Conceptualizing invisible labor. In M. Crain, W. Poster, & M. A. Cherry (Eds.), *Invisible labor: Hidden work in the contemporary world* (pp. 3–27). University of California Press.

Prouteau, L., & Wolff, F.-C. (2002). La participation associative au regard des temps sociaux. *Economie et Statistique, 352*, 57–80.

Roy, D. (2011). *La contribution du travail domestique au bien-être matériel des ménages : une quantification à partir de l'enquête emploi du temps*. Retrieved June 21, 2020, from https://www.insee.fr/fr/statistiques/1380932

Ruppanner, L., & Maune, D. J. (2016). The state of domestic affairs: Housework, gender and state-level institutional logics. *Social Science Research, 60*, 15–28. https://doi.org/10.1016/j.ssresearch.2016.04.006

Saraceno, C., & Keck, W. (2010). Can we identify intergenerational policy regimes in Europe? *European Societies, 12*(5), 675–696. https://doi.org/10.1080/14616696.2010.483006

Saxonberg, S. (2013). Defamilialization to degenderization: Toward a new welfare typology. *Social Policy and Administration, 47*, 26–49. https://doi.org/10.1111/j.1467-9515.2012.00836.x

Schmid, T., Brandt, M., & Haberkern, K. (2011). Gendered support to older parents: Do welfare states matter? *European Journal of Ageing, 9*(1), 39–50. https://doi.org/10.1007/s10433-011-0197-1

Schmidt, V. A. (2002). *The futures of European capitalism*. Oxford University Press.

Seiller, P., & Silvera, R. (2020). Sales boulots. *Travail, genre et sociétés, 43*(1), 25–30. https://doi.org/10.3917/tgs.043.0025

Sevenhuijsen, S. (2003). The place of care: The relevance of the feminist ethic of care for social policy. *Feminist Theory, 4*(2), 179–197. https://doi.org/10.1177/14647001030042006

Sjoberg, O. (2004). The role of family policy institutions in explaining gender-role attitudes: A comparative multilevel analysis of thirteen industrialized countries. *Journal of European Social Policy, 14*, 107–123. https://doi.org/10.1177/0958928704042003

Sofer, C. (1999). Modélisation économique de la prise de décision dans la famille. In B. M. d'Intignano (Ed.), *Egalité entre femmes et hommes : aspects économiques* (pp. 147–160). La Documentation Française.

Stafford, R., Backman, E., & Dibona, P. (1977). The division of labor among cohabiting and married couples. *Journal of Marriage and Family, 39*(1), 43–57. https://doi.org/10.2307/351061

Sullivan, O., & Gershuny, J. (2013). Domestic outsourcing and multitasking: How much do they really contribute? *Social Science Research, 42*(5), 1311–1324. https://doi.org/10.1016/j.ssresearch.2013.05.004

Sullivan, O., Gershuny, J., & Robinson, J. P. (2018). Stalled or uneven gender revolution? A long-term processual framework for understanding why change is slow. *Journal of Family Theory & Review, 10*(1), 263–279. https://doi.org/10.1111/jftr.12248

Swiebel, J. (1999). *Unpaid work and policymaking: Towards a broader perspective of work and employment*. DESA discussion paper ST/EAS/1999/DP.4. Retrieved March 7, 2022, from https://www.un.org/esa/desa/papers/1999/esa99dp4.pdf

Treas, J., & Widmer, E. D. (2000). Married women's employment over the life course: Attitudes in cross-national perspective. *Social Forces, 78*(4), 1409–1436. https://doi.org/10.1093/sf/78.4.1409

Triandaifyllidou, A. (Ed.). (2013). *Irregular migration and domestic work in Europe: Who cares?* Routledge.

UN Commission on the Status of Women. (1977, December 22). *Working women and the sharing of household duties.* 6/613.

United Nations (UN). (2020). *The world's women 2020 trends and statistics.* Retrieved March 7, 2022, from https://worlds-women-2020-data-undesa.hub.arcgis.com/

Van der Lippe, T., Treas, J., & Norbutas, L. (2018). Unemployment and the division of housework in Europe. *Work, Employment and Society, 32*(4), 650–669. https://doi.org/10.1177/0950017017690495

Veltman, A. (2004). The Sisyphean torture of housework: Simone de Beauvoir and inequitable divisions of domestic work in marriage. *Hypatia, 19*(3), 121–143. https://doi.org/10.1111/j.1527-2001.2004.tb01304.x

Warde, A., & Martens, L. (2000). *Eating out: Social differentiation, consumption and pleasure.* Cambridge University Press.

West, C., & Zimmerman, D. H. (1987). Doing Gender. *Gender & Society, 1*(2), 125–151. https://doi.org/10.1177/0891243287001002002

Williams, R. (1976). *Keywords: A vocabulary of culture and society.* Oxford University Press.

Williams, F. (2001). In and beyond new labour: Towards a new political ethics of care. *Critical Social Policy, 21*(4), 467–493. https://doi.org/10.1177/026101830102100405

Windebank, J. (1991). *The informal economy in France.* Avebury.

Windebank, J. (2001). Dual-earner couples in Britain and France: Gender divisions of domestic labour and parenting work in different welfare states. *Work, Employment and Society, 15*(2), 269–290. https://doi.org/10.1177/09500170122118959

Windebank, J., & Martinez-Perez, A. (2018). Gender divisions of domestic labour and paid domestic services. *The Service Industries Journal, 38*(11–12), 875–895. https://doi.org/10.1080/02642069.2018.1484110

Zimmerman, M. K. (2013). Theorizing inequality: Comparative policy regimes, gender, and everyday lives. *The Sociological Quarterly, 54*(1), 66–80. https://doi.org/10.1111/tsq.12003

CHAPTER 2

Domestic and Care Work in France: Legacies of the Twentieth Century

This chapter discusses the evolution of domestic and care work over the course of the twentieth century in France. In so doing, it has two aims. The first is to illustrate how the organisation of domestic and care work, its sites of production, and divisions of labour shift over time and that the current configuration of this work in France is a snapshot in a continuously developing process. The chapter discusses why these changes took place, and in so doing fulfils its second aim which is to identify the historical legacies and path dependencies in French politics, bureaucratic institutions and cultural norms that help explain contemporary configurations of domestic and care work. The discussion is divided into three periods: the Third Republic, including some discussion of the Vichy regime; the *Trente Glorieuses*[1] (1945–1975); and the period of post-Fordist economic restructuring after 1975 to the end of the century.

[1] The *Trente Glorieuses* refers to the "thirty glorious years" of strong economic growth in France following the Second World War, similar to the West German *Wirtschaftswunder* (economic miracle).

J. Windebank, *Domestic and Care Work in Modern France*, French Politics, Society and Culture,
https://doi.org/10.1007/978-3-031-33564-8_2

The Third Republic: Familialism and Pronatalism

In the early years of the twentieth century, women were responsible for the majority of domestic and care work, both unpaid work within the marriage contract and in their obligations to kin, and paid work as domestic servants. Women's relationship to domestic and care work was dependent on their social class, which determined the extent to which they undertook unpaid domestic and care work themselves or employed servants to carry out all or some tasks, or indeed whether they were employed as servants themselves. In the middle and upper classes, on marriage women were confined to the role of *femmes au foyer* (women in the home), but they were not expected also to be *ménagères*, that is someone who physically undertakes *le ménage* (housework). Rather, they used paid services to get this work done, most usually in the form of one or more live-in servants (Chatot, 2017), the management of whom was their responsibility (Clarke, 2011). Domestic technology at this time was rudimentary, and cleaning, laundry and food preparation were time-consuming and physically demanding jobs. The degree of responsibility of the housewife for any practical tasks, the cognitive aspects of domestic and care work, or indeed the emotional work of childrearing and other care tasks was dependent on the wealth of the family and the number and range of servants it could afford.

Prior to the First World War, significant social inequalities and a limited welfare safety net ensured a cheap labour supply composed of urban working class and rural single young women for paid domestic and care services (MacBride, 1976). Most of this work was organised on a live-in basis (Dussuet, 2017). Young girls working as domestic servants were often paid in kind with board and lodging. They had no set hours and in more modest middle-class households worked alone as a *bonne à tout faire* (maid of all works) (Fraisse, 1979). Domestic service work, hidden and invisible within the private home and out of reach of labour inspections, did not benefit from the legislation regarding for example night work or protection following workplace accidents that had begun to be enacted at the beginning of the twentieth century in France (Alexsynska & Schmidt, 2014). The first collective agreement for *employés de maison* (household workers) was not signed until 1980 (Lecomte, 1996). Domestic service of the early twentieth century was imbued with relations of servitude (Coser, 1973) and of economic and cultural domination (Foucault, 1975), a situation that constructed a cultural reference that impacts attitudes to home-based housekeeping services into the present day.

Among the urban working-class and in rural *familles paysannes* (peasant-farming families), most domestic and care work was undertaken unpaid by women for their kin with some input from out-of-home commercial services such as bakehouses or launderers, and from charities, mainly organised by the Catholic Church for welfare and childcare, and by the state, particularly as concerns education. A considerable proportion of the French population continued to work the land in the first half of the twentieth century and live in multi-generational households engaging in polyculture practices requiring a large workforce. Farms were run by a patriarchal head of the family, and other family members worked as *aides familiaux* (family helpers). In these households, economic activity was indivisible from family relations. The divide between a public and private sphere, and breadwinning and homemaking characteristic of middle-class households was absent (Barthez, 1986). Gender divisions of labour were better conceptualised as between inside and outside work with women being primarily responsible for inside work which included domestic and care activities but also tending kitchen gardens and looking after small livestock. In these rural families, there were high degrees of self-provisioning for food and clothing (Lagarve, 1997). This social structure survived longer among a greater percentage of the population in France than in comparable countries (Boinon, 2011) which contributed to the construction of a social norm accepting a dual role for women as participants in production and reproduction. The relatively high rates of women's economic activity in the country at the beginning of the twentieth century are the result of rural family helpers being included in the figures. In 1906, 3.3 million of the 7.6 million economically active women in France worked in agriculture (Tilly & Scott, 1987, p. 142).

However, by the beginning of the twentieth century, industrialisation was disrupting the rural economy and delocalising work into the public sphere of employment for an increasing proportion of the French population. In the early industrialisation of the nineteenth century in France, the wages available to urban working-class families were very low, and it was necessary for multiple members of a family to be employed in order to earn enough to survive. Alongside children, working-class women were obliged to find employment as well as be responsible for domestic and care work. However, the degree of poverty experienced by many urban working-class families, poor housing conditions and lack of access to varied foodstuffs meant that they had few material possessions to maintain or cooking to do in comparison with middle-class households for whom presentation of the self and the home were vital components of their social and cultural capital. Lack of outdoor space in many if not all working-class communities limited possibilities for self-provisioning for vegetables or keeping of livestock (Mendras, 1991). Investment in children's education was not a developed cultural norm in these communities at the time. Life expectancy was low, and lack of health care meant that work connected to caring for frail dependent adults was limited.

By the beginning of the twentieth century, improved productivity in manufacturing and trade union pressure had increased wage rates, and legislation preventing child labour alongside compulsory education had removed children from the factories. However, across Europe high infant mortality rates among the urban working class were of concern to governments. In the late nineteenth and early twentieth century, France was not only grappling with high infant mortality rates but had also experienced a birth rate that was lower than in comparable countries. The birth rate in France started to decline around a century before similar trends were witnessed elsewhere and significantly before improvements in health care and hygiene had enabled compensatory increases in life expectancy. The prospect of depopulation and the relative size and growth of the French population in comparison with its nearest neighbours and rivals were sources of concern across the political spectrum. By 1896 French demographers had discovered that the rate of population growth was declining so rapidly that an absolute reduction seemed possible (Offen, 1984). The defeat of the country in the Franco-Prussian War in 1871 was widely blamed on the weakness of the French population and birth rate, and the very high loss of life in the First World War further exacerbated fears of depopulation and weakness on the world stage. In 1900, France recorded 22 births per 1000 inhabitants as compared with 35 in Germany (Debord, 2020, p. 5). Between 1850 and 1910, the French population increased from 35.7 to 39.1 million[2] while that of Germany grew from 33.4 million to 58.4 million and that of England and Wales from 17.9 million to 36.0 million (Offen, 1984, p. 652).

The French Revolution had played a significant part in this situation. It gave individuals more freedom from the Catholic Church to make decisions regarding fertility. Married couples in France were practising birth control throughout the nineteenth century (King, 1998). The Revolution also led to years of political upheaval which further dampened the birth rate. In addition, discourses deriving from Malthusianism, which posited that population growth would outstrip the capacity to cater to human need and lead to hardships and catastrophes, provided cultural narratives

[2] During this period, France lost the population of Alsace-Lorraine to Germany. However, the size of this population is only a small fraction of the relative sizes and rates of growth of the population of the two countries.

to justify fertility decisions. Within the property-owning classes, Malthusianism was particularly influential as a justification for limiting the number of children in a family. Such practices had, however, an economic basis. The 1804 Napoleonic Civil Code had abolished primogeniture. Large numbers of children all with the right to inherit were considered problematic in that they would dilute and weaken the family property legacy (Debord, 2020).

These concerns over the birth rate and size of the French population informed how the French state dealt with questions of women's employment and caring responsibilities throughout the twentieth century, and to some extent continue to do so in the twenty-first century. They have also influenced cultural norms in France around the importance of children and the duty of the state to support families. As Reynolds (1990, p. 173) suggested in the 1990s: "there must be at least some correlation between the comparatively high provision of various forms of day-care for French children (of all ages) and the comparatively widespread concern for the birth-rate which also distinguishes France from other West European countries". During the early years of the twentieth century, two positions regarding women's employment, the family, the birth rate and infant mortality existed, expounded by two influential social movements that had emerged during the first years of the Third Republic. These were the natalist and familialist movements (De Luca Barrusse, 2009). They belonged to the two main political factions that had been in opposition to one another in France since the Revolution: the natalists were secular Republicans and the familialists were Catholic monarchists. Both viewed the family as the fundamental building block of French society.

French Republicanism, the philosophy that informed the French Revolution and derived from Jean-Jacques Rousseau's notion of a general will, promotes the individual citizen in their direct relationship to the state without intermediary affiliations. Universal equality under this model is associated with the rejection of claims to difference, viewed negatively as communitarianism. Furthermore, special treatment for particular groups is seen as unequal. The French Revolution in 1789 attributed human rights to individuals (men) as natural rights. This had the consequence of undermining the social body of the time based on feudal orders, corporations and other intermediary institutions. Some factions of Revolutionaries in the first years of the Revolution argued that these individual rights should be extended to women and be introduced into the private sphere of the home. Olympe de Gouges in her *Declaration of the Rights of Woman and the Female Citizen* of 1791 called for equal property rights and rights over children for women and was executed for treason for its publication (Reuter, 2019). The Thermidorians, who took power in 1794, were concerned with reconstructing the social, and selected the family as the best mechanism to manage and stabilise social cohesion in France. The Napoleonic Civil Code achieved this objective (Robcis, 2013). The Napoleonic Civil Code emphasised domesticity and the patriarchal family as the greatest source of social stability with marriage construed as a social rather than a religious act, and the family a social institution rather than a natural grouping or product of moral obligation. The withholding of individual rights from women was justified in that sex/gender differences were not considered to be susceptible to abstraction. They were symbolic of a fundamental division that could not be integrated into the concept of the indivisible nation (Robcis, 2013). French Republicanism therefore developed into a political model that promoted the equality and freedom of the individual in the public sphere and promoted the patriarchal family as the institutional model for the private sphere (Commaille, 1993).

The association of the Catholic Church with the monarchy and its defence of hereditary privilege attracted the wrath of the revolutionaries and their political descendants, the Republicans. The Church was involved in politics, gaining influence during the restorations of the monarchy in the nineteenth century and losing it when Republican constitutions were in place. However, even when weak in terms of influence within political structures, the Church could still exert direct influence over the populace, particularly through its social roles in charitable works and education (Lenoir, 2003). Following the collapse of the Empire of Napoleon III precipitated by the defeat of the French in the Franco-Prussian War in 1871, the Third Republic began. This was an era in which secular Republicans gained power in national and local politics. One of the reactions of the Catholic Church to its loss of political power was to devote more effort to the cause of the family, which became a "symbol and means" of "political conservatism" and "revival of morality" (Lenoir, 1991, p. 146). The hope was that if more traditional family forms could be encouraged, they would eventually lead to a change in political structure.

In the years before the First World War, a Republican natalist narrative held sway among policy stakeholders and philanthropists as regards solutions to the demographic problems of the country. The natalists based their opinions on scientific studies in demography and believed raising the

French birth rate was vital to increasing French military and economic strength, particularly in comparison with Germany (Lenoir, 1991). They were primarily concerned with number of births and tended to be indifferent to moral concerns about family forms or to working-class women's employment. They did not believe that increasing the birth rate and reducing infant mortality were incompatible with women's employment. Indeed, their overriding interest in the economic and military strength of France meant that they needed as large a workforce as possible. Women therefore had to produce babies, but also needed to be employed as and when required (Jenson, 1986). In 1906, 37 per cent of the labour force was composed of women. Of the 7.6 million women who were economically active, 2 million worked in industry and 2.1 million worked in the tertiary sector (Tilly & Scott, 1987, p. 142).

Although most employed women were single, married working-class women in France were slower to withdraw from the labour market than in comparable countries such as Germany and Britain (Tilly & Scott, 1987), particularly in Paris and in textile towns such as Lille, and a significant minority of women continued to work after childbirth (Reynolds, 1990). This tacit acceptance of women's and mothers' employment by the natalists was shared by the French labour movement. Whereas in some countries, the labour movement was dominated by trades unions with their roots in guilds that sought to protect the interests of particular trades and occupations and worked to remove women from the labour force as part of campaigns for a male family wage, the French labour movement was committed to class revolution. Consequently, the *Confédération Génerale du Travail (CGT)* chose to organise employed women rather than block them from participation in paid labour (Jenson, 1986). It should be noted that employment was not synonymous with women's independence and liberation at this time. Until 1965 married women were treated as minors as regards their civil rights and their husbands controlled their finances. The normative expectations around marriage meant that for most women, wage-earning was for the family and not for themselves and as such, not a source of emancipation.

The French state supported working mothers at this time in two ways: by providing paid maternity leave and by providing childcare in the form of crèches and through nursery schooling within the state education system. Health campaigners, philanthropists and demographers had identified that a principal cause of infant mortality was the early return of working-class mothers to work after childbirth and the resulting inadequate care for very young babies. By the beginning of the twentieth century, many European countries had enacted legislation to prohibit women from working in industry around the time of childbirth, sometimes as part of a wider strategy to remove women from the workplace more comprehensively and informed by a narrative that motherhood and employment were not compatible (Jenson, 1986). Consequently, none provided wage-replacement benefits for maternity leave. France was a latecomer to enacting legislation to remove women from industry around the time of childbirth, an indicator of the reluctance to limit women's employment on the part of the Republican state. In 1909, women were given the opportunity, but not obliged to take up to eight weeks' unpaid maternity leave (Armengaud, 1973). However, in 1913 France became the first European country to introduce paid maternity leave at the rate of 50 per cent of salary, the accompaniment to making the leave compulsory (Jenson, 1986). This payment represented a recognition that women's earnings were necessary to the family. The payment also symbolised the recognition that the leave was temporary and not part of a wider plan to take women out of the labour force. Jenson (1986, p. 19) notes that in the parliamentary debate on this legislation, although there were opposing voices as concerns the payment of the leave, few "wanted to discourage or forbid women to engage in paid labour that they might bear more and healthier children".

The provision of both crèches and nursery schools in France had grown out of the social welfare actions of the Catholic Church in the nineteenth century. From the beginning of industrialisation, employed working-class mothers had to rely on girl children or women relatives who did not have a place in the labour market to care for very young children during working hours, but where such kin support was not available, they used *nourrices*[3] (wet nurses) (Coulon & Cresson, 2013). It is estimated that up to 20 per cent of infants in Paris in 1913 were in the care of wet nurses (Reynolds, 1990, p. 176). Wet nurses often worked in insanitary conditions or provided the babies only with cows' milk and were viewed as a significant factor in high infant mortality rates by philanthropists. Philanthropic efforts on the part of social Catholic organisations therefore sought to replace the wet nurses with crèches on the grounds of child welfare (Morgan, 2002). The first crèche was opened in the 1840s in Paris. By 1913 there were 113 crèches in Paris, and workplace crèches

[3] *Nourrice* is used today as a colloquial term for a childminder.

began to emerge in towns such as Lille (Reynolds, 1990, p. 177). When women were called into munitions factories in the First World War crèches gained prominence in public discourse. Provision of crèches began to move to local authority control at this time, this development being part of the ideational struggle between Republicans and the Catholic Church. Local authority provision of crèches was supported by Republicans in order to undermine the power of the Church.

The Catholic Church had also run institutions originally known as *salles d'asile* (refuge halls) throughout the nineteenth century, the first being opened in Paris in 1826 (Morgan, 2002). In similarity to crèches, the *salles d'asile* were institutions providing support for working-class children of any age, rather than just for infants, who were left alone when their parents were at work. However, over the course of the nineteenth century the middle classes increasingly sent their young children to the *salles d'asile* for a moral education. When the Republicans took power in the 1870s, one of their principal objectives was to break the hold of the Catholic Church on the family and on education. This objective informed the introduction in 1879 of a national education system making schooling compulsory and free for children between the ages of seven and thirteen. Importantly from the point of view of parenting and childcare work, free nursery schools for children below the mandatory school age were also created at this time where there was local demand, often by integrating the *salles d'asile* into the state education system. This strategy of incorporating nursery provision into the national education system was seen in other Catholic countries with anticlerical governments in this period (Morgan, 2002). In the school year 1882–1883, although in principle under the jurisdiction of local authorities, 71.5 per cent of *écoles maternelles* were run by members of the Church. However, further Republican reforms sought to replace these Church members with anticlerical Republican inspectors. By the academic year 1912–1913, only two per cent of children were in church-run nursery schools (Prost, 1981, p. 153).

The fact of being part of the institutional framework of the national education system, and their history of providing education for middle-class children and not primarily as childminding facilities, protected nursery schools over the long term. The National Education Ministry has been one of the most powerful national bureaucracies in the country (Morgan, 2002; Reynolds, 1990). This institutionalisation of early years education is a key factor in the historical legacies influencing present-day childcare and work-family reconciliation in France. Although nursery schools were not established as a source of childcare for working women at their inception and were and have always been used by parents regardless of childcare needs because of their role in educating and socialising young children, they underwent a process of "institutional conversion" (Streeck & Thelen, 2005, p. 21) in the 1970s to act as childcare provision for employed parents when women's employment rates started to rise.

After the First World War and its significant losses of human life compounding existing demographic problems, and later the effects on unemployment of the 1929 crash and ensuing Great Depression, the familialists gained the upper hand over the natalists in France. In contrast to the natalists, the familialists were Catholics who viewed the low birth rate and potential depopulation of the country as evidence of the moral degradation of the country, and the result of the weakening of patriarchal family structures (Pedersen, 1993). The familialist movement subscribed to the Catholic Church social doctrine, set out by Pope Leon XIII's 1891 encyclical De Rerum Novarum that "it is primarily at home, [....] and among domestic occupations, that mothers' work resides" and that "it is therefore a harmful breach, that must at all costs be eradicated, that mothers, because of the father's limited income, are forced to look for paid work outside the house and thus neglect their very special duties, first of which is the education of children" (cited by Collombet, 2021, p. 199). Promotion of large families therefore went hand in hand with the promotion of what were viewed as traditional families structured around a patriarchal head of household and the woman at home responsible for bringing up children and domestic work. In practical policy terms, the efforts of these political actors were focused on obtaining family benefits favouring large families in the first instance, and later single-earner families.

The centrist and conservative post-First World War government, known as *Chambre Bleu Horizon*,[4] was receptive to these arguments. Among the deputies were members of the Alliance nationale pour l'accroissement de la population française *(*ANLPM*)* created in 1896, who called for taxation measures to increase fertility. The principle at the centre of this movement was the idea of equal burdens. Citizens have three responsibilities to the nation: to perpetuate it; to defend it; and to contribute to it through

[4] At the end of the First World War in 1919, 369 deputies were elected for the first time, and the *Bloc national*, an alliance of centrist and conservative forces were in the majority. Many were veterans of the war, led by Georges Clemenceau, who coined the nickname "*Bleu Horizon*" in reference to the blue uniforms of the French army.

taxation. The logic went that if you did not contribute by perpetuating the population, you should compensate for your lack of fertility by paying more tax. In January 1920 the Conseil supérieur de la Natalité (*CSN*) was created with a mission to research all measures needed to combat depopulation (De Luca Barrusse, 2009). The policies which ensued crystallised the symbolic power of the production of the third child to shape policy, a phenomenon that persists in certain family and childcare policies in contemporary France. In 1920 families of three or more children under 16 were allocated daily bread vouchers at reduced prices, and local authorities were funded to pay non-means tested *primes de natalité* (birth benefits) for the third child onwards. In 1923 the *Loi d'Encouragement aux Familles Nombreuses* (Law promoting large families) gave families of three or more children under 13 who did not reach the tax threshold a benefit. The *CSN* also supported the *fête des mères* (Mothers' Day) and the creation in 1920 of a *Médaille de la Famille Française* (French Family Medal) for mothers of five children or more—a bronze medal was awarded to women with five legitimate living children, silver for eight and gold for ten or more (Duchen, 1994). The award was opened up to fathers only in 1983. An equivalent still exists today, entitled the Childhood and Families Medal that can be awarded to foster carers and residential social workers as well as parents and guardians. The incentives and financial support for larger families were accompanied by more repressive measures to increase the birth rate: laws in 1920 and 1923 outlawed abortion, information about contraception and the distribution of contraceptive materials.

Following the 1929 financial crash and the Great Depression with its high levels of unemployment and worsening of the population problem—the mortality rate exceeded the birth rate from 1935 to 1939 (Collombet, 2021)—family policy started to focus on dissuading married women and mothers from remaining in or entering the labour market. After a long struggle the familialists had eventually gained support from a wide spectrum of political and economic interest groups in this regard (Pedersen, 1993). This culminated in the creation of a specific allowance for stay-at-home women in 1938, based on the family allowances for the whole population that had been introduced in 1932. The executive order of 11 November 1938 increased the rate of family allowances for families where the mother did not work, and to finance this measure, allowances for families with only one child were cut. Excluding families with one child from policy provisions, or offering them significantly reduced support, remains a feature of policy today, for example, as regards parental leave benefit entitlement (Collombet, 2021). The 1939 Family Code, voted on the eve of the Second World War, went further and replaced these increased family allowance rates for mothers at home with a specific benefit—the Allocation de la mère au foyer (*AMF*) (benefit for mothers at home). The *AMF* can be considered to be the forerunner of present-day parental leave in France (Collombet, 2021). The *AMF* was only paid to women living in urban areas because it was thought that in rural areas, women could work and look after their children at the same time (Fagnani, 2001). Young couples in agriculture could obtain loans to set up a farm on marriage, the repayments on which would reduce with the birth of each child. There was nothing to repay if you had five children. Family allowances were also increased to represent a significant proportion of average income: 10 per cent for two children, 30 per cent for three, 50 per cent for four and 70 per cent for five. The Code also included tax reductions for those with children (Pedersen, 1993).

Initially at the outbreak of the Second World War, women were recruited to replace men in the labour market. However, with the defeat of 1940 they were laid off. The collaborationist Vichy regime that controlled the south of the country, the north being under Nazi control, started an immediate campaign to raise the birth rate and return women to the home, further glorifying the housewife. In 1940 a law was passed severely restricting the employment of married women and in 1941 the *AMF* was transformed into the Allocation de salaire unique (*ASU*) (benefit for single-earner families), and the benefit level raised. The *ASU* was available for two years after marriage to allow the wife to stay at home in the hope she would produce children quickly. If a child remained an only child at age five, the benefit was lost.

By the 1930s, we see a prelude to the more unified class model of unpaid domestic and care work that would take shape during the *Trente Glorieuses* in France. This was not only because the state was attempting to make it financially possible for lower-earning families to adopt a single-earner model in similarity to the middle classes. This was also because the model of the housewife undertaking most domestic and care duties herself began to make its way up the income and social scale with the number of domestic servants declining in the first decades of the twentieth century. For example, between 1911 and 1921, there was a reduction in live-in domestic servants identified by the census of 15.3 per cent (from 929 548 to 787 385) (MacBride, 1976, p. 112). This was because the supply of domestic servants decreased, and costs increased. There were increasing job opportunities for young single women replacing men lost in the war in factories and in administrative jobs, and in the developing retail sector. Family allowances and other benefits as discussed above also reduced the financial incentive for married women to take on live-out domestic service work. The reduction in labour supply in metropolitan France[5] was not compensated by migration from the French overseas territories and colonies, despite the early twentieth century having seen significant French colonialism. In part, this situation reflects the racist preference of the time for white servants (Beal, 2020), either from the French countryside or from European countries such as Spain or Poland. There was strict state control of colonial citizens coming to the Metropole (Noiriel, 2006). In contrast, in the overseas territories and colonies the entire domestic workforce was composed of people of colour (Stoler, 2013) and colonial civil servants were allowed to bring servants with them to France, but only for a determined period.

The lack of demands to allow colonial migration to fill the gaps in the supply of domestic servants should also be viewed in the light of the reduction in demand for this labour following the financial crash of 1929. The Great Depression that followed severely reduced the ability of households to pay for the level of domestic service they had previously enjoyed. In addition, improvements in domestic technology (Clarke, 2011) alongside the increase in the cost of domestic service labour were changing the balance of the costs and benefits of self-provisioning (Gershuny, 1979). These material changes were supported by ideational developments. In the 1930s cultural narratives that sought to establish norms and a theoretical framework around the middle-class home without servants and the acceptability of middle-class women undertaking practical household work for themselves were promoted by members of the Taylorist domestic science movement such as Paulette Bernège through domestic science lessons in schools and articles in women's magazines (Clarke, 2011; Duchen, 1994). These narratives elevated the status of domestic and care work, encouraging the acquisition of Taylorist techniques for rationalising one's own domestic work with the help of technology. In these ways, the conditions

[5] La *France Metropolitaine* (Metropolitan France) is the part of the French Republic that is situated in Europe, in contrast to la *France d'Outre Mer* (Overseas France) which are the departments and territories situated outside France as a result of colonialism.

were prepared that would lead to the dominance of a more unified model across the social spectrum in which married women undertook domestic and care work unpaid, with the support of state services for education and healthcare, and technology for domestic work during the *Trente Glorieuses*.

The *Trente Glorieuses*: The Rise and Fall of the Breadwinner-Homemaker Model, Fordism and the Welfare State

During the *Trente Glorieueses,* the breadwinner—homemaker model of a different-sex married couple in which men were employed in the public sphere and women stayed at home in the private sphere undertaking most domestic and care work themselves became dominant across the population. The year 1962 was the year with the lowest percentage of women in the labour force in France in the twentieth century at 34 per cent (Duchen, 1994, p. 133). Esping-Andersen (2009, p. 8) has termed this social contract the "post-war equilibrium". Time-use studies of the 1940s (Stoetzel, 1948) and 1950s (Girard, 1958; Girard & Bastide, 1958) revealed just how demanding the role of full-time homemaker was. The 1947 time-use study of urban women found that a woman without children devoted 47 hours a week to domestic and care work, and with 3 children, 76 hours (Stoetzel, 1948, p. 52 Table 1). The objective of these studies was to ascertain the economic value of the unpaid work of women, and to compare urban and rural women at a time when many families were leaving the land and agriculture to relocate to cities. These studies demonstrate the early interest of the French state in the economic value of unpaid work.

Economic factors explain much of the spread of the breadwinner-homemaker model through the population. Rapid industrialisation and urbanisation during this period, encouraged by the state planning system[6] (Lagarve, 1983), led to the decline of the rural peasant family structure and lifestyle as increasing numbers of rural dwellers migrated to the towns, and integrated into the working class (Mendras, 1991). Between 1955 and 1980 the percentage of workers active in agriculture had more than halved from 5.5 million to 2.7 million (Barthez, 1986, p. 209). This industrialisation of France was taking place within the context of Fordism.

[6]The *Commissariat General du Plan* was created in 1945 and charged with drawing up five-year indicative and incentive-based plans to orientate state investments into priority sectors in agreement with the social partners

Fordism encapsulates the relationship between a way of organising mass production (large-scale Taylorist assembly lines) and a type of economic regulation (Keynesian demand-side management) which increases productivity and distributes a greater share of the wealth created to workers to facilitate mass consumption of, for example, cars, standardised household goods or leisure services (McDowell, 1991). The wage growth characteristic of Fordism meant that more households could rely on one family wage earned by the husband meaning that working-class women could stay at home as dependents of their husbands to take responsibility for unpaid domestic and care work and replicate the lifestyle of the middle-class housewife.

The gender politics of the time fitted with this model of economic dependency of married women. Women did not enjoy full equality in terms of their civil rights or economic independence for most of this period despite the constitution of the Fourth Republic[7] enshrining the principle of equality between men and women and giving women the vote in 1944. Until 1965 elements of the Napoleonic Civil Code remained in force, such as married women being treated as minors and not having control of their finances, as discussed in the previous section. Paternal authority over the children of a marriage was only abolished in 1970. The laws on contraception enacted in the 1920s remained in force until 1967, and abortion until 1975. French society in this period was characterised by early marriage and first births, and low rates of divorce, singlehood, and childlessness.

The construction of the welfare state in France following the Second World War was based on state familialism, that is, the defence of the interests of the family through the formation of institutions and state bureaucracies charged with this mission, that had been developing since the 1920s. These institutions were important in promoting the single-earner family model during much of the *Trente Glorieuses* and continued to influence work-family reconciliation policy subsequently. The family and family policy were placed at the heart of the welfare state and social security system. Distributive mechanisms transferred wealth between individuals with and without children, more than between rich and poor (Debord, 2020). At the beginning of the period, family policy was still heavily influenced by

[7] The Third Republic ended with the Occupation and Vichy Regime in 1940. The Fourth Republic is the constitution that was introduced after the Liberation and continued until 1958.

familialist pronatalism (King, 1998). In a speech on 5 March 1945 President de Gaulle told the French people that France needed 12 million babies in the next 10 years and supported legislation aimed at helping large families. Although not all politicians expressed their natalist views in such a direct way for fear of replicating too closely the rhetoric of the Vichy regime, there was widespread consensus about the need to strengthen the population (Reynolds, 1990). A discourse held sway that the German occupation would not have happened if France had been stronger demographically, echoing narratives that had developed following earlier military defeats.

Nearly all politicians, activists and interest groups agreed that the best way of supporting families and increasing the birth rate was to give women and mothers the means to stay at home (Duchen, 1994). A range of measures was enacted in the first 15 years of the *Trente Glorieuses* to make the homemaker model more affordable for working-class families and to encourage multiple births. The *ASU* was translated from the Vichy regime to the Fourth Republic by the Law of 4 October 1945 and its rate increased. The *quotient familial* (family quotient) was introduced into the taxation system to lower income tax in relation to the number of children in the family. Family allowances were extended for the first time to families with no economically active members and regardless of whether children were legitimate or of French nationality. Until 1962, family benefits for couples with at least two children made it economically rational for women to remain out of the workforce (Fagnani, 2001).

Furthermore, the welfare state created a powerful corporatist institutional structure around the family which gave and continues to give political opportunities to particular stakeholders, such as family associations. These structures have acted as a barrier to influences from other stakeholders, such as feminist lobbies in later years. A decree of 3 March 1945 gave the *Union nationale des associations familiales* (*UNAF)* (National Union of Family Associations) an institutional role within the corporatist structure of the French social security system to represent families and exclusive rights to represent all family organisations in the country with public authorities at the national and local level. The *UNAF* represents over 100 organisations but has been dominated by Catholic family associations (Minonzio & Vallat, 2006). The *UNAF* constituted a very powerful lobby in the 1950s with delegates on the administration of the social security board, the family allowance board, and other national consultative bodies. The *UNAF* has been regularly asked by Parliament for its opinion on all family matters (Minonzio & Vallat, 2006) and remains a powerful force in childcare policy and family policy to this day (Debord, 2020). Other bodies created at the time were explicitly pronatalist in their missions. For example, in October 1945, the *Institut National d'Etudes Démographiques* (*INED*) (National Institute for Demographic Research) was created with a mission to increase quantitatively and improve qualitatively the population and ensure the diffusion of demographic knowledge (Drouard, 1992). Alfred Sauvy, its founder, supported the widely held view that gender roles were "established in nature" (cited in Duchen, 1991, p. 7) and that a young woman's vocation was marriage, home and motherhood.

The Fordist social contract, the welfare state and social trends in the post-war period combined to further reduce the supply of labour for domestic service. The trend for early marriage, and the development of jobs in other parts of the service sector, such as retail, office work, health and education, further decreased the pool of young, single women prepared to work as live-in domestic servants. Moreover, the Fordist male family wage alongside family welfare benefits reduced the number of married women willing to undertake low-paid work as daily helps. The cost of home-based housekeeping services rose, making the hiring of help more and more socially exclusive and reducing the amount of help that could be purchased. Middle-class women could no longer afford live-in servants, even if they continued to have some daily or weekly help with heavier domestic tasks in the earlier part of the period: in the 1950s many middle-class housewives still had help for washing and cleaning, often in the absence of technology. The *INED* time-use study of married women in 1947 showed that 80 per cent of households in the liberal professions had paid help at that time, allowing middle-class housewives to devote their time to tidying, making beds, cooking and supervising children, activities defined as the "crowning glory of a woman's work" (Duchen, 1994, p. 82). With little regulation of migration during this period, migrant workers provided a domestic workforce with surveys in 1968 and 1975 showing that that workers from Portugal and North Africa, particularly Morocco, had replaced the Spanish and Polish as domestic service personnel (Moulier & Silberman, 1982).

A new form of paid domestic and care services emerged in the post-war period to respond to the needs of adults, in particular, the elderly with LTC needs. Increased life expectancy and better public health and healthcare in this period meant that more people could live with ongoing health conditions that required direct or indirect care. However, with the demise of the multi-generational rural family, and extension of pensions after the war, elderly people were more likely to remain living in their own household rather than with adult children or other extended family members than in previous eras. Furthermore, particularly with the increased geographical mobility of the workforce they could no longer necessarily rely on informal kin networks for care and support as they may have done in the past. Therefore, this period saw the rise of the phenomenon of elderly people in need of care living alone. Although much of this care was provided by kin, mainly by daughters, daughters-in-law or other female relatives who remained outside the labour market, local authorities began to provide institutional and home-based care services for this population (Debonneuil & Lahidji, 1998). After the war, associative networks had begun to develop social services to households in France to respond to these needs, providing *aides à domicile* (home helps). These associative initiatives were gradually taken under the auspices of the state. To guarantee a certain level of quality of service within the state sector, new qualifications developed for these workers, and sector-level collective agreements were concluded (Debonneuil & Lahidji, 1998).

Not only was the breadwinner-homemaker model constructed on the basis of the Fordist social contract and a pronatalist and familialist welfare state in France after the Second World War. This model was also reinforced by cultural gender norms expressed in public discourses in the media, advertising and politics. Political discourse lauded the noble pursuit of the housewife in creating a better life for her family rather than pursuing financial gain for herself. Women were told that they were indispensable and were contributing to the household income by staying at home and saving the cost of services that would have to be paid for if they were not there to do them. Furthermore, the figure of the ordinary housewife was presented as a social leveller, a unifying force of common goals and aspirations for material comfort and family happiness. There was little opposition to the model of the housewife and mother at home in the 1950s, and dissatisfaction with housework was not addressed. This included even the Communist Party who did not want to appear hostile to stay-at-home women and their families, the family wage being a symbol of working-class victory (Duchen, 1994).

By the early 1960s the success of earlier pronatalist policies and the positive effects of post-war prosperity on the birth rate alongside a tightening labour market meant that planners began to look at married women as potential employees and started to move away from the active promotion of the homemaker model. As discussed in the previous section, pronatalism in its Republican form had not precluded women from fulfilling a role as employee alongside that of parent (Collombet, 2021). Furthermore, the survival of the rural family model into the mid-twentieth century normalised the contribution of women to economic activity as family helpers on farms. In 1955 the government of Prime Minister Mendes-France called for the reform of the *ASU* and encouragement of part-time work for married women. The *ASU* was the policy most explicitly aimed at keeping married women and mothers out of the workforce and was therefore viewed as an impediment to easing labour shortages (Martin, 2008). One of the stated aims of the 1958 time-use study by the *INED* was to assess the extent to which married women's labour power could be liberated from the home for use in the labour market (Girard & Bastide, 1958). In *CGP* Plans for the late 1950s and early 1960s the question of childcare arose, as did issues around what would come to be termed work-family reconciliation. The *CGP* recommended in the Third (1958–1961) and Fourth (1962–1965) plans that early childhood care facilities should be developed and savings from reforms to the *ASU* used to finance them.

The objectives for women's labour-market participation of the Third and Fourth Plans were not met, however, even if there were modest increases in women's labour-force participation rates from the mid-1960s onwards (Marchand, 2010). Furthermore, the *ASU* survived but was made more restrictive in 1959 and allowed to reduce in value in real terms from 1962 onwards to the extent that it no longer acted as a real financial incentive for mothers of two children to remain inactive by the end of the decade (Martin, 2008). The *ASU* remained of value only to those women with larger families or who were the least qualified and skilled, the two groups who still have lower economic activity rates in France today. The *ASU* was eventually abolished in 1978 but continued to produce echoes in the parental leave policies developed in the 1980s and 1990s. The lack of success of the Third and Fourth Plans in increasing women's employment rates substantially and the survival of the *ASU*, even in reduced form, has been explained by the cultural strength and popularity of the housewife model as a symbol of prosperity in this period and by the strength of the family lobby within the state bureaucracy (Fagnani, 2001).

Nursery school did expand during the 1950s but more on the basis of their educational function than as childcare provision, although the two are not mutually exclusive. They were supported by a strong political consensus spanning Left and Right. Middle- and upper-income parents began to demand places for their children for pedagogical reasons and the Ministry for Education made every effort to meet growing demand. Highly unionised teachers also pressured the Ministry to expand access to nursery schools (Morgan, 2002). By 1960, 91 per cent of five-year-olds, 63 per cent of four-year-olds, and 35 per cent of three-year-old children were attending a free nursery school from 8.30 in the morning until 4 or 4.30 in the afternoon (Fagnani, 2001, p. 150). By the 1970s, the French nursery school had become a universal right of citizenship and played a significant part in allowing both parents of younger children to participate in the labour force.

From the end of the 1960s, proponents of married women participating in the labour force were starting to gain the upper hand in France. Continued economic growth, particularly in feminised areas of the service sector, required more women in the labour market. The dominant view of the mother at home started to become that of a luxury that the country could no longer afford. The core domestic work tasks of cleaning, laundry and food preparation had become less time-consuming by this era. This was due to the increased availability and affordability of domestic appliances (e.g., the refrigerator, vacuum cleaner and semi-automatic washing machine), more easy-care materials (e.g., nylon and Formica), and expansion of the range of end-consumption goods (off-the-peg clothing; ready-made food) that was replacing unpaid production. This meant that women who did not have direct care responsibilities for children because they were at school, or indeed for adults, were not considered to have a full-time occupation in domestic work. Although family associations and the *UNAF* still supported women staying at home to look after pre-school-age children, even the most conservative among them accepted that they could work outside the home without harm whilst children were at school (Debord, 2020).

At the same time as economic factors were undermining the breadwinner-homemaker model, cultural gender norms had also started to question women's vocation as homemaker. The boredom of being a housewife as discussed in Betty Friedan's book *The Feminine Mystique* resonated in France (Duchen, 1994). For example, Michel's 1966 study on women's professional status and its impact on the urban couple took as its starting point the hypothesis that women's employment was a key factor in the restructuring of the couple towards greater equality in decision-making and in domestic and care tasks. Following the events of May 1968, this dissatisfaction crystallised into a political lobby. The *Mouvement pour la liberation des femmes (MLF) (Women's liberation movement)* had as its political ideology second-wave feminism, inspired by the much earlier writings of Simone de Beauvoir (1989 [1952]) which rested on a set of fundamental principles: men and women only exist as social categorisations in relation to one another; nature is not an explanatory concept for gender differences; and the material basis of women's oppression is embedded in the mode of domestic production which confronts two patriarchal classes—men and women (Dunezat, 2016). Feminist theorists and activists therefore began to emphasise the contribution of women to society through their unpaid work in the home for the family at the same time as arguing that in order to gain liberation, women needed to be freed from domestic and care work and confinement in the private sphere (Dussuet, 2017).

By 1972, these combined social, economic and political pressures had translated into policy change. The Law of 3 January 1972 created the *Allocation de Frais de Garde* (Childcare expense allowance) for two-parent dual-earner families, or single-parent families in employment to sit alongside the *ASU*. The benefit covered the actual costs incurred in childcare up to a ceiling that was the equivalent of the monthly value of the *ASU*. In this way, family policy in France decisively moved away from a paradigm of support for the single-earner family alone and towards the paradigm that would inform policy until the 2010s and influence the organisation and divisions of labour of domestic and care work. This paradigm was based on two premises: first, the equal support by the state for families where one parent stays at home to look after pre-school-age children and for families where both parents are employed; and second, the implicit understanding that women have a natural role in parenting and caring more generally but can be enabled to engage in employment by the state assuming some aspects of this role (Chauffaut & Lévêque, 2012).

The End of the Twentieth Century: Post-Fordism, the Woman-State Contract, and the Development of Personal and Household Services

In the late 1960s and early 1970s, the emerging political ideologies and cultural norms in France around women's right to be present in the public sphere and the labour market, free from the constraints of the patriarchal family, had coincided with the need for women's labour power in the growing French economy. However, France was confronted by an economic critical juncture in the mid-1970s in the shape of the 1973–1974 oil crisis, or first oil shock.[8] The oil crisis was a catalyst in a far-reaching economic restructuring that would impact the organisation and divisions of labour of domestic and care work. This economic shock did not result in the removal of women from the labour market as had occurred in previous eras when jobs became scarce or even in rolling back the small advances in their employment participation rates that had been made in the late 1960s and early 1970s. Rather, the economic restructuring that followed the oil crisis led to the demise of the working-class family wage, and hastened the disappearance of the single-earner family model and French women's confinement to the homemaker role.

The oil crisis precipitated the decline of manufacturing and mass production in traditional industries in France, and thus a reduction in demand for semi- and unskilled industrial manual workers, who were in the majority men. Many of the jobs that replaced those lost in manufacturing for lower-skilled workers were in low-paid services in traditionally feminised sectors such as the retail, hospitality and care sectors. The lack of well-paid occupations in manufacturing for lower-skilled men brought about the demise of the family wage. Coupled with the reductions in the real value of family benefits (see above), this made dual-earning in lower-skilled couples increasingly necessary from a financial viewpoint. Furthermore, changes in family structures were coming about following modifications to divorce and birth-control legalisation and in social norms concerning family formation. These resulted in more single-person and single-parent households. For example, in 1980 the marriage rate was 6.2 but had almost halved to 3.6 by 2013 whereas the divorce rate increased from 1.6 to 1.9 over the same period.[9] Taken together, these labour market and social changes meant that fewer women could rely on a male breadwinner (Gross, 2015). Changes in gender norms meant that they did not necessarily want to do so (McDowell, 1991).

[8] Between October 1973 and March 1974, the Organisation of Petroleum Exporting Countries (OPEC) imposed an export embargo on oil to states that had supported Israel in the Yom Kippur War. This caused oil prices to rise sharply and caused severe recession throughout the Western world. The first oil shock heralded the end of the *Trente Glorieuses* and beginning of the period of economic restructuring in the West that saw manufacturing in traditional industries and of mass consumption goods move to other global regions.

[9] This is the number of inhabitants of metropolitan France out of 1000 who marry or divorce in a given year. https://www.insee.fr/fr/statistiques/1906665?sommaire=1906743

Not all workers displaced from manufacturing were able to find alternative employment. Over this period, the unemployment rate in France increased very significantly, and remained high in comparison with competitor countries for the ensuing decades. During the *Trente Glorieuses*, there had been full employment for much of the time. In 1974 the unemployment rate was 2.5 per cent.[10] Unemployment began to rise rapidly after the oil crisis, exceeding one million in 1977 (4.3 per cent of the workforce) and rising to two million in 1984 (8.4 per cent of the workforce). Unemployment rates hit nine per cent in 1987 and exceeded ten per cent on a number of occasions thereafter (Marchand & Minni, 2019, p. 91). However, these figures should be contextualised within the rates of economic inactivity of married women. In 1968 52 per cent of women aged 20–59 were economically inactive, a percentage that had fallen to 12 per cent by 2018.[11] Unemployment became one of the primary problems facing French governments, and eventually became more important than pronatalism as an influence in the construction of work-family reconciliation policy (Fagnani, 2001).

Due to the problem of unemployment following the oil crisis, labour migration stopped. To allow those workers already in France to settle, a policy entitled *regroupement familial* (family reunification) was implemented in November 1977. Family members, in the majority women, were allowed to join a breadwinner in France but were prohibited from gaining a work permit (Lebon, 1978). This situation lasted until 1984 (Chaib, 2008). The only work that was open to these family members was therefore undeclared (Moulier & Silberman, 1982). In 1982 and 1984 mass regularisations were undertaken of these undocumented migrants, 20 per cent of whom were women of whom over 40 per cent were working in domestic services (Laacher, 1998, p. 17).

As the economy moved away from mass production and demand for low-skilled labour in manufacturing declined, reducing employment opportunities for men, demand for highly skilled workers in the technological and knowledge economy grew. Highly educated women were able to join this workforce, benefitting from their investments in education and training (McDowell, 1991). Since reforms in the early 1960s that rid the

[10] This level is viewed as full employment and represents the number of people moving jobs and registering as unemployed on a short-term basis

[11] https://www.insee.fr/fr/statistiques/6047795?sommaire=6047805&q=femmes+emploi+enfants

education system in France of the vestiges of unequal treatment of boys and girls, women's human capital and qualification levels had risen considerably (Duru-Bellat, 1990). When entering into couples, these women often partnered with someone of similar professional standing. This expanding service class experienced rising salaries which they used to pay for services to facilitate their lifestyle, including a range of domestic outsourcing services (Gregson & Lowe, 1994).

In 1975, women composed only 36 per cent of the workforce, a figure that had risen to 39 per cent by 1982 and 44 per cent by 1991 (Marchand, 2010, p. 2). This increased participation in employment by women led to a reduction in their time availability for unpaid domestic and care work and increased their bargaining power to reduce their unpaid workload in comparison with men in their households if living in different-sex couples, leading to some equalisation of the gender division of unpaid labour. Between 1974 and 1986, women reduced the time they devoted to domestic and care work by four hours, and men increased theirs by three hours per week (Roy, 2011, p. 20). To facilitate these changes in women's relationship to the home and the labour market, the use of paid services for domestic and care tasks began to increase but on a different basis from the early twentieth century. Women were supported by the state through work-family reconciliation, LTC and PHS policies. By 2003 France had the highest proportion of dual-earner full-time working couples in the EU15, with 58 per cent of couples with at least one dependent child being in that category in comparison with 12 per cent of equivalent families in the UK, for example (Paihle & Solaz, 2008, p. 221). As Lewis et al. (2008, p. 264) in their comparison of France, Germany, the Netherlands, and the UK note: "France .... [had] one of the lowest gender employment gaps in Western Europe because women [were] more likely to be working full-time".

The principal reason for the spread of the dual-earner family in France was that by the international standards of the time, France had a significant and long-standing range of support in place for work-family reconciliation. This support took the form of in-kind provision (low-cost local authority crèches; free nursery schools) and cash-for-care benefits for childcare. By the end of the 1980s, a significant proportion of unpaid parenting work for very young children had been transformed into paid childcare work. By 1986, out of a population of 2.2 million children under three, 80,000 attended a classic, collective local authority run crèche, a figure that had increased from fewer than 17,000 full-time crèche places in 1960 and 30,000 in 1970 (David & Lezine, 1975, p. 72). A further 40,000 children were in *crèches familiales*;[12] 196,000 children were with childminders and 12,000 in a private kindergarten (*INSEE*, 1986). Due to the budgetary challenges for the welfare state brought about by economic restructuring and high unemployment, in the late 1980s and through the 1990s, policy to expand childcare provision for the under threes focused on new cash-for-care benefits to support parents paying childminders or home-based child carers through individualised direct employment rather than investing in new collective facilities. In 1986 the *Allocation de garde: employé à domicile* (*AGED*) (Childcare benefit: at-home employees) and in 1990 the *Allocation des frais de l'emploi d'une aide maternelle agréée* (*AFEAMA*) (Benefit for costs of employing a registered childminder) were introduced to subsidise the costs of individualised home-based childcare for children under six.

Throughout the latter part of the twentieth century and into the twenty-first century, work-family reconciliation policy in France was enacted within a frame of state familialism rather than of state feminism, that is, with the aim of responding to demands from the feminist movement to "produce feminist outcomes" in policy through women's policy agencies (McBride & Mazur, 2010, p. 64). Consequently, policy was shaped by the ideational frame of what could be described as a woman-state contract designed to relieve women of enough of their caring responsibilities by the provision and subsidy of care services to allow them to participate in the labour force rather than to be a catalyst of change in the gendered distribution of unpaid care and domestic work (Lewis et al., 2008; White, 2004). Due to the strength of state familialism, and the legacy of the natalists of the early twentieth century, the introduction of work-family reconciliation policies in France did not depend on the strength of feminist political actors or the existence of opportunity structures that would give them access to influence. Consequently, such policies could develop earlier in France than in many other Conservative states. The familialist framing of these policies garnered a wide partisan consensus spanning the bureaucratic family policy-making elite, organised interests such as family associations and women's groups, and indeed from the public (Bonoli, 2013; White, 2004). Even conservative stakeholders did not want to make women choose between employment and having

[12] This is a form of care combining home-based services provided by childminders, and collective care resulting from childminders working collaboratively with the local authority.

(more) children, lest they should choose employment. However, the lack of strong feminist underpinnings for work-family reconciliation policy in France made it vulnerable to be shaped by other agendas such as unemployment reduction, and entrenched traditional divisions of unpaid domestic and care work. Revillard (2006, p. 21) terms this situation the "French paradox".

Pronatalism had lost influence during the 1960s following the success of the post-war baby boom (King, 1998). However, the birth rate had dropped below the replacement rate of two children by 1976 and was only 1.87 by 1979.[13] Pronatalism started to re-emerge as an ideational driver in work-family reconciliation policy at this time. Similar groups of actors concerned with encouraging births earlier in the century instigated a pronatalist revival that peaked in the mid-1980s. Demographers and other intellectuals, using highly emotive language, declared that France was committing "*autogenicide*" (self-inflicted genocide) (Jobert, 1976) or "collective suicide" (Fourastie, 1979). Researchers from the prestigious *INED* published works such as *Marianne's Empty Cradles* (Biraben & Dupaquier, 1981) and *France's Tragedy* (Dumont & Sauvy, 1983). This group argued that the French welfare state would not be able to pay retirement and health benefits to its growing elderly population without a young workforce. In addition, the rise of the far-right *Front National* party during the 1980s focused debate on French national identity, culture and language, and national strength represented by a numerous French-born population to reduce reliance on migration. These pronatalism concerns informed the development of policy towards parental leave in the 1980s.

The support for childcare in the 1970s had been accompanied by equal support for parents (usually women) looking after their own very young children at home. From 1972 the *Allocation de Frais de Garde* and the *ASU* had existed alongside one another until being replaced by a single benefit, the *Complément familial* (CF) (family top-up allowance) (Martin, 2010). This allowance was given to families regardless of their employment status. The abolition of the *ASU* opened the door to the possibility of introducing an updated version of support for parents with children under nursery-school age for temporary withdrawal from the labour market. The *Congé parental d'éducation (CPE)* (parental leave) was first introduced into the Labour Code in 1977. The policy gave parents the right to

[13] https://www.insee.fr/fr/statistiques/serie/000436391

suspend their work contract for a maximum of two years with a guarantee to return to the same job or to a similar one with similar pay. Initially, the policy was aimed at mothers, with fathers only being able to take the leave if the mother waived her rights to it or was not eligible. Access was equalised between mothers and fathers in 1984 and the period of leave extended to three years. The 1984 reform added the possibility of half-time working and in 1991 the possibility of part-time working from 16 hours per week to an 80 per cent contract was put in place (Martin, 2010).

In its first years of operation, this right to parental leave in France did not attract financial support from the state. This changed in 1985 when the Socialist government introduced a wage-replacement benefit to supplement the right to parental leave—the *Allocation d'éducation parentale* (*APE*) (parental Leave benefit). However, not all parents were eligible to draw the benefit. It was reserved for the third and subsequent children of the family (Jenson & Sineau, 1995). Furthermore, the *APE* had two characteristics that reinforced traditional gendered caring roles in the family. First, the benefits were paid at a low flat rate, replacing less than 15 per cent of average earnings (OECD, 2014). When parental leave is paid at a flat rate, rather than indexed on previous salary, it makes it much more likely that the lower earner in a couple, mostly usually the woman in different-sex partnerships, takes the leave. Second, the benefit was payable for up to three years per child. Long parental leaves taken by women reinforce gender specialisation in domestic and care work and entrench a traditional gendering of caregiving roles (Moss & Deven, 2015). Furthermore, such absence from the labour market has long-term negative impacts on women's subsequent employment careers due to skills attrition and negative impacts on their human capital. Long paid parental leaves also have a symbolic and ideological effect in that they suggest that women's place is with the young child in the home. As Dex (2010, p. 85) asserts "[a]s soon as policies to allow or promote women to behave differently in terms of their employment participation or their hours of work are implemented, inequalities in the home and in domestic contributions are likely to emerge".

The reservation of the benefit for the third child makes clear the pronatalist inspiration of the policy. This was surprising as President Mitterrand's government had promised to modernise family policy and introduce non-patriarchal family legislation when it was elected in 1981. Electoral pressure from the successes of the *Front National* in the early 1980s played a part in this change of approach, as did support for the policy from the

Catholic-influenced family associations (Fagnani, 2000). The *APE* was denounced by feminist groups as a mothers' wage in disguise and a tool with which to remove women from the labour market to reduce unemployment. Revillard (2006) argues that the *APE* was constructed in a way that reinforced gender stereotypes both as regards employment and unpaid domestic and care work because feminist stakeholders found it difficult to influence work-family reconciliation policy due to the institutional structures in which it developed, namely within ministries and agencies charged with the family rather than those charged with women's equality. The governmental bodies that were created to promote women's equality in the late 1970s and through the 1980s by both Left and Right focused on the workplace and training, rather than on the home and family (Mazur, 1995). This was particularly the case for the 1982 Ministry for Women's Rights, under the Socialist Minister Yvette Roudy, which had a major influence on shaping succeeding structures (Lenoir, 2003). These bodies shied away from trying to compete with the powerful family-focused institutions, impregnated as they were with familialism and the defence of the family as an institution over and above the rights of women as individuals (Commaille, 1993).

In addition to the continuing influence of pronatalism, work-family reconciliation policy in France began to be influenced by employment policy which sought to de-activate certain sectors of the workforce, including parents of young children in pursuit of the goal of labour-shedding and work-sharing during the 1980s and 1990s (Bonoli, 2013; Martin, 2010). Bonoli (2013) asserts that the French response to the employment crisis of the late 1970s and early 1980s can be qualified as the archetypal version of the labour reduction route followed by Conservative welfare regimes. France looked to a combination of labour force shedding coupled with financial support for the unemployed and subsided employment to tackle the issue. For example, the retirement age was reduced from 65 to 60 in 1981, lowering the employment rate of the 55–64 age group from 74 per cent in 1970 to 47 per cent in 1985 (Morel, 2007, p. 623), and subsidised temporary jobs were created in the public and non-profit sectors.

The Socialist approach to unemployment reduction was also influenced by the *autogestionnaire* (self-management) movement of the 1960s in which key Socialist figures of the time such as Jacques Delors had been very active (Windebank, 1991). Delors argued that the *autogestion* (self-management) of society must be based on the self-regulation of time. It was necessary to reduce employment time to allow the population the freedom to engage in informal economic and leisure activities. Delors and Foucauld (1980, p. xiii) contended that such a revolution in the organisation of time centred on reduction of the working week and part-time work would also be "a successful formula for the sharing out of employment". Thereby unemployment would be reduced (Roustang, 1982). So developed the notion of the *revolution du temps choisi* (the chosen work-time revolution) and work-sharing—the idea that everyone should work less, improving quality of life, but also so that available employment could be better shared as technological advances created jobless growth.

As a practical step towards this goal, in 1982 the Socialist government reduced the statutory working week from 40 to 39 hours,[14] with a promise to reduce it further to 35 hours when economic circumstances allowed. This was achieved in 2002. They also introduced a fifth week of paid leave. More controversial as concerns gendered divisions of paid and unpaid labour was the encouragement of part-time work (Milner, 2010; Martin, 2010; Windebank, 2011). During the 1960s and 1970s, French women on the whole had been integrated into the labour market on a full-time basis because part-time work was not well developed in the country and actively discouraged by the Labour Code and by sectoral agreements. For example, part-time work was not allowed in the public sector until 1970 (Gregory & Windebank, 2000). The right-wing government of President Giscard d'Estaing had started to promote part-time work with the justification that women were calling for part-time options to better reconcile work and family life. This culminated in the Law of 28 January 1981 to facilitate part-time working. Right-wing politicians did not hide their view that part-time work was aimed at women because it fitted with their natural role as mothers and carers (Louis & Loos, 1982). Part-time work was vehemently opposed by feminists at the time who saw it as a retrograde step in women's integration into the workforce (Louis & Loos, 1982). Despite their feminist claims, the Socialists further promoted part-time work in ordinance 82271 of 26 March 1982 under the guise of *le temps choisi*, the gendered impacts of which had not been fully recognised by its proponents. Following these changes in policy, part-time work developed significantly for women in France. In 1983 20 per cent of employed

[14] In France work time is the subject of legal intervention and therefore a high-profile political topic (Gregory, 1991)

women worked part-time. This figure had increased to 30 per cent by the end of the 1990s (Afsa Essafi & Buffeteau, 2006, p. 86).

With the right wing in power in the 1990s, part-time work was further developed as part of an agenda to make the French labour market more flexible. In 1991 all employees were given the right to request a part-time contract. Furthermore, in 1994 the *APE* was extended to parents of two children. It was possible to draw the benefit on a part-time basis. Following this amendment to the *APE*, the employment rate of women with two children reduced significantly: in 1994, women with two children of whom the youngest was under three had an economic activity rate of 70.5 per cent. By 1998 this rate had declined to 55 per cent. This compared with a rate of 80.1 per cent in 1998 for women with one child who were not eligible to draw the *APE*, a figure that had increased from 77.1 per cent in 1994 (Algava et al., 2005, p. 4).

As discussed above, concerns over the birth rate were related in this period to the challenges and long-term care needs of an ageing population, rather than depopulation as had been the case earlier in the century. In 1900, 12.7 per cent of the French population was aged 60 or over, and 2.5 per cent 75 or over. By 1970 this had already increased substantially to 18 per cent over 60 and 4.2 per cent over 75. By the end of the century, a fifth of the population (20.6 per cent) were aged over 60 and 7.2 per cent over 75, almost trebling over the course of the century (*INSEE*, 2018). The changes in family structures brought about by the rural exodus and women's rising employment rates in France had reduced the provision of unpaid care by economically inactive women (Jonsson et al., 2011) creating a care gap. However, although the *CGP*, Parliament and the *Conseil Economique et Social*[15] (Social and Economic Council) were discussing the issues of an ageing population from the 1970s onwards, there was no bespoke policy regarding long-term care for the elderly in France until the 1990s (Martin, 2003). This was because of the Republican framing of policy that avoided the categorisation of French citizens into groups dependent on identities or personal characteristics such as age (Ledoux, 2011).

The needs of the dependent elderly were addressed alongside those of adults of working age with support and care needs. For both groups, the

[15] The *Conseil économique et social* was created in 1958 and is a consultative body that advises the government on economic and social matters. Its mission was revised, and it was renamed the *Conseil économique, social et environnemental* in 2008.

1970s witnessed a policy paradigm shift away from provision of care in institutions and towards care in the home of the recipient. This was justified by the idea that it is better for the social integration of LTC recipients to stay in their own home where possible and for those with care needs to have choice about how these needs are met. Furthermore, this was a less costly method of expanding LTC provision as support was offered through cash-for-care benefits rather than in-kind provision of services by the state. The shift from institutions providing in-kind care services to home-based services supported through cash-for-care benefits created the potential for the family to be implicated more in the practical activities and importantly the management of care for their family members. In this context it is relevant to note that local and national women's groups did not involve themselves in debates about adult care in the same way or to the same extent as they did in debates regarding childcare at the time (Ledoux, 2011).

In 1975, the *Loi d'orientation en faveur des personnes handicapées* (Framework law in favour of disabled persons) had the aim of supporting people with disabilities to live independently and be better integrated into society, and into employment where appropriate (Ennuyer, 2003). Introduced within this framework, the *Allocation compensatrice pour tierce personne* (*ACPT*) (Compensatory benefit for payment of a third party) was a cash-for-care benefit paid to adults with a high degree of incapacity, regardless of age, to cover the costs of having a third party to help with everyday life, whether this was the salary or fee of a professional care provider, or to compensate the loss of earnings of an informal carer, thereby reinforcing the implication of the family in care needs. There was no age criterion attached to the policy. It became increasingly apparent that a single benefit scheme for the elderly and the working-age population with LTC needs was not fit for purpose (Weber, 2010). Local councils noted the steep rise in requests for the *ACTP* as the result of an ageing population, and therefore in the costs of the policy. From the beginning of the 1980s, associations providing home-based care to older people had been lobbying for a service specifically for their constituency and those representing the working-age disabled also wanted a bespoke policy that would focus more on equality and social integration (Ennuyer, 2003). During the discussions on possible solutions to the LTC issue, policymakers on both the Left and the Right were widely agreed that there was a need to limit the cost of any new benefits and that raising social contributions to create a specific insurance scheme was not viable.

In 1997 a distinction was made in social care policy in France on the basis of age for the first time when the right-wing government of Prime Minister Alain Juppé introduced the *Prestation spécifique dependence* (*PDS*) (specific benefit for dependency) for the over 60s who would no longer be eligible for the *ACPT* which continued for the younger age group. The *PSD* defined the concept of *personnes agées dépendantes* (dependent older persons) (Ennuyer, 2003). The *PSD* benefit could be used for at-home care provided either by an organisation or within a direct employment relationship. Members of the family, with the exception of the spouse/partner could be employed. The *PSD* could also be used for residential care and be paid directly to the institution. Costs covered by the *PSD* could be reclaimed from the recipient's estate after their death. Prime Minister Lionel Jospin's Socialist government abolished the inheritance clause in the *PDS* on election.

At the beginning of the 1990s, support for LTC and childcare started to be merged with policies to encourage the use of PHS for domestic services for the general population in an effort to create jobs and reduce undeclared work in the sector (Cette & Diev, 2003). France was the pioneer country in Europe in its promotion of PHS as a new sector of activity and heavily influenced EU policy in this regard. There had been an early recognition by the *CGP* and its research partners such as the *INSEE* and *INED* of the economic potential of transforming unpaid domestic and care work into paid employment, and the interaction of paid and unpaid work in living standards (Jany-Catrice & Méda, 2011). The first attempt at estimating the value in terms of GDP of domestic and care work in France[16] was undertaken in 1981 by Chadeau and Fouquet (1981) on the basis of the first nationally representative *INSEE* time-use study of 1974/5. They calculated that unpaid work was worth between 32 and 77 per cent of GDP depending on the method of calculation (Chadeau & Fouquet, 1981). From the 1990s onwards, a strong political discourse developed around the idea of the commodification of unpaid domestic and care work being a *gisement d'emploi*, particularly for the lower qualified. Although this term might be best translated as "source of employment", the choice of the word *gisement* is significant as it refers to a mineral deposit, evoking the idea that domestic and care services were untapped and latent

[16] The first estimates of the GDP value of unpaid work were carried out at the beginning of the 1930s in Hungary, Italy and Sweden and showed results of between ten and thirty per cent.

opportunities for employment growth waiting to be uncovered (Devetter et al., 2009). Since the oil crisis, unemployment had remained high in France, ranging from 7 to 10.5 per cent of the workforce from 1985 until the end of the century (*INSEE*, 2016). Unemployment was particularly problematic for those with no or few qualifications and for school leavers. In 1990, the unemployment rate of those aged 15–24 was 15.1 per cent and of those without qualifications 11.3 per cent, (compared with the average rate of 7.6 per cent) (*Observatoire des Inégalités*, 2021). The government therefore sought job-creation opportunities for the lower skilled displaced from manufacturing, particularly jobs which could not be outsourced to lower-wage economies, hence the interest in domestic and care services.

The OECD (2012) identified France's unemployment problem as being the result of structural weaknesses in its Coordinated Market Economy (CME) based on the distinctive Republican model which attaches central importance to the state and results in a highly regulated and rigid labour market. The French labour market was, and remains, highly segregated, with a significant polarisation between labour-market insiders protected by these extensive labour-market regulations and a precariat of temporary and part-time workers (Castel, 2003). The social partners play a major role in defining labour contracts, social protection rights, wages and working conditions, leading to a compression of the wage structure and relatively low wage spread between more and less highly qualified and skilled workers. Income inequality has risen more slowly in France than in some other OECD countries, and France has had lower proportions of the working poor than elsewhere. However, the price paid has been a more stubbornly elevated unemployment rate (Milner, 2014; Vlandas, 2016) and strong exclusionary mechanisms relating to age and initial entry into the French labour market. These conditions hampered the development of the PHS sector in France, aside from those services subsidised through work-family reconciliation and LTC policy.

There were a number of stakeholders in France whose existence and efforts explain both the early adoption of PHS policies and their resistance to criticism and substantial change over the years. First and foremost, a number of professional associations were active in the 1990s in naming and defining PHS (Jany-Catrice, 2010). Since the 1950s in France, associations in the childcare and LTC sectors had been active in promoting home-based care services and defending the interests of their workers. However, it was the intervention of the *Conseil National du Patronat Francais* (*CNPF*) (National Council of French Employers) now the

Mouvement des Entreprises de France (*MEDEF*) (Movement for French Enterprises) in the 1990s that led to a step change in the success of their lobbying. In 1991, the Socialist Minister of Labour, Martine Aubry, had given households fiscal incentives to declare *emplois familiaux* (direct employees of the family/household) in an attempt to reduce undeclared work in the sector (Jany-Catrice, 2010). Interested by the possibilities of extending these tax breaks further, in the same year, the *CNPF* created the *Syndicat des Entreprises de Services à la* Personne (*SESP*) (Union of Services to Individuals Businesses) to lobby the government and EU actors to this end. This intervention galvanised other interested stakeholders to lobby governments for action to promote PHS, transforming the lobbying strategy from one of requesting improvements in welfare services via the home-based delivery of care to an employment logic of creating jobs in the care and domestic work markets.

In 1993, the right-wing *Rassemblement pour la Republique* (*RPR)* Minister of Labour Michel Giraud introduced the first scheme in Europe to simplify the process of hiring, paying and making social security contributions for a home-based direct employee: the *Cheque Emploi-Service* (*CES*). The direct employee could be paid for up to eight hours per week using a system of cheques purchased at the local bank. This was accompanied by a tax break in that the employer could claim an income tax reduction of 50 per cent of the sum spent on purchasing the cheques. The employee was paid at least the minimum wage and benefitted from social security cover and a ten per cent indemnity for paid leave. To complement the *CES*, the law of 29 January 1996 created the *Titre Emploi-Service* (*TES*). Workers could receive *TES* vouchers from their employer as part of their salary or from regional or local authorities or from associations if they were in need. The *TES* had to be used to pay for services provided in agency mode. This was an attempt to encourage the development of a tripartite system of service delivery in order to offer better guarantees both to workers (who received support from the organisation) and to users (who were guaranteed better quality of service). The schemes were also seen as encouraging the structuring of the often-chaotic supply system of domestic services in which one of the principal barriers to expansion was the difficulty of matching supply with demand. Policy instruments and tools to help keep dependent elderly people in their homes began to be subsumed into this wider PHS context (Jany-Catrice, 2010). This developing French approach to the PHS sector influenced EU policy. The 1993 European Commission White Paper, prepared by the then-French commissioner Jacques Delors, entitled *Growth, competitiveness, employment* (European Commission, 1994) had as one of its employment priorities the promotion of "services for everyday life" to provide employment to the low skilled, reduce the effect of high labour costs on fostering undeclared work and replacing expensive in-kind provision of social services.

Concluding Summary

The most fundamental change in domestic and care work that took place through the twentieth century in France was that advances in domestic equipment and materials and the development of commercial substitutes for home-based production improved the productivity of domestic work to the point where it no longer constituted a full-time occupation first for domestic servants in middle- and upper-class households, and then for housewives across the social spectrum. By the end of the century, responsibility for domestic work alone no longer represented an obstacle to participation in the labour market for women. However, caring for dependent children or adults remained an impediment to labour-market participation. Whereas in 1968 feminists had called for the liberation of married women from confinement in the role of unpaid homemaker, by the end of the century it was women's double burden of caring and related domestic duties alongside employment that was challenged (Delphy & Leonard, 1992). The development of women's employment during the last quarter of the century resulted in a care gap for children and for LTC that was filled by paid workers, providing either in-kind services on behalf of the state or, increasingly commonly, services as direct employees of the household partially or fully funded by in-cash benefits and/or tax and employer social security contribution deductions. Highly paid individuals and couples also started to increase their use of domestic services to ease their time pressures, encouraged by PHS policy. By the end of the twentieth century, France had one of the highest proportions of dual-earner full-time working couples with children in the EU15, enabled by a dense network of state support for childcare. Support for LTC and PHS was also starting to develop by the 1990s. However, as will be discussed in Chaps. 3–5, this more gender-equal division of employment in France was accompanied at the beginning of the twenty-first century by a relatively traditional gender division of unpaid domestic and care work.

One of the most important specificities of the French national case, as regards the development of policy towards women's role in the family and in employment, is the question of demography and the treatment of social problems through the prism of pronatalism. Dating back to the Revolution, the French had practised birth control within marriage and limited family size very much earlier than in competitor countries. Military and economic failures were blamed on the limited size of the population by both Republicans and the monarchy-supporting Catholic Church in the first half of the twentieth century. Concerns about demography re-emerged later in the century but focused more on how a low birth rate would lead to an ageing population and increase the dependency ratio in the country beyond a point that the welfare state would be able to manage. These concerns were shared by Left and Right alike. Furthermore, from the 1980s onwards, the far-Right evoked fears about the weakening of national identity that would ensue from a low birth rate. Concerns over the size of the French population have meant that women have been required to fulfil two roles: as employees, to compensate the lack of male workers, and as parents, to raise the new generation of citizens. Consequently, when the labour market required women as workers, the French state supported mothers' employment. This happened at the beginning of the century, with the introduction of paid maternity leave in 2013 and from the 1960s onwards with support for childcare for working parents. At times when there was less need for women in the labour force, particularly when more conservative political forces were in power, the state gave financial encouragement to French women to stay in the home and take responsibility for unpaid domestic and care work in the hope that in this way they would produce more children. This was the case from the 1920s until the 1960s when family benefits, particularly for larger families and single-earner families, were very generous. Furthermore, during the 1980s and the 1990s, parental leave benefits were only offered to those with multiple children.

The second notable specificity of the French case is the importance of the family to Republicans and the Catholic Church, who during the Third Republic battled for influence over the values and behaviours of the population. Throughout the nineteenth century, the Catholic church had provided welfare services in the form of crèches and *salles d'asiles*, that would become nursery schools, part of its strategy directly to influence the attitudes of the population. During the Third Republic, the state sought to remove the Church from this position of influence by co-opting these institutions. Although not originally created to facilitate women's employment, these institutions would undergo institutional conversion towards the end of the twentieth century to allow the collectivisation of childcare and facilitate women's participation in employment earlier than in comparable Conservative countries.

Furthermore, Republican interest in the family influenced the construction of the welfare state around a state familialist model that focused on horizontal distribution of resources towards families with children, rather than between rich and poor. The welfare state created a powerful bureaucratic infrastructure around the family, heavily influenced by family associations. These institutions reinforced the homemaker role for women in the mid-century with generous family benefits. Feminist stakeholders found it difficult to influence these powerful family institutions, and instead focused on influencing equal opportunities agendas in employment. This had the consequence of childcare, and subsequently LTC policy development that did not have the explicit aim of de-gendering the division of unpaid domestic and care work. Women were relieved of enough of these responsibilities in order for them to fulfil the dual roles of employees and carers in what can be termed a woman-state contract.

The third specificity of the French case is the stubbornly high unemployment rates that the country has suffered since the 1980s, the result of the high degree of regulation of the economy and labour market. This has resulted in a relatively low wage spread between more and less highly qualified and skilled workers. Attempts to tackle this unemployment problem had two consequences for domestic and care work: first, it led to policies encouraging the partial and/or temporary withdrawal of women with caring responsibilities from the labour market through part-time work or parental leave; and second, it necessitated policy to create the conditions for the development of paid domestic and care services to provide jobs for the young and lower qualified.

References

Afsa Essafi, C., & Buffeteau, S. (2006). L'activité féminine en France : quelles évolutions récentes, quelles tendances pour l'avenir ? *Économie et statistique, 398–399*, 85–97.

Alexsynska, M., & Schmidt, A. (2014). *A chronology of employment protection legislation in some selected European countries.* Conditions of work and employment series no.53. ILO. Retrieved August 9, 2022, from https://www.ilo.org/wcmsp5/groups/public/%2D%2D-ed_protect/%2D%2D-protrav/%2D%2D-travail/documents/publication/wcms_324647.pdf

Algava, E., Bresse, S., & Momic, M. (2005). Les bénéficiaires de l'Allocation parentale d'éducation : trajectoires d'activité et retour à l'emploi. *Etudes et Résultats de la DREES, 399*, 1–8.

Armengaud, A. (1973). L'attitude de la société à l'égard de l'enfant au XIXe siècle. *Annales de démographie historique*, 303–312. https://doi.org/10.3406/adh.1973.1197

Barthez, A. (1986). La famille-entreprise : l'exemple de l'agriculture. In Association internationale des démographes de langue française (AIDELF). In *Les familles d'aujourd'hui - Actes du colloque de Genève septembre 1984* (pp. 205–213).

Beal, M. (2020). Domesticité blanche et politiques raciales en France métropolitaine (1850-1930). *Travail, genre et sociétés, 44*(2), 31–47. https://doi.org/10.3917/tgs.044.0031

Biraben, J. N., & Dupaquier, J. (1981). *Les berceaux vides de Marianne : l'avenir de la population francaise*. Le Seuil.

Boinon, J. P. (2011). Les politiques foncières agricoles en France depuis 1945. *Economie et Statistique, 444–445*, 19–37.

Bonoli, G. (2013). *Origins of active social policy: Labour market and childcare policies*. Oxford University Press.

Castel, R. (2003). *L'insécurité sociale, qu'est-ce qu'être protégé ?* Seuil.

Cette, G., & Diev, P. (2003). L'impact de la réduction du temps de travail. *Futuribles, 285*, 59–66.

Chadeau, A., & Fouquet, A. (1981). Peut-on mesurer le travail domestique ? *Economie et Statistique, 136*, 29–49.

Chaib, S. (2008). Femmes immigrées et travail salarié en France. *Cahiers du CEDREF, 16*, 209–229. https://doi.org/10.4000/cedref.587

Chatot, M. (2017). Père au foyer: une nouvelle entrée au répertoire du masculine ? *Enfance, famille, générations : revue interdisciplinaire sur la famille contemporaine, 26*, 1–19. https://doi.org/10.7202/1041062ar

Chauffaut, D., & Lévêque, S. (2012). Femmes, mères, épouses et travailleuses : les représentations parlementaires des rôles sexués au travers des débats sur les politiques de conciliation (1965-2010). *Revue française des affaires sociales*, 12–31. https://doi.org/10.3917/rfas.122.0012

Clarke, J. (2011). *France in the age of organization: Factory, home and nation from the 1920s to Vichy*. Berghahn Books.

Collombet, C. (2021). French history of parental leave policies: A slow coming out of the stay-at-home mother compensation model. *Revue des politiques sociales et familiales, 4*, 195–207. https://doi.org/10.3917/rpsf.141.0195

Commaille, J. (1993). *Les stratégies des femmes. Travail, famille et politique*. La Découverte.

Coser, L. (1973). Servants: The obsolescence of an occupational role. *Social Forces, 52*(1), 31–40. https://doi.org/10.2307/2576421

Coulon, N., & Cresson, G. (2013). La parentalité et ses genres. Les sciences humaines et la place du père auprès du jeune enfant. In N. Coulon & G. Cresson (Eds.), *La petite enfance – entre familles et crèches, entre sexe et genre* (pp. 167–224). L'Harmattan.

David, M., & Lezine, I. (1975). *Early childcare in France.* Gordon and Breach Publishing Group.

de Beauvoir, S. (1989). *The second sex* (H. M. Parshley, Trans.). Vintage Classics (Original work published 1952).

De Luca Barrusse, V. (2009). La revanche des familles nombreuses : les premiers jalons d'une politique familiale (1896–1939). *Revue d'histoire de la protection sociale, 1*(2), 47–63. https://doi.org/10.3917/rhps.002.0047

Debonneuil, M., & Lahidji, R. (1998). Services de proximité, état et marché. In *Conseil d'Analyse Economique, Emplois de Proximité* (pp. 41–60). La Documentation Française.

Debord, R. (2020). L'UNAF face à la diversification des modèles familiaux. *Enfances Familles Générations, 35*, 1–19. http://journals.openedition.org/efg/10686

Delors, J., & Foucauld, M. (1980). *La Révolution du temps choisi.* Albin Michel.

Delphy, C., & Leonard, D. (1992). *Familiar exploitation: A new analysis of marriage in contemporary Western societies.* University of Chicago Press.

Devetter, F.-X., Jany-Catrice, F., & Ribault, T. (2009). *Les services à la personne.* La Découverte.

Dex, S. (2010). Can state policies produce equality in housework. In J. Treas & S. Drobnič (Eds.), *Dividing the domestic: Men, women & household work in cross-national perspective* (pp. 79–104). Stanford University Press.

Drouard, A. (1992). La création de l'INED. *Population, 47*(6), 1453–1466. https://doi.org/10.2307/1534080

Duchen, C. (1991). Occupation housewife: The domestic ideal in 1950s France. *French Cultural Studies, 2*(4), 1–11. https://doi.org/10.1177/095715589100200401

Duchen, C. (1994). *Women's rights and women's lives in France 1944–1968.* Routledge.

Dumont, G.-F., & Sauvy, A. (1983). *La tragédie de la France : un enjeu à surmonter. Non une fatalité.* Editions de L'A.P. R. D.

Dunezat, X. (2016). La sociologie des rapports sociaux de sexe : une lecture féministe et matérialiste des rapports hommes / femmes. *Cahiers du Genre, 4*(3), 175–198. https://doi.org/10.3917/cdge.hs04.0175

Duru-Bellat, M. (1990). *L'école des filles : quelle formation pour quels rôles sociaux ?* L'Harmattan.

Dussuet, A. (2017). Le « travail domestique » : une construction théorique féministe interrompue. *Recherches Féministes, 30*(2), 101–117. https://doi.org/10.7202/1043924ar

Ennuyer, B. (2003). Histoire d'une catégorie 'personnes âgées' dépendantes. In C. Martin (Ed.), *Histoire d'une catégorie: "personnes âgées" : la Dépendance des Personnes Agées : quelles politiques en Europe* (pp. 95–114). Open Edition Books.
Esping-Anderson, G. (2009). *The incomplete revolution: Adapting to women's new roles.* Polity Press.
European Commission, Secretariat-General. (1994). *Growth, competitiveness, employment: The challenges and ways forward into the 21st century.* White Paper. Publications Office.
Fagnani, J. (2000). *Petits arbitrages et grands dilemmes.* Bayard.
Fagnani, J. (2001). L'intégration progressive du modèle de la mère qui travaille. *Spirale, 18*(2), 1–14. https://doi.org/10.3917/spi.018.0139
Foucault, M. (1975). *Surveiller et punir.* Gallimard.
Fourastie, J. (1979, April 26). Le suicide collectif. *Le Figaro.*
Fraisse, G. (1979). *Femmes toutes mains. Essai sur le service domestique.* Seuil.
Gershuny, J. (1979). The informal economy: Its role in post-industrial society. *Futures*, 3–15.
Girard, A. (1958). Les budgets-temps de la femme mariée dans les agglomérations urbaines. *Population, 4*, 591–681. https://doi.org/10.2307/1525084
Girard, A., & Bastide, H. (1958). Le budget-temps de la femme mariée à la campagne. *Population, 2*, 253–284. https://doi.org/10.2307/1526410
Gregory, A. (1991). Patterns of working hours in large-scale grocery retailing in Britain and France: Convergence after 1992? *Work, Employment and Society, 5*(4), 497–514. https://doi.org/10.1177/0950017091005004003
Gregory, A., & Windebank, J. (2000). *Women and work in Britain and France: Practice, theory and policy.* Macmillan.
Gregson, N., & Lowe, M. (1994). *Servicing the middle classes: Gender and waged domestic labour in contemporary Britain.* Routledge.
Gross, M. (2015). L'homoparentalité et la transparentalité au prisme des sciences sociales : révolution ou pluralisation des formes de parenté ? *Enfances Familles Générations, 23*, 1–17. https://id.erudit.org/iderudit/1034196ar
Institut National des Statistiques et des Etudes Economiques (INSEE). (1986). *Femmes en chiffres.* INSEE.
Institut National des Statistiques et des Etudes Economiques (INSEE). (2016). *Chômage.* Tableaux de l'Economie Française Edition 2016. Retrieved November 17, 2022, from https://www.insee.fr/fr/statistiques/1906672?sommaire=1906743
Institut National des Statistiques et des Etudes Economiques (INSEE). (2018). *Population par âge.* Tableaux de l'Economie Française Edition 2018. Retrieved November 17, 2022, from https://www.insee.fr/fr/statistiques/3303333?sommaire=3353488
Jany-Catrice, F. (2010). La construction sociale du « secteur » des services à la personne : une banalisation programmée ? *Sociologie Du Travail, 52*(4), 521–537. https://doi.org/10.4000/sdt.15409

Jany-Catrice, F., & Méda, D. (2011). Femmes et richesse : au-delà du PIB. *Travail, genre et sociétés, 26*(2), 147–171. https://doi.org/10.3917/tgs.026.0147

Jenson, J. (1986). Gender and reproduction. Or babies and the state. *Studies in Political Economy, 20*, 9–46. https://doi.org/10.1080/19187033.1986.11675588

Jenson, J., & Sineau, S. (1995). *Mitterrand et les Françaises : un rendez-vous manque*. Presses de la Fondation Nationale des Sciences Politiques.

Jobert, M. (1976, March 24). Tribune Libre : L'autogénocide. *Le Monde*.

Jonsson, I., Daune-Richard, A.-M., Odena, S., & Ring, M. (2011). The implementation of elder care in France and Sweden: A macro and micro perspective. *Ageing and Society, 31*, 625–644. https://doi.org/10.1017/S0144686X10001327

King, L. (1998). "France needs children": Pronatalism, nationalism and women's equity. *The Sociological Quarterly, 39*(1), 33–52. https://doi.org/10.1111/j.1533-25.1998.tb02348.x

Laacher, S. (1998). *L'État et l'immigration clandestine. Entre la question du travail et celle des illégalismes.* Maison des sciences de l'Homme.

Lagarve, R.-M. (1983). Bilan critique des recherches sur les agricultrices en France. *Études rurales, 92*, 9–40. https://doi.org/10.3406/rural.1983.2932

Lagarve, R.-M. (1997). Les agricultrices : les oubliées de la recherche et du féminisme. *Lunes, 4*, 21–27. https://doi.org/10.3917/tgs.045.0031

Lebon, A. (1978). Présentation. In I. Taboada (Ed.), *Femmes immigrées. L'insertion des femmes immigrées en France* (pp. 7–13). La Documentation française.

Lecomte, S. (1996). *Les employées de maison : cadrage historique, juridique et statistique*. PhD thesis, Nantes University.

Ledoux, C. (2011). *L'Etat-providence et les mondes professionnels : la construction politique des métiers féminisés d'intervention dans la sphère privée. Une comparaison France-République fédérale d'Allemagne depuis les années 1970.* PhD thesis, Institut d'Etudes Politiques de Paris.

Lenoir, R. (1991). Family policy in France since 1938. In J. Ambler (Ed.), *The French welfare state: Surviving social and ideological change* (pp. 144–186). New York University Press.

Lenoir, R. (2003). *Généalogie de la morale familiale*. Seuil.

Lewis, J., Knijn, T., Martin, C., & Ostner, I. (2008). Patterns of development in work/family reconciliation policies for parents in France, Germany, The Netherlands, and the UK in the 2000s. *Social Politics, 15*(3), 261–286.

Louis, M.-V., & Loos, J. (1982). Femmes, travail, temps partiel. *Les temps modernes, 437*, 150–1166.

MacBride, T. (1976). *The domestic revolution: The modernisation of household service in England and France 1820–1920.* Croom Helm.

Marchand, O. (2010). 50 ans de mutations de l'emploi. *INSEE Première, 1312*, 1–4.

Marchand, O., & Minni, C. (2019). The major transformations of the French labour market since the early 1960s. *Economie et Statistique, 510-511-512*, 89–107. https://doi.org/10.24187/ecostat.2019.510t.1989

Martin, C. (Ed.). (2003). *Histoire d'une catégorie : "personnes âgées", La Dépendance des Personnes Agées : Quelles Politiques en Europe*. Open Edition Books.

Martin, C. (2008). Atouts et impasses du familialisme français. In S. Dauphin (Ed.), *Penser les politiques sociales* (pp. 153–158). Editions de l'Aube.

Martin, C. (2010). The reframing of family policies in France: Processes and actors. *Journal of European Social Policy, 20*, 410–421. https://doi.org/10.1177/0958928710380479

Mazur, A. G. (1995). *Gender bias and the state: Symbolic reform at work in Fifth Republic France*. University of Pittsburgh Press.

McBride, D., & Mazur, A. (2010). *The politics of state feminism: Innovation in comparative research*. Temple University Press.

McDowell, L. (1991). Life without father and ford: The new gender order of post-Fordism. *Transactions of the Institute of British Geographers, 16*(4), 400–419. https://doi.org/10.2307/623027

Mendras, H. (1991). *Social change in modern France: Towards a cultural anthropology of the Fifth Republic*. Cambridge University Press.

Milner, S. (2010). 'Choice' and 'flexibility' in reconciling work and family: Towards a convergence in policy discourse on work and family in France and the UK? *Policy and Politics, 38*, 3–21. https://doi.org/10.1332/030557309X445591

Milner, S. (2014). The politics of unemployment policy in an age of austerity: France in comparative perspective. *French Politics, 12*(3), 193–217. https://doi.org/10.1057/fp.2014.15

Minonzio, J., & Vallat, J.-P. (2006). L'Union nationale des associations familiales (UNAF) et les politiques familiales. *Revue française de science politique, 56*, 205–226. https://doi.org/10.3917/rfsp.562.0205

Morel, N. (2007). From subsidiarity to 'free choice': Child- and elder-care policy reforms in France, Belgium, Germany and The Netherlands. *Social Policy and Administration, 41*(6), 618–637. https://doi.org/10.1111/j.1467-9515.2007.00575.x

Morgan, K. J. (2002). Forging the frontiers between state, church, and family: Religious cleavages and the origins of early childhood education and care policies in France, Sweden, and Germany. *Politics and Society, 30*(1), 113–p148. https://doi.org/10.1177/0032329202030001005

Moss, P., & Deven, F. (2015). Leave policies in challenging times: Reviewing the decade 2004–2014. *Community, Work & Family, 18*, 137–144. https://doi.org/10.1080/13668803.2015.1021094

Moulier, Y., & Silberman, R. (1982). La montée de l'activité des femmes étrangères en France : une tendance qui ira s'accentuant. *Travail et emploi, 12*, 61–81. https://doi.org/10.2307/1535035

Noiriel, G. (2006). *Le creuset français : histoire de l'immigration, XIXe -XXe siècles.* Le Seuil.

Observatoire des Inégalités. (2021). *Le taux de chômage selon le diplôme et l'âge.* Retrieved November 17, 2022, from https://www.inegalites.fr/Le-taux-de-chomage-selon-le-diplome-et-l-age#:~:text=En%20trente%20ans%2C%20les%20in%C3%A9galit%C3%A9s,au%20milieu%20des%20ann%C3%A9es%201990

OECD. (2012). *OECD employment outlook 2012. La Situation de la France.* OECD.

OECD. (2014). *Use of childbirth-related leave by mothers and fathers, PF2.2.* Retrieved June 11, 2016, from www.oecd.org/els/fa,ily/database.htm

Offen, K. (1984). Depopulation, nationalism, and feminism in fin-de-siècle France. *The American Historical Review., 89*(3), 648–676. https://doi.org/10.1086/ahr/89.3.648

Paihle, A., & Solaz, A. (2008). Time with children: Do fathers and mothers replace each other when one parent is unemployed? *European Journal of Population/Revue européenne de Démographie, 24*(2), 211–236. https://doi.org/10.1007/s10680-007-9143-5

Pedersen, S. (1993). Catholicism, feminism, and the politics of the family during the late Third Republic. In S. Koven & S. Michel (Eds.), *Mothers of a new world: Maternalist politics and the origins of welfare states* (pp. 246–276). Routledge.

Prost, A. (1981). *Histoire générale de l'enseignement et de l'éducation en France. Tome 4. L'école et la famille dans une société en mutation (depuis 1930).* Nouvelle Librairie de France.

Reuter, M. (2019). Equality and difference in Olympe de Gouges : Les droits de la femme. *Australasian Philosophical Review, 3*(4), 403–412. https://doi.org/10.1080/24740500.2020.1840652

Revillard, A. (2006). La conciliation travail-famille : un enjeu complexe pour le féminisme d'État. *Recherches et Prévisions., 85*, 17–27. https://doi.org/10.3406/caf.2006.2227

Reynolds, S. (1990). Who wanted the crèches? Working mothers and the birth-rate in France 1900–1950. *Continuity and Change, 5*(2), 173–197. https://doi.org/10.1017/S0268416000003970

Robcis, C. (2013). *The law of kinship: Anthropology, psychoanalysis and the family in France.* Cornell University Press.

Roustang, G. (1982). *Le travail autrement, travail et mode de vie.* Dunod.

Roy, D. (2011). *La contribution du travail domestique au bien-être matériel des ménages : une quantification à partir de l'enquête emploi du temps.* Retrieved June 21, 2020, from https://www.insee.fr/fr/statistiques/1380932

Stoetzel, J. (1948). L'étude du budget-temps de la femme dans les agglomérations urbaines. *Population, 1*, 47–62. https://doi.org/10.2307/1523447

Stoler, A. L. (2013). *La chair de l'empire : savoirs intimes et pouvoirs raciaux en régime colonial.* La Découverte.

Streeck, W., & Thelen, K. (2005). Introduction: Institutional change in advanced political economies. In W. Streeck & K. Thelen (Eds.), *Beyond continuity: Institutional change in advanced political economies.* Oxford University Press.

Tilly, L., & Scott, J. (1987). *Women, work and family.* Routledge.

Vlandas, T. (2016). Labour market developments and policy responses during and after the crisis in France. *French Politics, 15*(1), 75–105. https://doi.org/10.1057/s41253-016-0008-3

Weber, F. (2010). Les rapports familiaux reconfigurés par la dépendance. *Regards croisés sur l'économie, 7*(1), 139–151. https://doi.org/10.3917/rce.007.0139

White, L. (2004). Ideas and normative instutitonalization: Explaining the paradoxes of French family employment policy. *French Politics, 2*, 247–271. https://doi.org/10.1057/palgrave.fp.8200061

Windebank, J. (1991). *The informal economy in France.* Avebury.

Windebank, J. (2011). Responses of French family and employment policy to the unemployment crises: Impacts on the gendering of paid and unpaid work. *Journal of Contemporary European Studies, 19*(3), 393–407. https://doi.org/10.1080/14782804.2011.610609

CHAPTER 3

Parenting Work and Childcare in Contemporary France

Although not all adults will have parenting responsibilities, and parenting for dependent children may only occupy a minority of an individual's life, the question of who cares for children is very important in understanding the organisation and divisions of labour of domestic and care work in France. This is for two reasons. First, caring for children is a full-time task in that at the very minimum children require constant supervision for the first six to ten years of their lives.[1] Given that in most cases it is not possible simultaneously to engage in employment and supervise young children, those with such parental responsibilities either have to modify their professional work time, outsource childcare to a paid or unpaid third party or parties, or engage in a combination of both strategies in order to reconcile professional and family life. A variety of types of work in differing social relations may be required to satisfy the educational, care, emotional and supervisory needs of a child across the course of a day, week or year. Furthermore, disengagement from the workforce to raise children

[1] French law does not stipulate an age at which children may be left alone, with Article 371-1 of the Civil Code rendering parents responsible for the safety of their children until the age of 18 but not providing further instruction. Child development specialists agree that children do not have the capacity to be left alone safely below the age of six, but after that, norms are culturally and historically variable, and practices among parents depend on material circumstances, risk assessments and the maturity of the child. The process of being able to leave a child unattended is gradual and may be lengthy.

J. Windebank, *Domestic and Care Work in Modern France*, French Politics, Society and Culture,
https://doi.org/10.1007/978-3-031-33564-8_3

increases an individual's availability for other kinds of domestic and care work and reduces their bargaining power to avoid these responsibilities. It also has long-term impacts on their career trajectories, lifetime earnings and pensions. If women are the ones to modify their employment for childcare reasons, essentialist gender stereotypes around women's suitability for caring and domestic roles more generally are reinforced. In consequence, welfare and labour-market policies relating to parenting, childcare and work-family reconciliation are central in framing individual decision-making on how domestic and care work beyond raising children is accomplished. These policies and the childcare infrastructure to which they give rise also influence the employment conditions of paid childcare workers.

Parenting and childcare work has three components. The first component is being present to supervise young children, alongside which it may be possible or expected to undertake other domestic or care work, leisure activities and under certain circumstances employment. The second component includes direct care (e.g., feeding, bathing, dressing), play, educational activities including the supervision of homework, and accompanying children when they go out of the home. The third is domestic work. Although domestic work will be the subject of Chap. 5, this chapter will reflect on the effect of presence of children on the volume and distribution of unpaid domestic work required in a household and the use of paid domestic services.

Parenting Work

The decrease in the number of families in which there is an economically inactive adult available to look after children full time begun in the 1970s continued in France into the contemporary period. In 2020, among those aged 25–49 living in couples[2] with at least one child under 18, 81.3 per cent of women were economically active, of whom 29.9 per cent worked part-time, alongside 95.5 per cent of men, of whom 4.5 per cent worked

[2] National data have a number of limitations as regards representing the diversity of families. They do not differentiate between *familles traditionelles* (traditional families) where the couple lives with their children only and *familles recomposées* (stepfamilies) where the couple lives with at least one child belonging to a different relationship. In 2020, 66.3 per cent of families in France were traditional families and 9 per cent stepfamilies. The remaining 24.7 per cent were single-parent families (Algava et al., 2021, Fig. 2). Furthermore, these data do not differentiate between different-sex and same-sex couples or represent the experiences of trans or non-binary parents.

part-time (*INSEE*, 2022, Fig. 1). In a *Caisse Nationale des Allocation Familiales* (*CNAF)* (National Fund for Family Allowances) study of 6000 parents, 28 per cent of women reported reducing their employment hours after the birth of a child as opposed to only 6 per cent of fathers (Laporte, 2019b, p. 22). It is clear from these figures that although women with young children are well integrated into the French labour market, they continue to reduce their employment commitments to liberate time for parenting more than men. This results in a parental employment gap. Men benefit from a "fatherhood labour participation premium" (ILO, 2018, p. 97) in that parenthood tends to increase rather than suppress their economic activity rates. In 2020, the economic activity rate for men aged 25–49 without children living in a couple was 93.8 per cent, of whom 5.4 per cent worked part-time. It was higher, however, for all men living in a couple with children under six with the exception of those with three children, one of whom was under three at 92.6 per cent, of whom 7.3 per cent worked part-time (INSEE, 2022, Fig. 1). All that said, it has been found that there is a degree of similarity in the proportions of men (11 per cent) and women (14 per cent) in France who make use of the possibilities for flexibility offered within their normal work hours to respond to parenting responsibilities (Bentoudja & Razafindranovona, 2020, p. 3).

Men who act as primary carers for children are a very small minority in France. Single fathers with sole custody and residence of children under 18 represented only 15.06 per cent of all single parents with sole custody in 2018. Over 99 per cent of these men were in employment or self-employment (Perivier, 2020, p. 13 Table 1.2). Very limited data is available for employment rates for fathers in same-sex families, but research suggests little differentiation between partners as regards modification of employment time and time devoted to parenting (see, e.g., Fossoul et al., 2013). Only a very small proportion of men who live in different-sex couples withdraw from the labour market to take on the primary carer role full- or part-time for children (Chatot, 2017b). Those who do tend to have less prestigious jobs and lower earnings than their partners and are more likely than average to work in the public sector (Pak, 2016).

In contrast to men, economic activity rates for French women are lower the younger their children are, and the more children they have in line with the intensity and volume of parenting work required of them. Part-time work for women, after increasing sharply between over the course of the 1980s, stabilised at around 30 per cent of women employees until 2014 and has since reduced slightly to around 28 per cent. For women aged 25–49 living in a couple but without children in 2020 in France 88.0 per cent were economically active with 16.5 per cent working part-time. For women with one or two children under eighteen all of whom were over three, economic activity rates were similar to those for women without children at 86.8 per cent and 89.3 per cent, respectively, but proportions of part-time workers were higher at 23.5 and 28.2 per cent. However, a third child in families with no under threes significantly reduces activity rates for women to 73.4 per cent and increases the proportion of part-time workers to 40.6 per cent (INSEE, 2022, Fig. 1).

The presence of a child under three in families has further impacts on women's activity and part-time work rates, as would be expected given the intensity of care needed for such young children, the availability of parental leave and the age at which nursery school starts. In 2020 for women with one child under three, activity rates remained relatively high at 82.2 per cent and the proportion of part-time workers similar to that for women with one older child, reflecting both the more limited volume of parenting and additional domestic work represented by a single child, but also the shorter period of parental leave available to these parents. The impact of having an under three was more significant for women with two children, with an economic activity rate of 74.9 per cent, with 37.3 per cent working part-time. The activity rate for those with three children including an under three was lower still at 47.5 per cent of whom nearly half (45.7 per cent) worked part-time (INSEE, 2022, Fig. 1). A survey in 2013 by the *Direction de la Recherche et des Etudes de l'Evaluation des Statistiques (DREES)*[3] found that 61 per cent of under threes were looked after by their parents between 8 a.m. and 7 p.m. Monday to Friday, 41 per cent being looked after by their mother alone, 4 per cent by their father alone, 16 per cent with both parents present the majority of the time. Where both parents are involved, this may be due to economic inactivity or unemployment. In 2021, 11 per cent of children aged under 17 lived in jobless households.[4]

Furthermore, children whose parents are separated tend to live either wholly or in the majority with their mother, further increasing the

[3] Regular surveys on childcare for young children have been carried out by the *DREES* in 2002, 2007 and 2013. See: https://drees.solidarites-sante.gouv.fr/sources-outils-et-enquetes/lenquete-modes-de-garde-et-daccueil-des-jeunes-enfants

[4] https://ec.europa.eu/eurostat/web/products-eurostat-news/-/edn-20220307-1#:~:text=In%202020%2C%2077%25%20of%20women,%25%3B%20%2D5%20percentage%20points)

proportion of parenting work accruing to women depending on custody and residence arrangements (Piesen, 2016). In 2020, 24.7 per cent of families with children were single-parent families, of whom 82 per cent were headed by a woman and 18 per cent by a man. Activity rates for single mothers were lower than those living in couples across all numbers and ages of children. In addition, the unemployment rate for single mothers was double (11.5 per cent) that of coupled mothers (5.5 per cent) (INSEE, 2022, Fig. 1). Furthermore, activity rates of women with family responsibilities vary significantly depending on socio-professional category.[5] Whereas 90 per cent of women in SPC 2 with family responsibilities were in employment in 2018, the figure was only 71 per cent for SPC 5 and 54 per cent for SPC 6 (Bentoudja & Razafindranovona, 2020, p. 2 Table 2).

National-level gender differences in the activity rates of those with parental responsibilities result from the sum of decisions individuals make about work-family reconciliation influenced by economic circumstances, cultural norms around gendered family responsibilities and policy provisions. France had a higher percentage of women aged 25–54 with children under 18 in employment in 2021 (76.2 per cent) than the EU average, (72.4 per cent). However, this figure was less than the 84.1 per cent recorded in Sweden. Even so, an ILO (2018, p. 88 Fig. 2.26,) review of maternal and paternal employment-to-population ratios by country

[5] Throughout this book, the French nomenclature for socio-professional categories will be used. This was created in 1982 and updated in 2003 and again in 2020 to include feminine versions of the professions where required. They are Socio-Professional Category (SPC) 1: *Agriculteurs exploitants / agricultrices* exploitantes (Agricultural and allied workers): agriculture, forestry and fishing own-account workers and family helpers for businesses with fewer than ten workers; SPC 2: *Artisans / Artisanes, commerçants / commerçantes et chefs / cheffes d'entreprise* (Trades and crafts persons, retailers and company owners); SPC 3: *Cadres et professions intellectuelles supérieures* (managers and higher intellectual professions); SPC 4: *Professions intermédiaires* (intermediary professions): a diverse group of professions situated between categories 3 and 5 and including primary and secondary teachers, health professionals other than doctors, social workers, intermediary administrative and security professionals in the public sector, and intermediary administrative and commercial professionals in the private sector, technicians and supervisors in industry; SPC 5 *Employés/Employées* (clerical, administrative and service workers): a diverse group of professions including administrative, commercial, security or home-based services occupations with the commonality of not having any management or supervisory component; SPC 6: *Ouvriers/*Ouvrières (manual workers) including those working in industry, services occupations such as cleaning or delivery, and undertaking manual jobs in retail or agriculture. https://www.insee.fr/fr/metadonnees/pcs2020/groupeSocioprofessionnel/1?champRecherche=true

situated France in a group with the lowest parenthood employment gap of between 10 and 20 per cent.

In national surveys and cross-national comparisons of attitudes towards questions of parents' employment in France, there are high degrees of approval of women's employment which are comparable with those seen in the Nordic countries (Brice et al., 2015). For example, Aboim (2010, p. 184 Table 3) compared attitudes towards work-family reconciliation across 15 European countries in 2002 and found that France had a greater proportion of its population (53.9 per cent) than the average for this group of nations (37.6 per cent) in favour of a dual-earner model for couples with children. Furthermore, Brice et al. (2015, p. 1) note that according to the 2015 *CREDOC* (*Centre de Recherche pour l'Etude et l'Observation des Conditions de vie*) survey *Conditions de vie et aspiration* (living conditions and aspirations), 75 per cent of the French population thought that women should work outside the home if they wish. However, these egalitarian views on employment sit alongside more traditional views on the priority that should be given to the interests of children. The opinion is widespread that the absence of a mother is detrimental to children's welfare (Papuchon, 2017) and support for the traditional two-parent family with a mother and father is as strong in France as that seen in countries with more traditional views on mothers' employment (Knight & Brinton, 2017). Meanwhile, in 2015 70 per cent of the French were in agreement that mothers should give priority to their young children rather than their career. It should be noted, however, that in 1992, 85 per cent of French respondents in a similar survey were in agreement with this opinion (Brice et al., 2015, p. 2).

Two major policy areas influence work-family reconciliation decisions. These are worktime regimes and the extent and type of support for childcare provided by the state to working parents. As concerns worktime, Hook (2006) suggests that long standard and maximum working hours encourage gender specialisation in parenting, and consequently unpaid domestic and care work more generally. The demands of long working hours render employment and care less compatible and favour a single-earner or one-and-a-half earner model in coupled parents. Regulations that decrease standard work time should therefore assist dual-earning and more symmetrical working hours for coupled parents, and employment for single parents and increase men's availability for unpaid work (Gornick & Meyers, 2003). It may therefore be assumed that in countries with shorter work times more equal shares of parenting and related unpaid domestic work would be seen.

Over the course of the twentieth century, worktime decreased across Europe, but at the beginning of the twenty-first century it began to rise again in most countries with the exception of France (Giminez-Nadal & Sevilla-Sanz, 2012). This was because France is an outlier in being the sole country in Europe to have used legislation to impose a collective reduction in working time in this period in the shape of the first and second *Reduction du Temps de Travail* (*RTT*) (Work-time reduction), or 35-hour-week laws passed in 1998 and 2002. Although dubbed the 35-hour week, the laws in fact annualised working hours to 1600 with the aim of creating flexibility for workers and businesses. These laws were the continuation of the *temps choisi* policy begun in the 1980s by the Socialists who had returned to power under Prime Minister Jospin in 1997 after 11 years out of government. On taking office, they made good on their 1982 promise to reduce the working week from 39 to 35 hours. It was one of the Jospin Government's four key elements of social policy, along with universal health cover, the creation of employment for young people and the reform of benefits for dependent elderly members of the population (see Chap. 4). The principal stated objective of the policy was to create jobs and reduce unemployment (Clift, 2006). The law gave state aid in the form of reductions in social security contributions to firms creating new jobs as a result of the reduction of the working week. Even though right-wing governments since 2002 have criticised the 35-hour week and made changes at its margins, the policy has remained substantially intact. The only substantive attempt to undermine the *RTT* law was the introduction of the law promoting *Le Travail, l'emploi et le pouvoir d'achat (TEPA)* (Work, employment and purchasing power) introduced by the right-wing government of Prime Minister Fillon in 2006 which reduced social security contributions on overtime payments for employees and employers and removed income tax on overtime.[6]

In the 1970s, women spent around half the time on professional activities, including commuting, studying and training, as men. The 1974 *INSEE* time-use study showed that the average daily time[7] women spent on professional activities was 2 hours 46 minutes, whereas for men it was 5 hours 23 minutes. By the 2010 study, these figures had not equalised completely, but were much more similar. Average daily time spent on professional activities had reduced to 2 hours 37 minutes for women, the sum

[6] In line with EU regulations, overtime is allowed in France up to a 48-hour week

[7] Taken across the sample population aged 18–64 and across 7 days per week

of the contradictory trends of increasing economic activity rates, increasing part-time employment rates and the reduction in the working week. The reduction for men was much more significant to 3 hours 53 minutes, brought about by both a reduction in weekly work hours and also increased economic inactivity due to early retirement or unemployment. Brousse (2015a, p. 92) calculates that 80 per cent of this reduction in professional work time for men was composed of fewer days being worked because of worklessness or underemployment, and 20 per cent by the shortening of work time. Between 1974 and 2010 the proportion of professional work time within total professional and domestic and care work time for women rose from 33 per cent to 39 per cent but fell from 72 per cent to 60 per cent for men, the reduction having taken place primarily between 1974 and 1986 (Brousse, 2015a, p. 103).

In addition to its job-creation objectives, the 35-hour week was also framed as part of the work–life balance and gender-equality agendas, promising to reduce the need for gender-segregated part-time work for parents which had been strongly encouraged by the preceding right-wing governments but had not received the support of the trades union movement and drawn strong criticism from feminist academics and activists (Goux et al., 2014). The reduction in working time was also deemed an opportunity for reorganising working time, and a way of better adjusting employees' demands to firms' needs for flexibility (Büttner et al., 2002). However, the 35-hour week did not lead to changes in the gendering of work time and work patterns to the extent that may have been hoped for, or indeed to men devoting the additional available time to unpaid domestic and care work (Goux et al., 2014). This is because the annualisation of work hours, the fact that employers were not permitted to reduce salaries in line with the worktime reduction, and the emphasis on flexibility resulted in a diversification and individualisation of working-time regimes, even within the same company, that did not necessarily benefit work-family reconciliation and produced differential results for men and women (Bouffartigue, 2010; Fagnani & Letablier, 2004). Depending on their relative power within the organisation, employees have had variable amounts of control over the flexibility offered by the *RTT* laws which has tended to deepen the existing segmentation of the workforce. A high proportion of those in management and professional occupations whose work patterns were already less rigid have tended to use the work-time reduction for longer vacations rather than reducing daily work hours. Those working in lower-level service and manufacturing jobs where work times were more strictly controlled have been more likely to see a daily reduction in work time but also more likely to be subject to the imposition of irregular hours that do not necessarily facilitate work-family reconciliation (Afsa et al., 2006).

Parental leave policies play a key role as regards activity rates for parents of children under three. As discussed previously, at the beginning of the twenty-first century parental leave benefit in France had been extended to parents of two children but was not available to parents of one child. However, in 2004 a further reform and renaming of the parental leave policy took place. The *APE* was renamed the *Complement de libre choix d'activité (CLCA)* (Supplement for free choice of activity) and extended to the parents of one child, but only up to the child's first birthday. For those with two or more children, the leave remained available until the child's third birthday when nursery school starts. The French scheme remained the longest parental leave in the EU. In similarity to the *APE*, the *CLCA* was paid at a low flat rate (around one-third to one-half of the minimum wage), rather than being indexed on previous salary. The uptake by men of the *CLCA* remained very low. Since the introduction of parental leave benefit in the 1980s, approximately 98 per cent of claimants have been women (Perivier & Verdugo, 2021a, p. 1). The level of gendering of parental leave in France placed it 15th out of 18 countries in an OECD ranking on this measure in 2013 (OECD, 2014, p. 3).

In addition to these problems of the gendering of parental leave in France, by the 2000s it had become clear that long parental-leaves played a large part in the bifurcation of the labour market between more highly qualified women who tended to work on a full-time or long-hours part-time and continuous basis through the early childhood years in contrast with more lowly qualified and younger women who tended to withdraw from the labour market after childbirth and take long parental leaves when they were entitled. In so doing, they risk becoming distanced from the labour market leading to future job insecurity, unemployment and likelihood of they and their children living in a jobless household and poverty (Thevenon, 2013).

Recognition of these twin problems of the very significant gendering of parental leave and its impact on the employability of low-qualified women gained momentum within the French welfare elite during the 2000s with reports published highlighting the need to review the existing parental leave policy.[8] These reviews eventually led to three reforms: the introduc-

[8] See for example a report by Michel Laroque, the General Inspector of Social Affairs in 2006 (Laroque, 2006)

tion of paid paternity leave in 2002; a further parental leave option with a shortened period of leave for families of three or more children accompanied by an enhanced flat-rate payment in 2006; and the introduction of a non-transferable element, or father quota, to the parental leave benefit in 2014. First, the right to paid paternity leave was introduced in France in 2002, initially for two weeks. Following its introduction, approximately two-thirds of fathers used at least some of this leave (Bauer, 2007). By 2021, 80 per cent fathers working on open-ended contracts took up the leave but only 50 per cent of those on fixed-term contracts did so (CAF, 2022). In July 2021 the government doubled the number of days of paternity leave to 28, making the taking of seven of these leave days compulsory immediately after the birth to address the disparity in take-up between different categories of workers. The rest of the leave can be taken over the ensuing six months.

Second, during the 2005 national annual *Conference des Familles*[9] (Families' Conference) where family-policy proposals are discussed and debated within the institutional policy elite, a working group led by the chair of the *UNAF* proposed what would become in 2006 the *Complément optionnel de libre choix d'activité (COLCA)* (Optional supplement for free choice of activity)—a one-year leave remunerated at a higher level than the *CLCA*, but still not indexed on previous income, which parents could choose instead of the *CLCA* for their third child and subsequent children (Milner, 2010). The scheme was criticised on a number of levels, for example, due to its pronatalist nature being limited to the third child, and as having the potential to worsen the bifurcation of the labour market for mothers, the assumption being that lower qualified women would continue to claim the *CLCA* and higher earning women (and men) would opt for the *COLCA* (Milner, 2010). However, the *COLCA* was not a success: by 2012, it was claimed by only 2400 people annually in comparison with 530,000 beneficiaries of the *CLCA* (Collombet, 2021, p. 206).

Third, a further and much more paradigmatic reform, and name change for parental leave benefit came about in 2014 when the *Prestation partagee d'education de l'enfant* (*PreParE*) (Shared childrearing benefit) was introduced by President Hollande's Socialist government. Whereas previous benefits had granted a family entitlement and given freedom of choice

[9] The *Conférences des Familles* bring together policy actors and stakeholders such as users, operators, and institutions collectively to exchange ideas on the direction of public actions towards the family.

to parents about how to distribute the leave between them, the *PreParE* stipulated individual entitlements to each parent that are not transferable if those parents are living in a couple. For coupled parents of one child, each is entitled to up to six months of benefit up to the child's first birthday. Single parents retain entitlement up to the child's first birthday. For coupled parents with two or more children, each parent has an individual entitlement to two years of paid leave until the child's third birthday with single parents retaining the right to up to three years' leave.[10] The outcome of this change is that if coupled parents want to retain their previous entitlement of one or three years of benefit, they have to share the leave (Perivier & Verdugo, 2021a).

The stated aims of the government in introducing the *PreParE* was first to encourage men to take up parental leave, thereby improving the gender division of parenting in different-sex couples, and indeed unpaid domestic and care work more generally, and second to reduce the time that women are out of the labour market. The *PreParE* was only one aspect of a wide-ranging piece of gender-equality legislation enacted by the Socialists very soon after coming to office, the 4 August 2014 *Loi pour l'égalité réelle entre les hommes et les femmes* (Law for real equality between men and women).[11] President Hollande's election campaign in 2012 had focused heavily on the Socialists *40 engagements pour l'égalité hommes-femmes* (40 promises for gender equality). The policy represented a paradigmatic shift in the French approach to work-family reconciliation policy in that it moved away from the woman-state contract model and the primacy of parental choice of how to care for very young children towards a more de-gendered model focusing on changing the behaviour of men and limiting family choice in the name of gender equality. However, the modalities of the policy have shortcomings that mean it has not achieved this objective: in similarity to the *CLCA* it is paid at a low flat rate which is not attractive or indeed financially viable for men living in different-sex couples given the persistent parental wage gap. In addition, the entitlement for those with two or more children remains long at up to three years in total. At the time of its introduction in 2014, some critics went so far as to claim

[10] For further details, see: https://www.caf.fr/allocataires/aides-et-demarches/droits-et-prestations/vie-personnelle/la-prestation-partagee-d-education-de-l-enfant-prepare

[11] For full details, see: https://www.gouvernement.fr/action/la-loi-pour-l-egalite-reelle-entre-les-femmes-et-les-hommes#:~:text=Adoption23%20juillet%202014La,et%20les%20hommes%20est%20promulgu%C3%A9e

that in making this change the government was more interested in reducing the cost of parental leave benefit rather than de-gendering it. It was estimated that if father take-up of the *PreParE* remained at previous low levels, the policy would save 70 million Euros by 2017, contributing to the 800 million Euros that the Hollande government aimed to save from its family budget as part of its planned spending cuts in the wake of the 2008 banking crisis (Windebank, 2017).

Such pessimistic predictions about the outcome of the policy have proved justified in that the *PreParE* has not increased the take up of the benefit by men but rather reduced the number of claims. Between 2014 and 2017, there was a 43 per cent reduction in the number of parental-leave benefit claimants overall (Laporte & Legendre, 2018, p. 1 Table 1), and an 83 per cent reduction in the number of families claiming for a child over two years old. The number of claimants whose child was under 2 fell by 25 per cent—accounted for in part by the reduction in entitlement for families of one child (Laporte & Legendre, 2018 p. 1 Table 1). In January 2018, 85 per cent of those who had started claiming during 2015 had ceased to claim in comparison with just 20 per cent for the generation of children born in 2014 over the equivalent time frame, with no difference being identified between part-time and full-time claimants (Laporte & Legendre, 2018, p. 2 Graph 1). The use of parental leave by men scarcely changed. In a comparison of parental leave uptake over the first three years of their life among those who had a child in December 2014, the last cohort to be eligible for the *CLCA*, and those who had a child in January 2015, that is, the first cohort of children born after the introduction of the *PreParE*, Perivier and Verdugo (2021a, p. 1) found that under the *CLCA*, 0.4 per of all fathers took at least one month of full-time leave during the eligibility period and 0.7 per cent part time leave, with a slight increase under the *PreParE* to 0.5 per cent and 0.9 per cent respectively. For those with two or more children, during the year that their children were two to three years old, the proportion of fathers taking at least one-month full-time leave was 0.6 per cent under the *CLCA* rising to 0.8 per cent under the *PreParE,* and part-time, 1.1 to 1.8 per cent respectively.

These rates fall well short of achieving the objective of encouraging fathers to take 25 per cent of leave days and means that France is still far behind the countries in Europe that have been most successful in encouraging take up of parental leave by men (European Institute for Gender Equality, 2019). For example, Swedish men took 25.1 per cent of all leave days related to childbirth and adoption in 2012 (Eydal et al., 2015, p. 172

Table 3). When the German government introduced a well-paid one-year leave package in 2007, men went from representing 3 to 32 per cent of claimants (Perivier & Verdugo, 2021b, p. 1). On the basis of these comparisons, it can be seen that individual non-transferable entitlement to parental leave benefits appears to be necessary but insufficient to encourage high levels of take up by men (Karu & Tremblay, 2018).

The *PreParE* has been more successful as regards its impact on women's employment patterns. In Perivier and Verdugo's (2021a) study, the percentage of all mothers of two or more children claiming the benefit when their child turns two reduced from 20.6 per cent to 5.7 per cent for full-time leave[12] and from 18.6 per cent to 5.0 per cent for part time leave by 2018. This led to a reduction in the wage gap between mothers and fathers in the three years after the birth of a child by 14 per cent as women returned to work earlier. In a survey of families having had a child in 2015 and no longer qualifying for the benefit by January 2018 because only one parent took the leave, it was found that of the women having claimed the benefit full time, 57 per cent took up or returned to employment and 43 per cent did not have employment at the end of the benefit period because they had transferred to unemployment benefit or became inactive (Laporte, 2019a, p. 3). These figures compare with the 36 per cent of women who were unemployed or inactive at the beginning of their leave. Given that children cannot normally start nursery school until the age of three, the lack of appropriate childcare that is affordable or accessible is likely to be an obstacle to returning to the labour force for some women. For others, their difficulties in securing employment encountered before having children and taking up the leave remain, and may worsen due to the leave.

It is important to note that discussions about reform of parental leave policy started under the right-wing administration of President Sarkozy and Prime Minister Fillon in the mid-2000s within the context of an active labour-market turn in policy, related to which was the introduction of the *TEPA* legislation (see above) (Windebank, 2012). As discussed in Chap. 1, the ALMP turn in labour-market policy, oriented towards the "social

[12] There are still women drawing the benefit after the child that they made the original claim for turns two because a subsequent birth gives rise to another period of entitlement to benefit.

investment state" (Jenson & Saint-Martin, 2003, p. 435), had begun as a response in the late 1990s to the post-industrial economic and social landscape of the "New Social Risks" (Taylor-Gooby, 2004, p. 2) of unemployment and an ageing population putting pressure on the welfare state in a context of increasing and intense global economic competition. Encouraging employment for low-qualified women was therefore promoted by Prime Minister Fillon's government within a social investment rather than a social rights or gender-equality frame, to promote the earning ability of women and act as a rampart against family poverty. Provision of childcare, and particularly creches and nursery education, can also be conceived within this social investment approach as a means to increase the human capital of the next generation and the productivity of the workforce (see discussion of Childcare below). President Sarkozy had been elected on a promise of increasing living standards by getting France back to work: "*travailler plus pour gagner plus*" (work more to earn more), in contrast with his Socialist rivals' slogan of "*travailler moins pour travailler tous*" (work less so everyone can work).

Within this activation paradigm, more radical changes to parental-leave benefit were discussed within the family-policy elite than were enacted in 2014 (see reports by Bousquet [2010], Clergeau [2009] and the *Haut Conseil de la Famille* [2009]). These included reducing the overall paid leave entitlement to one year offset by increasing the number of childcare places on offer for the under threes in crèches and with childminders and indexing the benefit on previous salary as well as introducing quotas of leave for each parent. Politicians on the left and feminist lobby groups such as the *Laboratoire d'Egalité* were in principle in favour of such a shorter, better paid and better shared parental leave for all (Morgan, 2013). However, the economic difficulties caused by the 2008 banking crisis limited the possibilities for funding the significant extensions of childcare provision that would be necessary if parental leave were to be shortened to one year for all families. The government ran out of time to act before the 2012 presidential elections. Furthermore, the attachment of public opinion to the notion of free choice in how to care for the under threes as revealed in opinion surveys and reactions to proposals for change on social media, opinions reinforced by groups such as those affiliated to the *UNAF* and centre-right politicians, made the governing administration hesitant to support a significant shortening of the leave so as to remove the option of looking after children at home until nursery school age in the run-up to the Presidential election (Windebank, 2017).

Gender differences are not only to be found in the ways individuals balance professional and parenting work time. There are significant gender disparities in the ways in which men and women engage with parenting work, whatever their employment status. Even when all adults in a family are employed and use some form(s) of childcare when children are not in school, the majority of direct and indirect caring work for children is undertaken in the private sphere by those who have parenting responsibility for them, and women undertake the majority of this unpaid work. The 2013 *DARES* study on childcare provision found that from Monday to Friday women living in dual-earner couples with at least one child under three spent between 71 and 81 per cent of their time outside employment in the presence of their child(ren) whilst fathers spent between 53 per cent and 65 per cent. Women in this group spent on average two hours per day alone with their children, whereas men spent shorter and more dispersed periods alone with them, averaging around 50 minutes per day (Briard, 2017, p. 4). The 2010 *INSEE* time-use study demonstrated similar gender disparities in time spent with children. In the category of 18–49-year-olds living in couples with children under 16, women spent more time doing any type of activity in the presence of children than men. Furthermore, regardless of the age and number of children, women spent significantly more time alone with their children (from 1 hour 54 minutes to 3 hours 47 minutes) than men (from 46 minutes to 1 hour 12 minutes) (Brousse, 2015b, p. 134 Table 4). In couple households where one or both parents work non-standard hours and have a split-shift childcare arrangement, men are found to spend more time alone with their children and are therefore obliged to take on more responsibilities for them, leading to a more egalitarian distribution of both parental and domestic work with their partner (Briard, 2017; Cartier et al., 2018; Windebank, 1999).

An intensification of parenting work has taken place since the 1980s and has increased the time that parents spend engaged in direct care, and educational, play and developmental activities with their children and accompanying them outside the home, often to improving activities (Sayer, 2010). In France, the amount of time spent in this way increased for both men and women over the period 1986 to 2010 according to the *INSEE* time-use studies for those years. Men aged 18–60 with children under 18 nearly doubled their parental time[13] from 22 minutes per day in 1986 to 41 minutes per day in 2010, whilst women, starting from a baseline that was four times that of men in 1986, increased this time from 82 minutes to 95 minutes per day (Champagne et al., 2014, p. 221) . Over the same time period both men and women decreased the time they spent on domestic work[14] resulting in the proportion of total domestic and care work time devoted to child-centred activities rising. This change in parenting practices is related to the shift to a post-industrial and post-Fordist economy and hypermodern society in which individuals have the possibility, but also the responsibility and necessity to define their own path in life and be high performing to compete in the globalised market system (Genest Dufault & Castelain Meunier, 2017). The family and parents are the prime source of support for that development for their children (Lacharité & Gagnier, 2010). Furthermore, individuals report finding satisfaction in parenting work. An add-on to the 2010 *INSEE* time-use study asked people to give a (dis)satisfaction score of -3 to +3 to the activities that they noted in their time diary. With an aggregate score of 1.9 across the population, time devoted to activities with children scored more highly that any professional or domestic activity (Brousse, 2015b, p. 128).

These general trends conceal differences in the types of activities undertaken with children by men and women. Men's parenting work tends to be more related to leisure (for example, outings, undertaking sports) and practised at the weekends and the holidays (Brachet & Salles, 2011; Brousse, 2015a). In addition, men increased the time spent taking children from place to place by 75 per cent between 1974 and 2010, in large part due to fears about children's safety increasing the age at which children are allowed out alone, the increase in extracurricular activities, the use of out-of-home childcare and women's unavailability for the task due to their employment (Brousse, 2015a, p. 100). Women spent more time on physical and medical care (Ricroch, 2012). It is not only those who live in different-sex couples who display these gendered practices: the 2010 *INSEE* time-use study showed that single fathers whose children lived

[13] This includes direct care, supervising homework, games and conversations, and transport as primary activities. Passive supervision while undertaking other primary activities is not included

[14] Defined for these purposes as including cleaning, cooking, washing up, laundry, shopping, administrative tasks, DIY and gardening

with them spent less than half the time on parental work as single mothers (Brousse, 2015b, p. 101).

It is noteworthy that the time spent on parental activities does not decrease with income according to the 2010 time-use study (Bittman, 2015). This finding is echoed across the EU (Lightman & Kevins, 2021). However, some differences are identified between socio-professional groups. Because they spent less time on domestic work, women in SPC 3 devoted a greater proportion of their overall domestic and care work time to parenting activities than other groups even though they had fewer children while men in SPC 3 devoted double the time to parental activities in comparison with men in SPC 6 (Brousse, 2015b, p. 134, Table 4). This class disparity in parental work time is explained by the fact that those in SPC 3 households have the financial means to outsource domestic work to free time for parental activities, work regular hours that coincide with school hours and put more emphasis on the need to develop the human and cultural capital of their offspring (Cartier et al., 2018).

Research to date suggests that in same-sex couples divisions of parenting work are more equal than in different-sex couples (Gross, 2009). However, even if not as pronounced as in different-sex couples, certain specialisations do arise in parenting work in same-sex families (Stambolis-Ruhstorfer & Gross, 2021). In lesbian couples parenting work may vary between the member of the couple who has given birth and her wife / partner. Research has shown that the partner who has given birth takes more responsibility for educational and medical matters for that child than their other parent, influenced both by the social and legal status of birthing parents and the cultural representations attaching to them, such as their rights to maternity leave, and the practicalities of breastfeeding for young babies (Descoutures, 2006; Vecho et al., 2011). In gay couples, divisions of parenting work have been found to vary less between the fathers. The take up of parental leave by fathers living in same-sex couples is higher than for men living in different-sex partnerships (Berton et al., 2017; Gross, 2009). Berton et al. (2017) argue that the use of parental leave among gay fathers of young children may be an attempt to counter the continued lack of acceptance of men in primary parenting and caregiving roles by enacting a traditional stay-at-home role. The social landscapes of parenting are still dominated by women, and for this reason, men with primary parenting responsibilities express a sense of unease as they negotiate this domain (Chatot, 2017b).

In addition to inequalities in the gender division of supervision and direct activities for and with children, the presence of children in a household increases the volume of domestic (indirect care) work to be done, reduces the time available to do it because of the demands of parental work, and results in a more unequal gender division of unpaid domestic and care work in households of different-sex couples. The 2010 *INSEE* time-use study found that hours spent on core domestic work (cleaning, cooking, washing up, shopping and laundry) in different-sex couples were unequal regardless of the presence and age / number of children in the family, but became more unequal from the arrival of the second child. Women with no children spent an average of 2 hours 54 minutes per day on these activities, compared with 1 hour and 2 minutes for men. There was a decrease in time spent on these tasks in couples with one child in response to the time needed for parental work, but the time women devoted to domestic activities increased to 3 hours and 3 minutes a day with two children, and 4 hours 19 minutes per day with three. In contrast, the highest amount of time devoted to these activities by men was for those with three children at 1 hour 10, but even so, this was only 8 minutes longer than for childless men. Furthermore, in households with two or three children, three out of ten fathers declared not to have done any domestic tasks, alongside three out of four who declared not to have done any parental work (Brousse, 2015b, p. 134 Table 4).

Studies have found that even when men are stay-at-home carers, they view and enact the relationship between parenting work and domestic work differently from women in a similar situation (Boyer, 2016; Chatot, 2021). Although in different-sex couples where the man stays at home full or part-time to look after young children they do take on a greater share of certain domestic tasks than their partners alongside parental tasks, particularly cooking, washing up and shopping, they rarely envisage themselves in a traditional homemaker role as responsible for all domestic and care work, and often do not engage in the most feminised domestic tasks of cleaning and laundry (Boyer, 2016; Chatot, 2017b). Rather, they undertake traditionally masculine domestic activities during their time at home such as DIY and gardening, engage in some form of economic activity, either related to their employment or as a secondary occupation, or participate in training or in sport. They express the opinion that responsibilities for parenting and domestic work do not necessarily go hand in hand. Men as primary carers for children seem, therefore, to be in a site of "circumscribed transgression" (Merla, 2007, p. 158) between a caring masculinity and the need to signal aspects of traditional masculinity.

Descoutures (2006) compared the role of parents in domestic work in same-sex lesbian couples and different-sex couples, finding a more egalitarian division of domestic work among the same-sex parents. This egalitarianism took the form of the parents more often undertaking tasks together, or if it was necessary for the one parent to undertake direct care tasks such as breastfeeding the other parent compensated by taking on more domestic tasks alone. Collective activity was only rarely witnessed in the different-sex couples. The use of paid services was higher for cleaning in the same-sex than in the different-sex couples after controlling for socio-professional status. Indeed in general, the use of paid services for domestic work is often justified by the desire to liberate time for the intensified needs of parenting and parental activities among higher-earning dual-earner families, whether this be cleaning, laundry or gardening and small household repairs (Burikova, 2016; Cox, 2015; Kilkey, 2010) and permitted by the decline of social norms that require women to undertake duties for their families that do not require higher thinking or emotional involvement (Bereni et al., 2001).

In all Western countries, a similar pattern of men increasing their involvement in parental work more than in domestic work has been witnessed (Altinas & Sullivan, 2017). However, the ways in which parents respond to the increased expectations of parenting alongside the need to be economically active, and the extent to which men and women share these responsibilities, are shaped by the work-family landscape in particular countries. French men have been found to spend less time looking after their children than men in countries that have comparable levels of publicly supported childcare and integration of mothers in the labour market but whose policies are more explicitly de-gendering, such as Sweden and Denmark. They have also been found to engage less with parenting and related domestic work than men in Liberal countries where lack of state support obliges men to take more responsibility for parenting work to liberate the labour power of their partners which is necessary for the economic wellbeing of the family (Geist, 2005; Windebank, 1999). For example, Craig and Mullan (2010) compare the paid and unpaid work of different-sex couples with and without children in the United States, Australia, Italy, France and Denmark using national time-use studies.[15]

[15] For France the 2010 INSEE time-use study is used.

French men spent the least amount of time looking after their children: 0.8 hours on a weekday in comparison with 1.3 hours for men in Australia and the United States, and 1.5 hours in Denmark. This was in the context of France being the country, alongside Denmark, where professional worktime demands differed the least between families with and without children, reflecting the wide availability and use of childcare and nursery-school provision to relieve families of parenting work in both countries. However, in Denmark this support was accompanied by a more equitable gender division of parenting work, whereas in France it appeared to relieve men more than women of parenting duties.

However, French men have been found to participate more in direct and indirect care for children than men in other Conservative regimes, and in Southern and Eastern European countries. For example, Solera and Mencarini (2018, p. 532), conducting a comparative-longitudinal study on the gender division of housework before and after the birth of the first child in different-sex couples using the first two waves of the Gender and Generations Survey[16], compared Bulgaria, France and the Netherlands. They found that in all three countries, the birth of a first child triggered a re-traditionalisation of domestic and care work (defined as the woman doing more than 75 per cent of the total household chores), but this was less pronounced in France than in the other two countries. In France, the percentage of couples falling into the traditional category rose from 21 per cent before the birth of the child to 29 per cent afterwards; from 43 to 53 per cent among the Bulgarian couples; and from 29 to 39 per cent in Dutch couples. It should be noted, however, that in France the arrival of the first child has less of an effect both on women's employment and domestic work time than the arrival of subsequent children, so replicating this study on larger families may result in differing comparative results.

Childcare

In order for both parents of young children to be able to be at work at the same time, or undertake leisure or social activities without their children, they need to access childcare. The forms of care required are varied. They depend on the intensity of the care needs of the child, the length of time care is required and whether the care required is regular or sporadic in nature. In selecting types of care, not only will availability, accessibility and

[16] https://www.ggp-i.org/

affordability be important for parents, but also the quality of the care in terms of safety, affection and stimulation for the child as appropriate to their stage of development and in line with cultural expectations and norms.

Unpaid Childcare Work

In 2018 29 per cent of dual-earner families and 53 per cent of single-parent families with a child under three did not use any form of formal childcare or work-family reconciliation policy in France, including the *PreParE* (Béradier, 2021, p. 2). In these households, childcare was managed either between the parents or with the input of informal support from the extended family, friendship, neighbourhood or other community groups. Working parents whose primary source of childcare is formal may also call on these informal unpaid sources of support as a secondary or occasional form of childcare, as may non-working parents. Looking after children by friends and family may also be construed as leisure or sociability time by the individuals concerned depending on the circumstances.

By far the most important source of unpaid non-parental childcare is provided by grandparents. Because of increased life expectancies and improved health status of older people, grandparents and grandchildren share a longer period of their lives together. Childcare by grandparents is constructed within the context of functional intergeneration solidarity, that is family obligations and long-term reciprocity based on the giving and receiving of money, time and space (Bengston & Roberts, 1991). Opportunity structures, such as grandparents' employment and health status, geographical proximity and financial and capital resources, and the contextual frame of tax, labour market and welfare policies influence this intergenerational solidarity. The 2010 *INSEE* time-use study demonstrated that between 1974 and 2010 grandparental involvement in childcare work increased, with grandparents living in cities devoting 2.5 times more hours to looking after their grandchildren in 2010 than in 1974 (Brousse, 2015a, p. 101). Of all children under 6 in 2013, 70 per cent were minded at least occasionally by family members, mostly grandparents, who provided 16.9 million hours of childcare for that year (Kitzman, 2018, p. 3).

This does not necessarily mean that grandparents or family members provide the principal mode of childcare when parents are at work. In 2013 in France grandparents were the principal mode of childcare for only three per cent of all children under three during business hours (Monday to Friday 8 a.m.–7 p.m.) and two per cent of under sixes. This represented a one-point reduction from the proportions observed in 2002 and 2007 (Kitzman, 2018, p. 3 Table 1). This is unsurprising given the range of paid childcare options in France and possibilities for parental leave. Grandparents and family members more often act as the main secondary source of childcare for this pre-school age group: 9 per cent of children aged 3–5 and 13 per cent of children aged 0–2 were looked after in this way in 2013. Furthermore, 14.6 per cent of children of nursery-school age (3–5) were minded by grandparents on a Wednesday when there is no school or a reduced number of classes (Kitzman, 2018, p. 3 Table 1). Even more children were looked after at least once a week by grandparents when evenings and weekends are included: 18.9 per cent of 0–2-year-olds during the week (average 6 hours per care session) and 6.9 per cent at the weekend (average 8 hours 17 minutes per care session); and 23.4 per cent of 3–5-year-olds during the week (average 4 hours 2 minutes per care session) and 6.7 per cent at the weekend (average 9 hours 4 minutes per session) (Kitzman, 2018, p. 3 Table 1).

Grandparents are a particularly important source of support for single parents with twice as many of their children being minded by grandparents as children of coupled parents, all other things being equal. The geographical proximity of grandparents to grandchildren and mothers' employment increases the probability of grandparents looking after grandchildren on a regular basis (Charavel, 2016). There is a clear pattern of gendering of childcare by grandparents. On the one hand, children are more often taken care of by their grandmothers than their grandfathers (Kitzman, 2018), and on the other, mothers have been found to give precedence to maternal grandmothers in expecting help with children (Thalineau & Nowik, 2018). There exists, therefore, a network of matrilinear exchange for childcare within the extended family, demonstrating how expectations around the caring role for women extend beyond their own children. Much has been said in recent years in the media about the so-called squeeze generation of women who find themselves looking after their own children and elderly parents. However, in reality and due to the trend for later births and improved health and fitness of older people, it is more common to find women caring simultaneously for their grandchildren and their older parents (Herlofson & Brandt, 2020; Le Dantec, 2017). Research has found that providing help and care to elderly parents increases the probability of providing childcare for grandchildren, not the contrary (Vlachantoni et al., 2019; Železná, 2018) as families characterised by strong intergenerational solidarity help both older and younger generations and those characterised by weak solidarity are more likely to not provide help to either.

Unpaid childcare is also undertaken within neighbourhood, friendship or other community groups, often for shorter periods, and exchanged on a short- to medium-term reciprocal basis between parents (Lowndes, 2006). Networks of parents based around their children's activities, childcare providers or schools are often involved (Gray, 2003; Windebank, 1999). In France, a nationally representative survey by Prouteau (1998, p. 60) showed that 48 per cent of those aged 15 and over reported undertaking informal voluntary work in the four weeks prior to the survey, 32.1 per cent for the extended family, 22.6 per cent for friends, neighbours and colleagues and 6.7 per cent for both. Shopping and childcare were the most frequently cited tasks, and the activities carried out reflected traditional gender norms with women undertaking care tasks, including for children, more frequently than men. For women, having children reduced the frequency of informal voluntary work for the extended family, but increased it for non-kin members of their entourage suggesting that obligations within the extended family are lessened when individuals have their own parenting responsibilities, but the norms of exchange mean that in non-kin networks to gain support with childcare, support has to be given. These exchanges of childcare are heavily gendered and constructed as an extension of mothering practices (Prouteau, 1998; Windebank, 2008). Furthermore, the 2018 *Mon Quartier, Mes Voisins* (My Neighbourhood, My Neighbours) survey carried out by the *INED* found that of the 68 per cent of respondents who reported doing favours for those living in their neighbourhood, 28 per cent reported looking after children, or accompanying them to or picking them up from school or other activities (Authier & Cayouette-Remblière, 2021). Men who are full-time carers for their children report difficulties in being able to integrate into these informal support networks (Chatot, 2017a).

In international comparisons of European or high-income countries France has a lower-than-average contribution of informal provision by kin and non-kin to childcare. This is because in countries with less formal childcare provision, informal unpaid carers, particularly grandparents, help dual-earning or single-parent families much more intensively so that they can access employment (ILO, 2018). Such high-intensity care is crowded out by the professional childcare infrastructure in France. However, levels of such informal childcare are substantially higher in France than in the

Nordic countries, particularly Sweden, Finland and Denmark (ILO, 2018, Fig. 2.5 p. 52). In 2014, the proportion of children cared for by unpaid carers (non-parents) for at least one hour during a-typical week in France was 20 per cent of 0–2-year-olds (OECD average 28 per cent; lowest average Denmark at 0 per cent); for 3–5-year-old, 22 per cent (OECD average 29 per cent; lowest average Denmark at 0 per cent); and for 6–12-year-olds 15 per cent (OECD average 21 per cent; lowest average Finland at 1 per cent).

Professional Childcare Work

A very substantial amount of work looking after children is undertaken within the social relations of employment, both within the education system and by childcare providers in France. There is a wide range of types of employment and workers involved, from teachers, and creches and nursery professionals working in large organisations to childminders working in their own home as direct employees of their clients. Each type of employment entails differing types of relationship between the worker and the families they serve, demands varying levels of qualification, and brings diverse levels of professional and social status.

The principal form of out-of-home care for children is school where they are looked after for free within the state system or for a fee in the private sector. Schools are staffed by teaching and other educational professionals who have specific and well-recognised qualifications and professional status. Pay and conditions in the public sector are set by the Ministry for Education and teaching is a highly unionised profession. Teaching is also a highly feminised profession particularly for younger children with 83 per cent of nursery and primary school teachers being women in 2019 in contrast with 58.6 per cent in secondary education.[17] School is compulsory in France for children aged six to eighteen, and non-compulsory free nursery schooling within the state system is taken up by over 97 per cent of all children aged three to five, although 19 per cent of three-year-olds, 14 per cent of four-year-olds, but only 1 per cent five-year-olds attend on a mornings-only basis (Charavel, 2016, p. 2 Table 1). France therefore scores very highly in international comparisons of childcare coverage for three–five-year-olds (ILO, 2018, p. 136 Fig. 3.12). Nursery and primary school children receive 24 hours of classes per week

[17] https://donnees.banquemondiale.org/indicator/SE.PRM.TCHR.FE.ZS

and secondary pupils receive a minimum of 26 hours of classes over a 36-week school year.

The school day in France is relatively long between 8.30 a.m. and 4.30 p.m. with a lunch break of between 1.5 and 2 hours with canteen facilities provided—exact school times are decided locally. Until 2014, nursery and primary age children had no school on a Wednesday, this originally being a concession when secular education was introduced to allow Catholic children to attend catechism. Since 2014 the norm has been to have school on Wednesday morning, but local authorities have the right to reorganise school hours within certain limits, including to have no school on a Wednesday. The lack of school on Wednesday or on Wednesday afternoon is related to the popularity of long-hours part-time work among parents in France who often work on an 80 per cent contract so they can be at home on Wednesday (Windebank, 1999).

Parents therefore have to make arrangements for children when they are not at school if they cannot be present due to their work hours, inflexibility of their job, commuting time or other commitments. As discussed above, informal arrangements with grandparents, other kin or members of the community may have to be made. As concerns formal provision, extended hours are available for nursery-school children at low cost for an additional two hours per day (Fagnani & Math, 2011). Childcare allowances available to the under threes such as the *AFAEMA*, *AGED* and since 2004 their replacement, the *Complement de libre choix de mode de garde (CMG-MG) (Supplement for the free choice of childcare arrangements)* are also available for children up to the age of six to support parents with out-of-school care costs. Parents of children of any age employing a childminder or babysitter through direct employment can also benefit from the subsidies available for PHS under the Borloo Plan (see below and Chap. 5). Lastly, *centres de loisirs* (leisure facilities) and *colonies de vacances* (holiday camps) regulated by the local authority can be used for out-of-school care. The *DREES* childcare survey found that in 2013, 61 per cent of three–five-year-olds at nursery school were looked after by someone other than their parents outside school hours and during the holidays. Thirty per cent of these children were minded by grandparents, 30 per cent were in some form of formal care, more usually childminders but also *halte-garderies* (see below for definition) and 12 per cent were looked after by friends, neighbours or babysitters, either on an unpaid or an undeclared paid basis. Dual-earner and higher paid families were more likely to use formal care (Charavel, 2016, p. 3 Table 2).

For the under threes, parents in France have a very wide range of formal childcare options at their disposal, both in collective facilities and provided by individuals, all supported by the state. This range of options is wider in France than in nearly all other high-income countries in keeping with the emphasis in work-family reconciliation policy on choice (Thevenon, 2013). These formal childcare options are used in the majority by parents due to their employment commitments but are also used by some economically inactive parents. There are several different types of collective childcare establishments available to parents in France (*Etablissements d'accueil du jeune enfant [*EAJE*]*). First, traditional crèches, which trace their roots back to the nineteenth century (see Chap. 2) have between 20 and 60 children, are run by professional staff qualified in early years care and education and managed by local authorities, associations or more rarely within the private sector. *Micro-crèches* (micro-crèches) are a more recent phenomenon and provide a half-way house between traditional crèches and individual care, accommodating up to ten children. They are normally privately run. *Halte-garderies*[18] provide occasional part-time care and *crèches multi-accueil* (multi-functional crèches) provide the services of both a traditional crèche and a *halte-garderie*. In addition, there are a limited number of workplace crèches which may be subsidised by employers. In the late 1960s, as part of the counter-culture movement *crèches parentales* (parent-run crèches) developed in France, that is, crèches run on a self-management basis by parents. A small number of these crèches still exist. Local authority crèches are the cheapest childcare option for the under threes. They are particularly advantageous for lower-earning families because the fees are set dependent on income. However, places in these crèches are limited, and availability varies widely across the country. Parents using private-sector micro-crèches can claim the *CMG-micro-crèches* which refunds up to 85 per cent of the cost depending on income and number of children (Observatoire National de la Petite Enfance [ONAPE], 2019).

Individualised forms of care are often based on a relationship of direct employment by the parent of an *assistante maternelle agréée* (registered childminder) in whose homes children are cared for, or for an individual providing *garde à domicile* (at-home childcare) where the child carer works in the child's home. These individualised childcare options are

[18] There is no English equivalent to this term that denotes a form of childcare for occasional, irregular or short-term care.

subsidised by the state. The *Prestation d'accueil du jeune enfant (PAJE) (Benefit for young children)* was introduced in 2004 by the right-wing government of Prime Minister de Villepin. The *PAJE* brought all existing childcare and parental leave benefits under one umbrella, and these were renamed to emphasise the choice for parents offered by work-family reconciliation policy and the equal support by the state to help parents with the costs either of reducing their employment to look after very young children or of paying for childcare. The *AFAEMA* and *AGED* were merged and replaced with one childcare allowance, the *CMG* which has three permutations—the *CMG (Assistantes Maternelles)* (childminders), the *CMG (Garde a domicile)* (home-based care) and the *CMG (Micro crèches)* (micro creches) depending on the type of care provider used. These benefits used to sit alongside the *CLCA* and later the *COLCA* and now are paired with the *PreParE*. The allowances can be claimed on behalf of children up to the age of six, and up to a ceiling of 85 per cent of costs. The exact amount of subsidy available is dependent on income and the number of children in the family, and subject to economic activity conditions. Additionally, the 2005 Borloo Plan (see Chap. 5) extended the social security and tax exonerations that had previously been on offer to those employing home-based workers to parents employing a childminder through direct employment (Thevenon, 2013).

The parliamentary debates on the *PAJE* represented the first time that work-family reconciliation had been discussed without an underlying concern for demographic issues being expressed (Chauffaut & Lévêque, 2012). There was a consensus among parliamentarians that employment for all parents should not just be tolerated, but that it was positive for women, children and the economy. The term mother had been replaced with parent in the vast majority of interventions. Although preferential treatment for the third child did not disappear from French work-family policy, it was justified more by the issue of the relatively low labour-market participation of mothers of three children, and insistence that no-one should have the size of their family curtailed by financial considerations, rather than population concerns. This change may well be the result of altered cultural norms, but it should be noted that in the twenty-first century just as during the *Trente Glorieuses*, the fertility rate in France has been very strong ranging from 1.87 and 2.03 children. France had the highest or second highest fertility rate in Europe alongside Ireland between 2000 and 2015, and since has been in the top three with Sweden joining the ranks (*INSEE*, 2020).

In response to the increasing birth rate and participation of mothers in employment, there have been very substantial increases in the number of childcare places available for the under threes. From 1995 to 2010, available places increased from 880,000 to 138,000. Until 2004, the number of places with registered childminders represented the vast majority of this increase, with little to no increase in the numbers of places on offer in collective facilities. Given the increased birth rate in the twenty-first century, this represented a decline in collective childcare coverage for this age group (Fagnani & Math, 2011; Thevenon, 2013). As discussed in Chap. 2, this focus on individualised forms of childcare was the result of policy decisions to develop them as a cheaper option than crèches within the context of the post-industrial pressures on the welfare state. This policy preference for childminders was criticised in terms of its impact both on childcare workers and on its affordability for low-income families.

The creation of the status of *assistant maternel agréé* (registered childminder) in 1977, an attempt to eradicate the undeclared work of traditional *nourrices*, and subsequent measures to provide support and training for home-based child carers professionalised childminding, improved the pay and status of this occupation to some extent (David-Alberola & Momic, 2008). However, there remains a number of aspects of the pay, career and working conditions of childminders and nannies who work as direct employees for households that are less favourable than for those working as employees in crèches and other collective facilities. Child carers working in collective facilities must have a minimum qualification of a relevant *Certificat d'Aptitude Professionnel* (*CAP*), a nationally recognised vocational qualification that gives access to studying for higher levels of diploma and may qualify the holder to work in other fields. Childminders or nannies do not need any qualifications to apply for registration. They can become registered by following 120 hours of training, 60 of which must be undertaken before they start to work. This training does not have the same recognition or validity outside childminding as a *CAP*. Furthermore, working within an organisation gives creche employees the opportunity for career progression, and a regular salary. For childminders and nannies working as direct employees there is no clear career path, and income is dependent on the children that can be recruited.

Working in your own home as a childminder or in the child's home as a carer also has a number of drawbacks in comparison with working in an institution. Direct employees often have to provide services for several employers leading to role strain and instability of income. Working alone in the home environment can be isolating which impacts on day-to-day mental health. Working alone also increases the level of responsibility that childminders and home-based carers must bear in comparison with creche workers who can share responsibilities with their peers and rely on supervisors and managers for support (Unterreiner, 2018). Despite the difficulty of the job, childminders in particular may find that their work is not viewed as a *bone fide* profession by family and friends because of the lack of distinction between the home and workplace and the proximity of the work to its unpaid familial equivalent (Cartier, 2015). Meanwhile, child carers who work in the homes of their employers may find it difficult to refuse to undertake domestic tasks that are not specified in their contract of employment or work unpaid overtime. Live-in workers, particularly those without the independent right to reside or work in France, are especially vulnerable to unfair treatment and even abuse. The inability to delegate responsibility also means that childminders and home-based child carers have little control over their work rhythms (e.g., rest breaks) and must sustain high levels of attention over long periods. That said, Avril (2012, p. 92) found that 20 per cent of childminders in their survey had access to help for complicated tasks from staff at the local *CAF* or *Protection maternelle et infantile* (*PMI*)[19] (mother and child protection) service. Childminders may also belong to independent professional associations or informal neighbourhood networks that organise meetings and group activities during or outside work hours (Mozère, 1988) and encounter their colleagues in public spaces (Pande, 2012).

The French Labour Code explicitly excludes those working in direct employment relations from many of its general provisions (Ledoux & Krupka, 2020). For example, in order to have the right to representatives who can negotiate with the employer, there must be enough employees to organise a group, and the more employees a business has, the more rights those workers can obtain. Direct employees therefore have few opportunities to act collectively in support of their rights. That said, those working as direct employees on a declared basis in France have had protections under the *Convention collective nationale des salariés du particulier employeur* (collective national agreement for direct employees) of 2000 (Sohler & Levy, 2013, p. 49), which was updated in January 2022. However, even

[19] The *PMI* is service based in departmental local authorities responsible for the health and wellbeing of mothers and children.

with this agreement in place, there is less scrutiny of the work conditions of home-based workers than other types of workers by the state because labour inspectors do not have the right to enter private residences in the same way they do other workplaces in France without the owner's authorisation or a judicial order. France has not yet ratified the ILO Convention 189 on domestic work which has been in existence since 2011. The convention aims at ensuring decent work conditions for home-based care and domestic workers and requires ratifying member countries to implement a range of legal protections including labour inspections and penalties for employers contravening regulations.

The socio-demographic profile of home-based childcare workers, particularly childminders, in France suggests that this is not necessarily a first choice of profession for many. The 99.5 per cent of registered childminders in France are women (Havard Duclos, 2018, p. 30), such a majority that often the generic term used, even in academic research and policy documents, is in the grammatical feminine, and many studies of childminders do not even bother to give statistics for the gender distribution of these workers. Furthermore, older workers are overrepresented among childminders, the average age in 2014 being 47.1 years in comparison with an average of 43.2 years for the economically active population as a whole in France (Vroyland, 2016, p. 3). This is because childminding is a profession that women often take up after a period of inactivity due to their own parenting responsibilities or after losing their jobs in traditional, declining industries or occupations (David-Alberola and Momic (2008). Those living in couples with a manual worker and migrant or second or third-generation citizens with a migrant heritage are also overrepresented among childminders (Avril, 2012; Unterreiner, 2018).

There has been a recalibration of policy towards increasing childcare places in crèches in France. However, it was not concern for the working conditions of childcare workers that prompted this change. Rather it was concerns over the employment rate of low-qualified mothers. As discussed in relation to the *PreParE* there was concern in the early years of the new century about the bifurcation of mothers' labour-market participation in France. In 2002, the Barcelona agreement[20] had set targets for childcare

[20] The EU Barcelona agreement 2002 stipulated that "Member States should remove disincentives to female labour force participation and strive, taking into account the demand for childcare facilities and in line with national patterns of provision, to provide childcare by 2010 to at least 90% of children between 3 years old and the mandatory school age and at least 33% of children under 3 years of age" (European Council, 2002).

coverage in the EU for the under threes and three- to five-year-olds. Although France met these targets, this EU framework highlighted to French policymakers the obstacle to improving women's activity rates further, which was lower qualified women's labour-market position (Thevenon, 2013). The structure of support for formal childcare played a part in this bifurcation because it provided more childcare options for higher qualified and better paid women than for lower qualified women whose job opportunities were fewer, who were lower paid and who were often required to work non-standard work hours. Individualised forms of childcare are more expensive than collective care in traditional crèches, despite the fact that childcare allowances were and are calculated on ability to pay. Furthermore, fees have to be paid by the user and then claimed back which can be financially challenging for those on low incomes (Evertsson, 2014). Traditional crèches are financed directly by the local Caisse des Allocations Familiales and fees means-tested, making them more affordable and accessible for low-income families. However, demand for places in these traditional crèches outstrips supply in many areas, and their geographical spread is not consistent. Furthermore, even though the hours offered by creches are relatively long (often from 7 a.m. to 6 p.m.), many do not cater for those working a-typical hours.

From the mid-2000s onwards, French family bureaucratic institutions and politicians began to place more emphasis on meeting the needs of lower qualified and lower paid parents, particularly those living in deprived areas with a limited childcare infrastructure, and who may work or need to work non-standard hours (Fagnani, 2012; Thevenon, 2013). Among the ways to achieve this end was the provision of more places in crèches better suited to the needs of these parents. In 2006 the objective of increasing the accessibility of childcare services for families receiving social assistance was set into law. There was to be an obligation for local authorities to reserve at least five per cent of creche places for these families. Furthermore, the 2009 law on social assistance stipulated that local authorities should give priority to parents engaged in processes of social inclusion (whether receiving benefits or not) in the allocation of crèche places. In the same year, the *Plan Crèches Espoir Banlieues*[21] (Hope for the estates - creche plan) aimed to create 10,000 childcare places in deprived estates with

[21] For further details, see: https://travail-emploi.gouv.fr/IMG/pdf/LIVRET_ESPOIR_BANLIEUE.pdf

extended opening to cater for those working a-typical hours (Boyer & Céroux, 2012). The 2012 Conference on Poverty set the objective of delivering more childcare places for children from poor families, with a target of them representing ten per cent of all children in local-authority collective facilities (Thevenon, 2013). Lastly, both left- and right-wing administrations changed the conditionality of the *CMG*: in 2010 Prime Minister Fillon's right-wing administration increased the *CMG* by 10 per cent for those working a-typical hours (*Haut Conseil de la* Famille, 2011) and in 2014 Prime Minister Valls' Socialist government reduced the *CMG* for those earning above an income ceiling leading to 6.1 per cent of claimants for childminders and 1.9 per cent of claimants for home-based carers experiencing a reduction in their benefits (Boisnault & Fichen, 2015, p. 5).

In addition to concerns over childcare options for the low paid, governments also had to respond to parents across the social spectrum who were beginning to voice a preference for crèches over childminders due to the enhanced educational experience parents believed their child would receive by trained staff. Creche provision also corresponded better to a social investment approach to early years care than childminding. In 2021, the preferred childcare option even of parents of children aged six to twelve months was a creche (Crepin & Boyer, 2022). Strategies for the general expansion of childcare places therefore put more emphasis on collective facilities. The Fillon government's *Plan Petite Enfance* (Early Childhood Plan) 2007–2012 aimed to generate an extra 100,000 childcare places by 2012, half in collective and half in individual provision, in part by loosening regulations regarding child-to-carer ratios and ensuring full occupancy of crèches. However, by the elections of 2012, only 13,160 extra places had been created. The Hollande administration had plans to create an extra 275,000 places for the under threes between 2013 and 2017, again split equally between individual care and collective care and to provide more places for the under threes in nursery schools (75,000 places) to increase the childcare coverage rate for this age group from 54 per cent to 65 per cent. The aim was also to correct the territorial inequalities in childcare coverage which in 2012 ranged from 9 to 80 per cent in different *départments*. Furthermore, and echoing the *Plan Crèches Espoir Banlieue*, urban regeneration policy was to be harnessed to improve cover for the most deprived areas (*Haut Conseil de la Famille*, 2014). However, progress was slow with only 19 per cent of the hoped-for increase having been realised by 2015 (*Haut Conseil de la Famille*, 2015).

Chiefly to blame for these shortfalls was the post-2008 economic situation. Just as France was starting to debate significant change to its work-family reconciliation policy within the context of the adoption of ALMP and desire to activate the labour power of lower qualified mothers, the 2008 economic banking crisis hit, and in its wake came a sovereign debt crisis and recession leading to austerity measures (Ollier-Malaterre et al., 2013). This economic situation increased the existing pressures on welfare (Ferrangina & Seeleib-Kaiser, 2014). Work-family reconciliation policy in France and elsewhere demonstrated resilience in the face of these pressures. Indeed, across Europe childcare provision was able to withstand budget cuts because it was regarded as a social investment rather than a welfare cost (Kvist, 2013), and brought electoral advantage to parties in government at a much lower cost than other types of welfare expenditure (Bonoli, 2013). Increasing mothers' employment rates was deemed even more important in difficult economic times as a protection against poverty and benefit dependency. However, the economic situation did make it difficult to make significant, costly and paradigmatic changes to work-family reconciliation policy in France such as introducing a shorter parental leave, indexed on previous income accompanied by a significant expansion of formal childcare as envisaged by the Sarkozy administration. For example, the *Haut Conseil de la Famille* reported that reductions in standards of living after 2008 meant that families had to reduce their childcare expenditure; local authorities who are in charge of implementing the improvements in collective care had suffered budget cuts and demand for childcare fell due to the recession since more parents and grandparents were unemployed[22] and available for childcare within the family limiting the expansion of childminding services (*Haut Conseil de la Famille*, 2015).

By 2018, 52 per cent of families (1.3 million) with a child under three in France benefitted from at least one form of work-family reconciliation for a minimum of one hour per month (Béradier, 2021, p. 1). There has been some equalisation of the use of individual and collective care with 25 per cent of families (636,4000) using childminders or home-based child carers and 22 per cent (548,900) using some form of crèches. Ten per cent claimed the *PreParE* (Béradier, 2021, p. 1) with some families using multiple options. As regards childcare places and childcare coverage for children under three, the balance between collective and individualised

[22] The unemployment rate in 2008 in France as 7.4 per cent but had risen to 10.4 per cent by 2015. By 2020 it had returned to 8 per cent.

care remains uneven. In 2019, there were in principal 1,345,700 childcare places representing 59.8 places per 100 children, an improvement on the 2014 situation but short of the objective of a 65 per cent coverage rate of the Socialist administration. Childminders provided the majority of places (55 per cent) and collective care facilities the next largest share at 35 per cent of places. Home-based child carers working in private homes only contributed marginally to this global offer: 2.1 per cent of all places (*Observatoire de la Petite Enfance* [ONaPE], 2019, p. 2).

The number of places offered in crèches continues to rise (2.5 per cent overall between 2018 and 2019), particularly in micro-crèches with a rise of 13.6 per cent between 2018 and 2019. However, micro-crèches do not necessarily deliver the financial benefits to low-paid families that traditional crèches do as they are funded in the same way as childminders and home-based child carers through the *CMG*. The socio-demographic and socio-professional characteristics of families continue to have a significant influence on the extent to which they can access work-family reconciliation support and what types of support they claim. In 2018 for those families whose income was below the poverty line, 24 per cent used at least one type of childcare or parental leave benefit, whereas this was the case for 64 per cent of those with incomes above the poverty line. This is particularly marked for individualised forms of care (childminders and nannies) with seven per cent as opposed to thirty-three per cent of users respectively in these two categories, respectively (Béradier, 2021, p. 3). It is often the least well-off families with at least one child under three who do not use any form of childcare or parental leave benefit (Béradier, 2021, p. 3).

Levels of inequality of access to childcare by socio-economic and socio-professional group for zero–three-year-olds in France are some of the highest in Europe. There remains a significant gap between the participation rates of zero–two-year-olds in formal childcare in low-income households (38 per cent in 2017) in comparison with middle-income (78 per cent) and high-income (82 per cent) households (OECD, 2020, p. 5 Fig. 3). The gap between low- and middle-income households is much larger in France than in other EU countries where, when a significant gap exists, it is more usually between high earners on the one hand, and low- and middle-income earners on the other caused by the lack of public subsidy and high cost to the consumer of childcare services (OECD, 2020). In France, the particular position of low-income families despite the high expenditure and extensive range of work-family reconciliation policies on offer is due to the lack of accessibility of cheaper collective childcare particularly in more deprived areas, very patchy geographic childcare coverage across the country, lack of provision for those working non-standard hours and lack of childcare support for the high numbers of young and low-qualified unemployed parents seeking work. Despite the efforts in the 2010s, many local authorities have continued to give priority to dual-earner families rather than those looking for work for crèche places (Taylor, 2016). In addition, the diversity of the French childcare landscape makes it difficult to navigate for those who are not well informed or have cultural reticence about using childcare (Collombet, 2018). In this regard, it is interesting to note that there is negligible difference between socio-economic groups for attendance at nursery school for three– to five-year-olds suggesting that free and universal in-kind provision leads to more equal outcomes than the fragmented and partially cash-for-care system in operation for the under threes (OECD, 2020).

Some argue that these material factors interact with ideational factors such as class-based differences in values regarding parenting to explain these disparities in France and that cultural norms persist in working-class households that favour a breadwinner-homemaker family model in different-sex couples. *Cartier* et al. (2018, p. 73) found that women in households in SPC 6 were more likely to agree (54 per cent) with the statement "a pre-school age child risks suffering if their mother is employed" than those in SPC 5 (45 per cent), SPC 4 (31 per cent) or SPC 3 (28 per cent). Meanwhile, Beque (2019) found that all things being equal as concerns work conditions, women in SPC 5 and 6 were more likely than those in other socio-professional groups to suffer from their friends and family reproaching them for working whilst raising children. It has also been found that in different-sex couples if the male partner cannot secure a job, the female partner remains outside the labour market (Taylor, 2016). Given the emphasis on parental choice, and historic lack of attempt by the state to persuade its population that certain forms of work-family reconciliation are preferable to others, these more traditional attitudes have been able to persist. These attitudes may also be informed by the more limited employment opportunities for the individuals, families and communities concerned, and the material obstacles to accessing childcare and employment mean that there is less of a positive feedback loop concerning the compatibility of parenting and employment than among groups where such obstacles are lesser.

Concluding Summary

During the first decades of the twenty-first century, trends in parenting in France that had begun in the latter part of the twentieth century have continued and, in some cases, amplified. Parenting work falls disproportionately on the shoulders of women, whatever the household type in which they live. A parental employment gap persists. Women modify their employment to accommodate parenting responsibilities, whether this be by withdrawing temporarily from the labour market using parental leave or becoming economically inactive, or partially by working part-time. That said, employment rates of women with parenting responsibilities are high in France in comparison with other high-income countries, and rates of part-time work average, the result of long-standing de-familialising work-family reconciliation policies and childcare provision in the country. However, this overall positive picture hides a bifurcation of the labour market among women with parenting responsibilities, with low-qualified and low-skilled and younger mothers being much less likely than average to be employed. In international comparisons, levels of inequality of access to childcare by socio-economic and socio-professional group for zero–three-year-olds in France are some of the highest in Europe. In contrast, on becoming parents, most men increase their employment commitment, and both uptake of parental leave and adoption of part-time work remain marginal choices for them. French men have had very low rates of take-up of parental leave in comparison with other high-income countries. This situation is explained in part by the fact that work-family reconciliation policy until 2014 had few deliberately de-gendering elements.

Social norms concerning the intensity of parenting, the extension of the period of dependence of children, and the responsibility of parents to develop their children's human, social and cultural capital through education and developmental activities, have led to increases in the time spent on parental work. Although the time devoted to parental work by French men has increased proportionately more than the parental work time of women and more than for other forms of unpaid work (see Chaps. 4 and 5), women still spend more time on these activities than men. Despite the 35-hour-week laws in France giving men the opportunity to participate more in parenting and family life than in countries with longer working hours, in international comparisons, parenting and related domestic work remains more gendered in France than in countries with comparable levels of work-family reconciliation provisions. Policies offering the opportunity for men to take a more involved approach to parenting work without specifically de-gendering measures appear insufficient to bring about higher levels of gender equality in this regard.

The optional de-familialisation of parenting work within the women-state contract without an explicit de-gendering strategy for parenting in France led to a situation in which men did not develop internal identities as carers even when external constraints on their opportunities to engage in parenting were removed (Himmelweit & Sigala, 2004). However, starting in the mid-2000s, the woman-state contract in work-family reconciliation policy has been increasingly questioned due to problems of the parental employment gap, the labour-market marginalisation of low-skilled mothers and the continued gendering of parenting work. The call of the feminist lobby to put more emphasis on the de-gendering of parenting responsibilities in work-family reconciliation policy began to gain ground within the bureaucratic institutions surrounding the family at this time because it chimed with the social investment approach to welfare and the activation paradigm within labour-market policy promoted by the right-wing governments of President Sarkozy. Change came about in two aspects of work-family reconciliation policy. First, there were changes to paternity leave and parental leave policy to include more coercive measures to encourage men's participation in parenting responsibilities. In 2002 paternity leave was introduced, and in 2021 extended, and one week of leave made compulsory. In 2014 the *PreParE* was introduced which shortened the period of leave that one parent in a couple can take so that if a couple wants to make use of the full benefit entitlement, they are obliged to share the leave. These policy changes are significant because they represent the first attempts in France to curtail the choice of parents over how to look after very young children in the name of gender equality.

The introduction of the *PreParE* had two objectives, only one of which has been successful to date. The first was to reduce the amount of time women remain absent from the labour market by shortening the leave period that one parent can take. This is important because the take-up of long parental leaves are more prevalent among young and low-qualified mothers than average, leading to their medium- to long-term marginalisation or indeed exclusion from the labour market. In this respect, the policy has had some success. The second objective was to increase men's take-up of parental leave. In this regard, the policy has so far failed with only marginal increases having been achieved. A major reason for the lack of impact on men's behaviours lies with fact that the benefit is still paid at a low flat rate, rather than indexed on previous salary. Schemes that have been more successful in increasing men's participation, such as that introduced in Germany in 2007, index benefit payments on previous salary, the cost of which is offset by maximum leave periods being much shorter, usually one year. A scheme with similar provisions had been proposed in France in the late 2000s, but due to a combination of the impacts of the 2008 financial crisis and the resistance by stakeholders to curtailing parental choice, the degree of policy change that was eventually implemented was more tempered.

Furthermore, the French state has attempted to change the balance between provision of childcare places in crèches and provision of childcare places by childminders for the under threes. During the last decade of the twentieth century, expansion of childcare places was achieved through cash-for-care benefits for the direct employment of childminders with little support for increasing the number of creche places. Not only was this policy less expensive but it was also justified within the frame of giving parents choice over childcare options. Furthermore, childminding was viewed as a source of employment particularly for lower qualified women. The need for more crèche places arose from two sources. The first was demand from parents, who viewed crèches as providing more educational and developmental opportunities for their children than childminders. The second was the need to provide cheaper childcare options for low-income parents to overcome the problem of the bifurcation of the labour market among mothers. However, a number of plans to increase childcare places, particularly in crèches in deprived areas, failed to meet their targets, mainly because of the effects of the 2008 financial crisis. These failures help explain why parental leave was not shortened further in 2014, as such a change would had to have been accompanied by a significant expansion of childcare places.

References

Aboim, S. (2010). Gender cultures and the division of labour in contemporary Europe: A cross-national perspective. *The Sociological Review, 58*(2), 171–196. https://doi.org/10.1111/j.1467-954X.2010.01899.x

Afsa Essafi, C., & Buffeteau, S. (2006). L'activité féminine en France : quelles évolutions récentes, quelles tendances pour l'avenir ? *Économie et statistique, 398–399*, 85–97.

Algava, E., Bloch, K., & Robert-Bobee, I. (2021). Les familles en 2020 : 25% de familles monoparentales, 21% de familles nombreuses. *INSEE Focus, 249*. Retrieved August 26, 2022, from https://www.insee.fr/fr/statistiques/5422681

Altinas, E., & Sullivan, O. (2017). Trends in fathers' contribution to housework and childcare under different welfare policy regimes. *Social Politics, 24*(1), 81–108. https://doi.org/10.1093/sp/jxw007

Authier, J.-Y., & Cayouette-Remblière, J. (2021). *Les formes contemporaines du voisinage. Espaces résidentiels et intégration social.* Retrieved October 4, 2022, from https://mon-quartier-mes-voisins.site.ined.fr/fichier/s_rubrique/31550/les.formes.contemporaines.du.voisinage_authier_cayouette_vf.fr.pdf

Avril, C. (2012). Ressources et lignes de clivage parmi les aides à domicile. Spécifier une position sociale : quelles opérations de recherche? *Actes de la recherche en sciences sociales, 191–192*(1), 86–105. https://doi.org/10.3917/arss.191.00869

Bauer, D. (2007). Entre maison, enfant(s) et travail: les diverses formes d'arrangement dans les couples. *Etudes et Résultats de la DRESS, 570*, 1–8.

Bengston, V. L., & Roberts, R. E. L. (1991). Intergenerational solidarity in aging families: An example of formal theory construction. *Journal of Marriage and the Family, 53*(4), 856–870.

Bentoudja, L., & Razafindranovona, T. (2020). Être parent : des cadres aux ouvrières, plus de conséquences sur l'emploi des femmes. *INSEE Première, 1795*, 1–4.

Bèque, M. (2019). Conciliation difficile entre vie familiale et vie professionnelle. Quels sont les salaries les plus concernes ? *DARES Analyses, 045*, 1–8.

Béradier, M. (2021). Le recours aux modes d'accueil des jeunes enfants en 2018. *L'e-ssentiel, 199*, 1–4.

Bereni, L., Marry, C., Pochic, S., & Revillard, A. (2001). Le plafond de verre dans les ministères : regards croisés de la sociologie du travail et de la science politique. *Politiques et management public, 28*(2) http://journals.openedition.org/pmp/4141

Berton, F., Bureau, M.-C., & Rist, B. (2017). Father figures and cultural diversity in France. *Men and Masculinities, 20*(5), 552–569. https://doi.org/10.1177/1097184X17727799

Bittman, S. (2015). Ressources économiques des femmes et travail domestique des conjoints : quels effets pour quelles tâches ? *Economie et Statistique, 478-479-480*, 305–338.

Boisnault, D., & Fichen, A. (2015). Enfants, politique familiale et fiscalité : les transferts du système social-fiscal aux familles 2014. *Lettre Trésor-Eco, 142*.

Retrieved April 17, 2016, from http://www.tresor.economie.gouv.fr/File/409076

Bonoli, G. (2013). *Origins of active social policy: Labour market and childcare policies*. Oxford University Press.

Bouffartigue, P. (2010). The gender division of paid and domestic work. Some remarks in favour of a temporal perspective. *Time and Society, 19*(2), 220–238. https://doi.org/10.1177/0961463X09337855

Bousquet, D. (2010). *Rapport au nom de la Commission des Affaires Sociales sur la proposition de loi relative à la modernisation du congé maternité en faveur de la protection de la santé des femmes et de l'egalite salariale et sur les conditions d'exercice de la parentalité*. 1468. Retrieved November 23, 2011, from www.assemblee-nationale.fr/13/rapports/r2344.asp

Boyer, D. (2016). Les pères en congé parental à temps partiel en France : vers un modèle égalitaire ? *Revue des politiques sociales et familiales, 122*, 63–76. https://doi.org/10.3406/caf.2016.3163

Boyer, D., & Céroux, B. (2012). Le congé parental dans les trajectoires professionnelles féminines. *L'e-ssentiel, 119*, 1–4.

Brachet, S., & Salles, A. (2011). Être père en France et en Allemagne : entre représentations et pratiques. *Informations sociales, 163*(1), 62–70.

Briard, K. (2017). L'articulation des temps parental et professionnel au sein des couples : quelle place occupée par les pères ? *DARES Analyses, 58*, 1–10.

Brice, L., Daudey, D., & Hoibian, S. (2015). Une société qui aspire à plus d'égalité entre les femmes et les hommes. *Notes de synthese du CREDOC, 15*, 1–4.

Brousse, C. (2015a). La vie quotidienne en France depuis 1974. Les enseignements de l'enquête Emploi du temps. *Economie et Statistique, 478-479-480*, 79–117.

Brousse, C. (2015b). Travail professionnel, tâches domestiques, temps « libre » : quelques déterminants sociaux de la vie quotidienne. *Economie et Statistique, 478-479-480*, 119–154.

Burikova, S. Z. (2016). Exploring the demand for paid domestic workers in Slovakia through the intersection of welfare and gender regimes. *Laboratorium, 8*(3), 28–51.

Büttner, O., Letablier, M.-T., & Pennec, S. (2002). *L'action publique face aux transformations de la famille en France*. Rapport de recherche 02, Centre d'études de l'emploi.

Caisse des Allocations Familiales (CAF). (2022, May 13). Un congé de paternité deux fois plus long. *Vies de familles*. Retrieved November 18, 2022, from https://www.caf.fr/allocataires/vies-de-famille/articles/un-conge-paternite-deux-fois-plus-long

Cartier, M. (2015). *Les assistantes maternelles ou la subordination chez soi ? Sociohistoire d'une relation d'emploi depuis 1977 en Loire-Atlantique*. PhD thesis, University of Nantes.

Cartier, M., Letrait, M., & Sorin, M. (2018). Travail domestique : des classes populaires conservatrices ? *Travail, genre et sociétés, 39*, 63–81. https://doi.org/10.3917/tgs.039.0063

Champagne, C., Paihlé, A., & Solaz, A. (2014). 25 ans de participation des hommes et des femmes au travail domestique : quels facteurs d'évolution ? *Documents de travail de l'Institut National des Etudes Démographiques, 203*, 1–45. https://doi.org/10.3917/reof.149.0101

Charavel, C. (2016). Avant et après l'école, qui prend en charge les jeunes enfants scolarises ? *Etudes et Résultats de la DREES, 0959*, 1–6.

Chatot, M. (2017a). Profiter des enfants ou s'offrir du temps ? Les conditions auxquelles les pères prennent un congé parental. *Revue française des affaires sociales, 2*, 229–246. https://doi.org/10.3917/rfas.172.0229

Chatot, M. (2017b). Père au foyer : une nouvelle entrée au répertoire du masculine? *Enfance, famille, générations : revue interdisciplinaire sur la famille contemporaine, 26*, 1–19. https://doi.org/10.7202/1041062ar

Chatot, M. (2021). Learning to be a "stay-at-home father": Full-time parental leave as temporal socialisation. *Revue des politiques sociales et familiales., 141*(4), 161–176. https://doi.org/10.3917/rpsf.141.0161

Chauffaut, D., & Lévêque, S. (2012). Femmes, mères, épouses, travailleuses : les représentations parlementaires des rôles sexues au travers les débats sur les politiques de conciliation (1965-2010). *Revue française des affaires sociales*, 12–31. https://doi.org/10.3917/rfas.122.0012

Clergeau, M.-F. (2009). *Rapport d'information en conclusion des travaux de la mission d'évaluation et de contrôle des lois de financement de la sécurité sociale sur la prestation d'accueil du jeune enfant.* Retrieved November 23, 2011, from assemblee-nationale.fr/13/rap-info/i1801.asp

Clift, B. (2006). The French socialists, dirigisme, and the troubled Europeanisation of employment policy. In E. Godin & T. Chafer (Eds.), *The French exception* (pp. 106–120). Berghahn Books.

Collombet, C. (2018). Les inégalités sociales d'accès aux modes d'accueil des jeunes enfants. Une comparaison européenne. *Revue des politiques sociales et familiales, 127*, 71–82. https://doi.org/10.3406/caf.2018.3289

Collombet, C. (2021). Égalité entre hommes et femmes et politiques familiales : un sujet prioritaire pour l'Union européenne et l'OCDE. *Informations sociales, 203–204*(2), 134–142. https://doi.org/10.3917/inso.203.0134

Cox, R. (2015). Competitive mothering and delegated care: Class relationships in nanny and au pair employment. *Studies in the Maternal 3*(2). https://doi.org/10.16995/sim.66

Craig, L., & Mullan, K. (2010). Parenthood, gender and work-family time in the United States, Australia, Italy, France and Denmark. *Journal of Marriage and the Family, 72*(5), 1344–1361. https://doi.org/10.1111/j.1741-3737.2010.00769.x

Crepin, A., & Boyer, D. (2022). Baromètre de l'accueil du jeune enfant 2021 La crise sanitaire n'a guère modifié les représentations, les aspirations et les recours aux modes d'accueil. *L'e-ssentiel, 209*, 1–4.

David-Alberola, E., & Momic, M. (2008). Le métier d'assistante maternelle. *Etudes et Recherches de la DREES, 636*, 1–6.

Descoutures, V. (2006). Les « mères non statutaires » dans les couples lesbiens qui élèvent des enfants. *Dialogue, 173*(3), 71–80.

European Council. (2002). *Presidency conclusions Barcelona European council 15 & 15th March 2002.* Retrieved November 18, 2022, from https://www.consilium.europa.eu/uedocs/cms_data/docs/pressdata/en/ec/71025.pdf

European Institute for Gender Equality. (2019). Work-life balance. *Gender Equality Index 2019.* Retrieved November 18, 2022, from https://eige.europa.eu/publications/gender-equality-index-2019-report/parental-leave-policies

Evertsson, M. (2014). Gender ideology and the sharing of housework and childcare in Sweden. *Journal of Family Issues, 35*, 927–949. https://doi.org/10.1177/0192513X14522239

Eydal, G. B., Gíslason, I. V., Rostgaard, T., Brandth, B., Duvander, A.-Z., & Lammi-Taskula, J. (2015). Trends in parental leave in the Nordic countries: Has the forward march of gender equality halted? *Community, Work & Family, 18*(2), 167–181. https://doi.org/10.1080/13668803.2014.1002754

Fagnani, J. (2012). Recent reforms in childcare and family policies in France and Germany: What was at stake? *Children and Youth Services Review, 34*, 509–516. https://doi.org/10.1016/j.childyouth.2011.10.011

Fagnani, J., & Letablier, M.-T. (2004). Work and family life balance. The impact of the 35-hour laws in France. *Work, Employment and Society, 18*, 551–572. https://doi.org/10.1177/0950017004045550

Fagnani, J., & Math, A. (2011). The predicament of childcare policy in France: What is at stake? *Journal of Contemporary European Studies, 19*, 547–561. https://doi.org/10.1080/14782804.2011.639990

Ferrangina, E., & Seeleib-Kaiser, M. (2014). Determinants of a silent evolution: understanding the expansion of family policy in rich OECD countries. *Social Politics, 2*, 1–37. https://doi.org/10.1093/sp/jxu027

Fossoul, C., D'Amore, S., Miscioscia, M., & Scali, T. (2013). La transition a la parentalité chez les couples homosexuels : étude exploratoire. *Thérapie Familiale, 34*(2), 265–283. https://doi.org/10.3917/tf.132.0265

Geist, C. (2005). The welfare state and the home: Regime differences in the domestic division of labour. *European Sociological Review, 21*(1), 23–41. https://doi.org/10.1093/esr/jci002

Genest Dufault, S., & Castelain Meunier, C. (2017). Masculinités et familles en transformation. *Enfance, Familles, Générations : revue interdisciplinaire sur la famille contemporaine, 26*, 1–17.

Giminez-Nadal, J. I., & Sevilla-Sanz, A. (2012). Trends in time allocation: A cross-country analysis. *European Economic Review, 56*(6), 1338–1359. https://doi.org/10.1016/j.euroecorev.2012.02.011

Gornick, J. C., & Meyers, M. K. (2003). *Families that work: Policies for reconciling parenthood and employment.* Russell Sage Foundation.

Goux, D., Maurin, E., & Petrongolo, B. (2014). Worktime regulations and spousal labor supply. *American Economic Review, 104*(1), 252–276. https://doi.org/10.1257/aer.104.1.252

Gray, A. (2003). *Towards a conceptual framework for studying time and social capital (Families and Social Capital ERSC Research Group).* South Bank University.

Gross, M. (2009). Les familles homoparentales : entre conformité et innovations. *Informations sociales, 154*, 106–114.

Haut Conseil de la Famille. (2009). Le complément de libre choix d'activité : un état des lieux. *Lettre du Haut Conseil de la Famille, 1*, 1–5.

Haut Conseil de la Famille. (2011). *Architecture des aides aux familles : quelles évolutions pour les 15 prochaines années.* Note of 28th April. Retrieved February 17, 2014, from http://www.hcf-famille.fr/IMG/pdf/Architecture_des_aides_aux_familles___quelles_evolutions_pour_les_15_prochaines_annees-2.pdf

Haut conseil de la famille. (2014, October 9). *Point sur le développement de l'accueil des jeunes enfants : annexe.* Retrieved November 19, 2015, from http://www.hcf-famille.fr/IMG/pdf/Annexes_AJE_2014_10_09-2.pdf

Haut Conseil de la Famille. (2015). *Point sur le développement de l'accueil des jeunes enfants : Section 1 & 2 adoptées par consensus à la séance du 10 septembre 2015.* Retrieved September 28, 2016, from http://www.hcf-famille.fr/IMG/pdf/2015_09_10_AJE_1ere_partie_bilan-3.pdf

Havard Duclos, B. (2018). L'internet des assistantes maternelles : un outil pour faire vivre le metier. *Réseaux, 208-9*(2–3), 28–61. https://doi.org/10.3917/res.208.0025

Herlofson, K., & Brandt, M. (2020). Helping older parents in Europe: The importance of grandparenthood, gender and care regime. *European Societies, 22*(3), 390–410. https://doi.org/10.1080/14616696.2019.1694163

Himmelweit, S., & Sigala, M. (2004). Choice and the relationship between identities and behaviour for mothers with pre-school children. *Journal of Social Policy, 33*, 455–478. https://doi.org/10.1017/S0047279404007779

Hook, J. L. (2006). Care in context: Men's unpaid work in 20 countries, 1965–2003. *American Sociological Review, 71*(4), 639–660. https://doi.org/10.1177/000312240607100406

INSEE. (2020). *Natalité et fécondité. Tableaux de l'Economie Française.* Edition 2020. Retrieved November 18, 2022, from https://www.insee.fr/fr/statistiques/4277635?sommaire=4318291

INSEE. (2022). Articuler emploi et famille. *Femmes et hommes, l'égalité en question*. Retrieved November 17, 2022, from https://www.insee.fr/fr/statistiques/6047759?sommaire=6047805&q=familles

International Labour Office (ILO). (2018). *Care work and care jobs for the future of decent work*. Retrieved March 8, 2022, from https://www.ilo.org/wcmsp5/groups/public/%2D%2D-dgreports/%2D%2D-dcomm/%2D%2D-publ/documents/publication/wcms_633135.pdf

Jenson, J., & Saint-Martin, D. (2003). New routes to social cohesion? Citizenship and the social investment state. *The Canadian Journal of Sociology / Cahiers canadiens de sociologie, 28*, 77–99. https://doi.org/10.2307/3341876

Karu, M., & Tremblay, D.-G. (2018). Fathers on parental leave: An analysis of rights and take-up in 29 countries. *Community, Work & Family, 21*(3), 344–362. https://doi.org/10.1080/13668803.2017.1346586

Kilkey, M. (2010). Men and domestic labor: A missing link in the global care chain. *Men and Masculinities, 13*(1), 126–149. https://doi.org/10.1177/1097184X10382884

Kitzman, M. (2018). Les grands-parents : un mode de garde régulier ou occasionnel pour deux tiers des jeunes enfants. *Etudes et résultats de la DRESS, 1070*, 1–6.

Knight, C. R., & Brinton, M. C. (2017). One egalitarianism or several? Two decades of gender-role attitude change in Europe. *The American Journal of Sociology, 122*(5), 1485–1532. https://doi.org/10.1086/689814

Kvist, J. (2013). The post-crisis European social model: Developing or dismantling social investments? *Journal of International Comparative Social Policy, 29*. https://doi.org/10.1080/21699763.2013.809666

Lacharité, C., & Gagnier, J.-P. (2010). *Comprendre les familles pour mieux intervenir : repères conceptuels et stratégies d'action*. Gaetan Morin.

Laporte, C. (2019a). Les sortants de la PreParE : retour à l'emploi et mode de conciliation familiale. *L'e-ssentiel, 186*, 1–4.

Laporte, C. (2019b). Attentes, besoins et contraintes des parents en matière de conciliation vie familiale et vie professionnelle. *Collection des documents de la CNAF Dossier d'Etude, 208*, 1–61. Retrieved November 17, 2022, from https://www.caf.fr/sites/default/files/medias/cnaf/Nous_connaitre/Recherche_et_statistiques/Dossiers%20d'%C3%A9tudes/2019_DE_208_Enqu%C3%AAte_Embleme.pdf

Laporte, C., & Legendre, E. (2018). Bilan de la PreParE. Une prestation moins utilisée, rarement partagée et toujours peu attractive auprès des pères. *L'e-ssentiel, 183*, 1–4.

Laroque, M. (2006). *Congé parental fractionnable indemnisé. Report 2006–97.* Retrieved November 18, 2022, from http://www.ladocumentationfrancaise.fr/var/storage/rapports-publics/064000687.pdf

Le Dantec, E. (2017). Aider simultanément ses ascendants et ses descendants. Les ressorts et enjeux sociaux d'une situation en progression parmi les retraités. *Retraite et société, 78*(3), 91–116. https://doi.org/10.3917/rs1.078.0091

Ledoux, C., & Krupka, R. (2020). *PHS-QUALITY project job quality and industrial relations in the personal and household services sector – VS/2018/0041Country report France.*

Lightman, N., & Kevins, A. (2021). "Women's work": Welfare state spending and the gendered and classed dimensions of unpaid care. *Gender and Society, 35*(5), 778–805. https://doi.org/10.1177/08912432211038695

Lowndes, V. (2006). It's not what you've got, but what you do with it: Women, social capital and political participation. In B. O'Neill & E. Gidengil (Eds.), *Gender and social capital* (pp. 213–240). Routledge.

Merla, L. (2007). Masculinité et paternité à l'écart du monde du travail : le cas des pères au foyer en Belgique. *Recherches Sociologiques et Anthropologiques, 38*(2), 143–163. https://doi.org/10.4000/rsa.473

Milner, S. (2010). 'Choice' and 'flexibility' in reconciling work and family: Towards a convergence in policy discourse on work and family in France and the UK? *Policy and Politics, 38*, 3–21. https://doi.org/10.1332/030557309X445591

Morgan, K. (2013). Path shifting of the welfare state: Electoral competition and the expansion of work-family policies in Western Europe. *World Politics, 65*, 73–115. https://doi.org/10.1017/S0043887112000251

Mozère, L. (1988). Maman sérieuse cherche enfants à garder : Petits métiers urbains au féminin. *Les Annales de la Recherche Urbaine, 88*, 83–89.

Observatoire national de la petite enfance (ONAPE). (2019). *L'accueil du jeune enfant en 2017.* Retrieved January 25, 2022, from http://paternet.fr/wp-content/uplaods/pdf/2019/03/20190327-rapport-onpe.pdf

OECD. (2014). *Parents' use of childbirth related leave.* Retrieved August 26, 2022, from https://www.oecd.org/els/family/PF2-2-Use-childbirth-leave.pdf

OECD (2020). *Is childcare affordable? Policy brief on employment, labour and social affairs.* Retrieved May 14, 2022, from https://www.oecd.org/els/family/OECD-Is-Childcare-Affordable.pdf.

Ollier-Malaterre, A., Valcour, M., Den Dulk, L., & Kossek, E. (2013). Theorizing national context to develop comparative work-life research: A review and research agenda. *European Management Journal, 31*, 433–447. https://doi.org/10.1016/j.emj.2013.05.002

Pak, M. (2016). Du côté des pères à temps partiel familial. *Revue des politiques sociales et familiales., 122*, 123–131. https://doi.org/10.3406/caf.2016.3169

Pande, A. (2012). From "balcony talk" and "practical prayers" to illegal collectives: Migrant domestic workers and meso-level resistances in Lebanon. *Gender and Society, 26*, 382–405. https://doi.org/10.1177/0891243212439247

Papuchon, A. (2017). Rôles sociaux des femmes et des hommes : l'idée persistante d'une vocation maternelle de femmes malgré le déclin de l'adhésion aux stéréotypes de genre. *Insee Références*, 81–96.

Perivier, H. (2020). *Etudes sur la situation économique et sociale des parents isolés : niveau de vie, marche du travail et politiques publiques.* Report of the

OFCE. Retrieved August 27, 2022, from https://www.ofce.sciences-po.fr/pdf-articles/actu/helene.pdf

Perivier, H., & Verdugo, G. (2021a). Cinq ans après la réforme du congé parental (PreParE), les objectifs sont-ils atteints ? *OFCE / Sciences Po Policy Brief, 88*, 1–16. Retrieved March 17, 2022, from https://hal.archives-ouvertes.fr/hal-03382667/

Perivier, H., & Verdugo, G. (2021b). Can parental leave be shared? *Sciences Po OFCE working paper*, 06/2021. Retrieved November 18, 2022, from https://www.ofce.sciences-po.fr/pdf/dtravail/OFCEWP2021-06.pdf

Piesen, A. (2016). Une paternité à construire au quotidien : le cas de la résidence au père. *Revue des politiques sociales et familiales, 22*, 77–88. https://doi.org/10.3406/caf.2016.3164

Prouteau, L. (1998). Les différentes façons d'être bénévole. *Economie et Statistique, 311*, 57–73.

Ricroch, L. (2012). En 25 ans, moins de tâches domestiques pour les femmes, l'écart de situation avec les hommes se réduit. *INSEE Femmes et hommes – regards sur la parité édition 2012*. Retrieved March 16, 2019, from https://www.insee.fr/fr/statistiques/1372773?sommaire=1372781

Sayer, L. (2010). Trends in housework. In J. Treas & S. Drobnič (Eds.), *Dividing the domestic: Men, women and household work in cross-national perspective* (pp. 19–14). Stanford University Press.

Sohler, K., & Levy, F. (2013). Migration careers and professional trajectories of irregular domestic workers. In Triandaifyllidou, A. (Ed.), *Irregular migration and domestic work in Europe: who cares?* (pp. 43–70). Routledge.

Solera, C., & Mencarini, L. (2018). The gender division of housework after the first child: A comparison among Bulgaria, France and The Netherlands. *Community, Work & Family, 21*(5), 519–540. https://doi.org/10.1080/13668803.2018.1528969

Stambolis-Ruhstorfer, M., & Gross, M. (2021). Qui lave le linge sale de la famille? *Travail, genre et sociétés, 2*, 75–95. https://doi.org/10.3917/tgs.046.0075

Taylor, A. (2016). *An analysis of the work-care experiences of out-of-work partnered parents in France and the UK: Ideals, practice and policy learning*. PhD thesis, University of Sheffield.

Taylor-Gooby, P. (2004). Introduction: The post-industrial welfare state. In P. Taylor-Gooby (Ed.), *New risks, new welfare: The transformation of the European welfare state* (pp. 1–28). Oxford University Press.

Thalineau, A., & Nowik, L. (2018). Place des grands-parents après la naissance du nouveau-né. Les attentes des parents participant à la cohorte Elfe. *Revue des politiques sociales et familiales, 126*, 9–20. https://doi.org/10.3406/caf.2018.3259

Thevenon, O. (2013). Public childcare services in the European Union: The model of France. In Directorate General for Internal Policies Policy Department

C (Ed.), *Citizens' rights and constitutional affairs women's rights and gender equality. Barcelona targets revisited compilation of briefing notes WORKSHOP 25* (pp. 88–104) Retrieved August 30, 2022, from https://www.europarl.europa.eu/document/activities/cont/201311/20131128ATT75082/20131128ATT75082EN.pdf

Unterreiner, A. (2018). Les assistantes maternelles au quotidien. Un travail invisible rythmé par différentes fonctions d'accueil du jeune enfant. *Revue des politiques sociales et familiales, 126*, 75–82. https://doi.org/10.3406/caf.2018.3267

Vecho, O., Gross, M., & Poteat, V.-P. (2011). Partage des tâches parentales au sein des couples de mères lesbiennes françaises ayant eu recours à une insémination artificielle avec donneur anonyme. *Psychologie Française, 56*(1), 1–18.

Vlachantoni, A., Evandrou, M., Falkingham, J., & Gomez-Leon, M. (2019). Caught in the middle in mid-life: Provision of care across multiple generations. *Ageing & Society (Firstview)*. https://doi.org/10.1017/S0144686X19000047

Vroyland, T. (2016). Les assistantes maternelles gardent 80 pour cent d'enfants de plus en 2014 qu'en 2010. *Etudes et Résultats de la DREES, 0978*, 1–6.

Windebank, J. (1999). Political motherhood and the everyday experience of mothering: A comparison of the childcare strategies of French and British working mothers. *Journal of Social Policy, 28*(1), 1–25. https://doi.org/10.1017/S0047279499005486

Windebank, J. (2008). Volunteering and the gender division of labour: A Franco-British comparison. *Community, Work & Family, 11*(4), 457–473. https://doi.org/10.1080/13668800802349802

Windebank, J. (2012). Reconciling work and family life for French mothers in the Sarkozy era: Working more to earn more? *International Journal of Sociology and Social Policy, 32*, 576–588. https://doi.org/10.1108/01443331211257661

Windebank, J. (2017). Change in work-family reconciliation policy in France and the UK since 2008: The influence of the economic crisis and austerity. *Journal of International and Comparative Social Policy, 33*(1), 55–72. https://doi.org/10.1080/21699763.2017.1288160

Železná, L. (2018). Caregiving to grandchildren and elderly parents: Role conflict or family solidarity? *Ageing and Society, 38*(5), 974–994. https://doi.org/10.1017/S0144686X16001434

CHAPTER 4

Long-Term Care for Adults in Contemporary France

This chapter discusses the work involved in providing long-term care to adults in France, an aspect of domestic and care work that is set to grow substantially over the next 30 years as the population ages. LTC consists of a range of services for those with some degree of long-term dependency including personal (direct) care, or ADLs (e.g., washing or dressing); domestic (indirect care) work, or IADLs (cooking, cleaning or gardening); services to help with social activities (e.g., transport) and medical services to manage chronic health conditions, this latter lying outside the remit of this book (Oliveira Hashiguchi & Llena-Nozal, 2020). LTC needs are highly diverse and reflect the degree of dependency of the individual and range from requiring a few hours of assistance with IADLs per week through needing help with ADLs throughout the day to 24-hour supervision. There is no internationally agreed framework of disability or dependency to categorise these needs (Roy, 2019). Rather, there are a number of frameworks based on differing sets of indicators, for example, the *GIR* (*groupe iso-ressources*) framework, the Katz indicator, the Colvez indicator and the GALI (Global Activity Limitation Indicator) (Baradji et al., 2021; Brunel & Carrère, 2017). LTC services may be formal—that is, provided by professional workers within a residential institution (institutional care) or in the care recipient's home (professional home-based care)—or informal, that is provided by family members who live with the

J. Windebank, *Domestic and Care Work in Modern France*, French Politics, Society and Culture,
https://doi.org/10.1007/978-3-031-33564-8_4

care recipient (co-residency), this most often being their spouse/partner but also their parents or children, or by kin or non-kin from another household, most often adult children. Many individuals rely on a combination of types of care, both formal and informal, and multiple carers. For example, 53 per cent of the over 60s living at home requiring assistance with everyday activities in 2015 in France relied on two or more carers and 15 per cent on four carers or more (Brunel et al., 2019, p. 4). Family members may need to undertake the cognitive labour of managing care arrangements even when they do not carry out practical tasks themselves.

The *INSEE Statistiques sur les ressources et conditions de vie* (*SRCV*) (Statistics on resources and living conditions) survey, using the GALI, found that in 2017 4.9 million people aged 16 or over residing in metropolitan France and living in a domestic rather than an institutional setting had significant limitations in participating in everyday activities because of a health condition lasting for at least six months. This number represents 9 per cent of this category of the population. The proportion of those experiencing such limitations was higher in older age groups: 6 per cent of 16–64-year-olds in comparison with 20 per cent of those aged 65 and over (Baradji et al., 2021, p. 9). Furthermore, the *DREES* carries out surveys of LTC needs of the elder population in France every 7–8 years: the two most recent studies are the *Handicap-Santé Ménages (HSM)* survey, which was carried out in 2008, and the *Capacités, Aides et REssources des seniors* (*CARE*) (Capabilities, Assistance and Resources for Older people) study carried out in 2015. A new study is underway at the time of writing. In 2015, 10 per cent of the over 60 population living in a domestic setting in metropolitan France were dependent, according to the *DREES* definition of dependency[1] (Brunel & Carrère, 2017, p. 1). A higher percentage (21 per cent) declared that they were regularly helped with everyday activities[2]

[1] In France, the *DREES* applies three criteria to define an individual as dependent: they must find either one physical function impossible (e.g., walking), or experience limitations in a number of physical functions; they must find at least one everyday activity impossible (e.g., cooking) or experience restrictions in a range of everyday activities; and they must have experienced these issues for at least six months.

[2] The following activities were included in this category: assistance with washing, dressing, toileting, eating and drinking, food preparation, going to medical appointments, filling prescriptions, leaving the house, moving around the house, getting up from a chair or bed, managing household finances and administration, housework, washing up, laundry, shopping, DIY, and gardening, and monitoring during the day or overnight. Not included in this definition were moral support (emotional support and companionship) or financial support.

because of their age or health problems. Whilst only 8 per cent of 60–69-year-olds received such help, the proportion rose to 41 per cent for 80–84-year-olds and 80 per cent of those aged 90 plus (Brunel et al., 2019, p. 2). The most commonly cited tasks where assistance was required were housework, reported by 63 per cent of those requiring assistance, and shopping, required by 61 per cent (Brunel et al., 2019, p. 3).

Given the relationship between age, dependency and LTC, the volume of LTC work in a given society and the capacity of that society to respond to those needs, are determined to a great extent by the age profile of its population. In 2015, 34 per cent of the French population was aged 60 or over, compared with just 26 per cent in 1990 (INSEE, 2018). This trend will continue in years to come: the *INSEE* estimates that the number of people aged 60 or over in France will increase by 40 per cent between 2015 and 2040 and the rise will be even higher for those aged over 80 (78 per cent) (INSEE, 2017). This translates to an increase in potentially dependent older people from 3,268,000 in 2015 to 5,188,000 by 2050. However, between 2008 and 2015 there was a reduction of 3 percentage points in the proportion of the over 60s requiring help with everyday activities in France due to improving health in older age (INSEE, 2017). This offsets to an extent the care challenges posed by the increase in numbers of older people. Further evidence of the improving health and capacity of older people is that the average age at which individuals enter a care home in France rose from 82 in 1994 to 85 years and 2 months in 2015 (Muller, 2017, p. 2).

The decisions that individuals and families make about LTC are dependent to a large degree on the policy context in which they live. State support for LTC varies widely between countries in terms of both levels of public spending and financial support and the types of provisions offered. This influences the organisation of LTC work across different social relations of production, its divisions of labour, particularly its gendering, the work conditions of LTC employees and the degree to which it is delegated to migrant workers. The state may provide in any combination free or subsidised in-kind LTC services or cash-for-care benefits to pay for professional institutional or home-based care in service-provider, agency or direct employment mode. There may also be cash benefits to compensate informal carers for their time and loss of income paid via the care recipient or directly to the carer. Individuals may have employment rights giving them time to provide LTC.

LTC policy is influenced by the affordability of levels and types of state support in conjunction with social norms regarding the respective obligations of the family and the state to provide LTC. Policy frameworks in turn help shape these norms over the long term. Comparative research has shown that in the most familialist states, low levels of public spending for LTC often coincide with social norms that consider the family as the primary institution for its provision. Families assume responsibility for even the most intensive caregiving which is often delivered by a small number of people, in the majority of cases, women and often in a context of intergenerational co-residency (Herlofson & Brandt, 2020). Families who need to access professional care may use undeclared particularly migrant labour to reduce costs. Furthermore, the lack of an organised market in care services in such countries fosters undeclared employment in LTC (Picchi, 2016). In the most de-familialised states, high levels of public spending on LTC and comprehensive care services coincide with social norms that place a duty on the state to provide LTC according to the wishes of care recipients. However, this state provision does not crowd out informal care, not least because care needs are not finite (Haberkern et al., 2015; Igel et al., 2009). The less onerous and more optional nature of the caring tasks remaining with the family in these circumstances means that they are more often shared among a wider group of people than when more intensive informal care is required (Schmid et al., 2011). This lessens but does not eradicate gender specialisation in LTC by reducing the time women (spouses and daughters) spend on LTC but not necessarily increasing the time men, particularly sons, spend on care (Haberkern et al., 2015). Where policy encourages the use of LTC services provided by organisations rather than through direct employment, the work conditions of professional carers tend to be more favourable, and where cash-for-care benefits are highly regulated, undeclared work less prevalent.

This chapter discusses how France occupies an intermediate and to some extent singular position between the most familialist and the most de-familialised states in terms of how LTC has been provided in the twenty-first century. Referring to the relatively undeveloped pre-1997 LTC policy framework, France was deemed an explicit familialist state in Leitner's (2003) model as regards LTC. However, in the twenty-first century France could better be described as an optional familialist state as the country has developed a mixed model for LTC, based primarily on cash-for-care benefits alongside promotion of family care (European Commission, 2021). This is in similarity with other Conservative welfare regimes such as Austria and Germany (Schmid et al., 2011). The optional familialism of French LTC policy is mirrored in social attitudes concerning care for adults. For example, the 2004 Survey of Health and Ageing in Retirement in Europe[3] (SHARE) asked respondents to agree or disagree that the family and not the state should be mostly or exclusively in charge of caring for older people. The French population were divided on this issue with 52.1 per cent in agreement with the statement. In contrast, this was only a minority view in Social Democratic countries such as Denmark (11 per cent) and Sweden (33 per cent) while in Southern and Eastern European countries such as Greece (91 per cent) and Poland (91.7 per cent), the overwhelming majority of the population agreed with the proposition (Spasova et al., 2018, p. 65).

The family still bears legal responsibility for the care of dependent adults in France (Weber, 2006). Article 205 of the Civil Code stipulates that children have an *obligation alimentaire* (duty of support) towards their mother and father or other ascendants who are in need (Argoud, 2020). Even though legal interventions concerning lack of care for ascendants are very rare, the existence of these obligations has the symbolic power to define norms around filial responsibilities and reinforces an ideological and institutional adherence to the family as social carers at the political level (Fontaine et al., 2007; Mestheneos & Triantafillou, 2005). In deliberations on LTC policy, there has been agreement on left and right that the family should be encouraged to keep on caring, and there should be incentives for them to do so. This position has had a dual justification: undermining the role of the family would be harmful to the cohesion of society, and in view of the aging population, it would be too costly to provide care to all those in need without the informal and unpaid input of family members (Morel, 2007).

Spending on LTC is above average in France in relation to other high-income countries, but significantly lower than in the countries with the highest spending levels. The 2017 OECD (2018) annual health statistics on LTC for all age groups show that spending in France was 1.9 per cent of GDP (OECD average 1.4 per cent). However, the highest spending country, the Netherlands, devoted 4.3 per cent of its GDP to LTC. In contrast, some countries, such as Greece and the Slovak Republic, were

[3]The SHARE is a research infrastructure for studying the effects of health, social, economic, and environmental policies over the life-course of European citizens and beyond. http://www.share-project.org/home0.html

reported as spending nothing in this area. The most recent report on LTC for older people in France published in 2019 has recommended an increase in spending, suggesting a set of measures that would add 9.2 billion Euros to the LTC budget by 2030 funded through taxation. It also recommends recognising loss of autonomy as a universal social protection risk[4] (Libault, 2019). Implementation of the recommendations of the report has been delayed due to the COVID pandemic (European Commission, 2021). It should be noted, however, that the over 60s are the largest group of beneficiaries of tax and employer social security reductions to support direct employment in PHS in France, the funding for which may not be fully captured by statistics on spending on care benefits.

Since the 1960s the French state has been committed to home rather than institutional care for the working-age disabled and retired populations. It is assumed to be the preferred option of most care recipients, providing better quality care, and promoting integration into society. The latest expressions of this support for home care appeared in the 2016 *Adaptation de la Société au Vieillissement (ASV)* (Adapting to an aging society) law that committed to providing older people with the possibility to *vieillir chez elles dans de bonnes conditions* (grow old at home in comfortable conditions)[5] and in the Libault report, which also emphasises the commitment of the government to providing choice of options to LTC recipients (Libault, 2019). This narrative of freedom of choice for care recipients as rational-actor consumers of services is also used to justify the orientation of spending on LTC in France towards cash-for-care benefits (Jany-Catrice, 2010).

Informal Care

In similarity to caring for children, the majority of LTC work in France is carried out on an unpaid, informal basis by other household members (spouses, parents or children), and/or members of the family living in another household (often adult children particularly for the over 60s), and to a lesser extent the wider community of kin, friends and neighbours. The *INSEE SRCV* survey demonstrated that in 2017 whereas 21 per cent of

[4] The four existing risks are age, family, illness/pregnancy/invalidity/death, and workplace accidents/work-related illness.

[5] https://www.pour-les-personnes-agees.gouv.fr/actualites/la-loi-relative-a-ladaptation-de-la-societe-au-vieillissement

the population aged 16 and over with significant limitations in participating in everyday activities had had recourse to professional services, 79 per cent reported that they had not, 46 per cent of whom having stated that this was because they had been helped informally by family and friends. The rest either had not required assistance or could not access professional services (Baradji et al., 2021, p. 22, Table 8). Among the population under 60, 61 per cent of the 271,000 persons eligible for the *Prestation de compensation du handicap* (*PCH*) (Disability Compensation Benefit) (see below) in 2015 received payments for *aide humaine* (help from another person with everyday activities or regular monitoring), 70 per cent of whom used the payment to compensate family members (Baradji et al., 2021, p. 4 Table 2). For those under 20, the proportion was higher at 95 per cent and reduced with age (Baradji et al., 2021, p. 5, Table 3). Furthermore, the *CARE* survey shows that in 2015, 48 per cent of the 2,950,000 people in France aged 60 plus living at home requiring assistance with everyday activities reported being regularly helped only by family and friends. A further 34 per cent reported benefiting from a combination of professional and informal care, with only 19 per cent relying solely on professional services (Brunel et al., 2019, p. 5).

At all levels of dependency, the median number of hours of informal assistance with everyday activities is much higher than hours of professional care. For example, the *CARE* survey shows that in 2015 of those with the highest level of dependency the median total number of hours of assistance received was 54, 35 hours of informal care and 19 hours of professional (including medical) care. For those with lower levels of dependency (GIR 3) 8 hours of assistance per week were received in total, composed of 6 hours of informal care and 2 hours of professional (including medical) care (Brunel et al., 2019, p. 6, Table 5). The frequency of recourse to professional care increases with level of dependency—for example, in 2015 of the over 60s with a high level of dependency (*GIR* 1–2) living at home, only 36 per cent received informal assistance from family and friends alone and 48 per cent benefitted from a combination of professional and informal care. The remaining 22 per cent received professional care only (Brunel et al., 2019, p. 4 Fig. 3).

There are class and gender differences in care provision. The 2010 *INSEE* time-use survey finds that the over 75s living alone whose former professions placed them in SPC 5 and 6 were helped principally by their family, whereas those who had been in SPC 3 relied more on paid help. Differences in care provision across socio-professional groups are explicable by a combination of financial necessity and social norms. State support for professional care does not preclude all out-of-pocket expenses and more traditional social norms concerning familial responsibility for caring, and indeed women's responsibility for caring is found more frequently among those in SPC 5 and 6 than in SPC 3. Lower employment rates and higher part-time rates for women in SPC 5 and 6 also increase the pool of potential informal carers among these groups (Brousse, 2015, p. 86).

As concerns gender, fewer women rely solely on informal care than men, particularly in the over 60 age group. According to the *CARE* survey, in 2015 43 per cent of women in comparison with 58 per cent of men received informal care from family and friends only, and a further 36 per cent of women compared with 29 per cent of men received both professional and informal care (Brunel et al., 2019, p. 4, Fig. 2). There are also differences as regards the providers of informal care. The *CARE* survey found that in 2014 men were more likely to be looked after by their spouse alone (43 per cent) than women (22 per cent) (Brunel et al., 2019, p. 5 Table 2). This gender difference has a number of explanations. First, it is principally the result of the greater life expectancy of women[6] which means that women experience more years of potential infirmity than men. In 2019 69 per cent of the over 85s in France were women (INED, 2022). For those living in different-sex couples, this greater longevity in conjunction with the fact that in such couples, women are on average younger than men, means that women are more likely to live alone due to widowhood. In 2013, 75 per cent of women aged 80–89 lived without a spouse/partner, this percentage having nonetheless reduced from 86 per cent in 1999 (Ogg et al., 2015, Table 1). Living alone increases the likelihood of recourse to professional services (Brunel et al., 2019; Renaut, 2021).

A large number of people in France supply informal care. The *CARE* survey found that in 2014 3.9 million people regularly provided material, financial or moral support for everyday life to someone aged over 60 living in their own home due to their age or disability (Roy, 2019, p. 13). According to the 2015 *DREES* survey, 22 per cent of the French adult population regularly provided informal care to an older dependent person, with the majority (56 per cent) providing under three hours of assistance

[6] In 2019, life expectancy for women in France was 85.6 years as opposed to 79.7 years for men (INSEE, 2020).

per week (Perron-Bailly, 2017, p. 5, Fig. 5). In comparative studies, France has been found to have a high volume of care provided informally relative to countries with comparable levels of spending on LTC and/or women's employment rates. According to the 2004 SHARE survey France had the second highest percentage of dependent over 65s reporting having received informal care from their families (86 per cent) behind Italy (87 per cent) (Fontaine et al., 2007, p. 104, Table 1). Meanwhile, a Franco-Swedish comparison found that French families not only undertook more practical tasks to help with everyday life for their dependent relatives than Swedish families, but they also had to undertake much more cognitive and administrative labour in organising professional care for them than in Sweden where the management of care is part of the care service offered by the state (Jonsson et al., 2011).

The distribution of roles among family carers follows an "order of mobilisation" (Weber, 2010, p. 145) based on norms of mutual help. For those living in couples, the spouse/partner is usually the primary carer if they are physically able. Among the 16–64-year-old population, those with a disability are more likely to be single than the equivalent population with no disability. However, the majority still live in couples. In 2018 in France, 58 per cent of adults with a disability that significantly restricted their everyday lives were in a couple. Seven per cent lived in a single-parent family, 19 per cent lived alone and 15 per cent in other types of households, including cohabitation with their parents or other family members (Baradji et al., 2021, p. 10). The *CARE* survey finds that of the over 60 population receiving informal assistance with everyday activities, 28 per cent received spousal care alone and a further 10 per cent received spousal care alongside other types of informal assistance, for example, from children (Brunel et al., 2019, p. 5, Table 2). In the sample, 36 per cent of care recipients were co-resident with their caregiver, 76 per cent of whom were spouses and 23 per cent adult children (Roy, 2019, p. 13). If not able to undertake all or part of the care themselves, the spouse most often undertakes the cognitive labour of organiser of secondary forms of care, whether informal or professional (Banens et al., 2019). Even care recipients with the most severe functional limitations living at home more often have their partner as their primary carer than a professional (Renaut, 2021).

Men as well as women fulfil the spousal caring role. The qualitative follow up to the *CARE* survey among those living at home—*CARE-Ménages*[7]—found similar proportions of men and women in different-sex couples who declared that they cared for their dependent spouse (Thomas & Banens, 2020). Using the 2010 *INSEE* time-use study, Brousse (2015, p. 91) compared the domestic time (time spent on both domestic and care activities) of the 60–74 and 75 plus age groups. For both men and women,[8] the time devoted to these activities was lower in the 75 plus than the 60–74 age group, but the gender difference in this older age group was smaller. This reflects the need for men who live or have lived in different-sex couples to take on activities that they previously did not do, either as the result of widowhood or the incapacity of their partner.

The gendering of spousal care is complex and based on attempts to adhere to the norms concerning the functioning of the domestic unit established during the lifetime of the couple, both in terms of what work is deemed acceptable to outsource and under what conditions, and in terms of the division of labour between the partners (Calasanti & Bowen, 2006). These objectives can be in tension with one another. Men in different-sex couples may take over domestic or caring functions from their women partners in order to preserve the norms of the privacy of the couple and the household even if these are tasks that they did not previously undertake. Spousal care is also dependent on the skills of the partners, which to a great extent will be determined by prior experience. Daune-Richard et al. (2013) in a comparison of France and Sweden found that the likelihood and types of spousal caregiving were influenced by the gender distribution of roles through the lifetime of the couple. Fewer French men in their study took charge of the LTC needs of their women partners than Swedish men due both to a lack of skills resulting from their lesser participation in household work through their lifetime, a lesser normative expectation on them to breach former gender boundaries, and more willingness to outsource tasks.

For younger care recipients, the next in the order of mobilisation of carers are their parents and then siblings (Soullier, 2012). For older people, adult children follow spouses in the order of mobilisation. The 2015 *CARE* survey found that 55 per cent of the over 60s who received help for

[7] *CARE-Ménages* is a follow-up interview study carried out in 2015 with 15,000 over 60s living at home who declared 8000 informal carers, 6201 of whom were interviewed.

[8] These are aggregates of the population.

everyday activities did so from their adult child(ren) in comparison with 38 per cent from their partner, and a further 6 per cent received support from both (Brunel et al., 2019, p. 5 Table 2). A minority of adult children in France care for their parent(s) in a co-residency arrangement. The degree of co-residency differs very significantly between countries and is a marker of the strength of familialism and the more intensive care burden remaining with the family that it entails. The 2004 SHARE survey revealed that France occupied an intermediate position in this regard in that 11 per cent of individuals without a partner and with at least one limitation aged 65 or over lived with one of their children, in contrast to 2 per cent in Sweden and 35 per cent in Spain (Fontaine et al., 2007, p. 101).

By far the most usual mode of support of older parents by adult children in France is exchange of care between two separate households (Ledoux & Dussuet, 2020). Where there are siblings, the question arises of how and why each contributes to the informal care work needed by their parents. A number of factors come into play, the majority of which but not all are related to gender. Adult children without their own children or grandchildren may be the first expected by the rest of their family to look after parents (de Bony et al., 2020). Second, the ranking of children has been found to be a factor. The 2008 *HSM* survey found that in families with two or more children, the youngest often became the primary or sole carer for the parent(s) with the older child modifying their behaviour in relation to that of the younger sibling (Roquebert et al., 2018). All that said, daughters are over-represented among carers for their parents in comparison with sons all other things being equal: the *CARE-Ménages* survey found that there were three daughters helping their parents for every two sons (Thomas & Banens, 2020, p. 55). Both sons and daughters have less likelihood of caring for their parents regardless of other factors if they have a sister (Roquebert et al., 2018, p. 339).

Furthermore, the kinds of support provided by sons and daughters vary along traditional gender lines. Sons more often take care of the garden, do repairs in the house and take care of financial issues while daughters help with shopping, laundry and meal preparation (Morel, 2007). There is also a difference in the intensity of care provided by sons and daughters. Daughters spend more time caring for their parents and undertake ADLs more often than do sons (Herlofson & Brandt, 2020; Soullier, 2012). The reasons for this gendering of intergenerational care relate to the micro-level explanations for the configuration of domestic and care work discussed previously. According to a time availability and relative resources argument, daughters and sons have different opportunities to provide care and/or resources to be able to undertake it, or indeed avoid it. Due to their lesser engagement in employment, daughters traditionally have had more discretionary time to provide LTC for family members. The gender wage gap and higher rates of part-time work among women that have been discussed in Chap. 3 mean that there is still a likelihood that daughters will be in a weaker labour market position than sons, making them more available to care for their parents and with fewer resources to bargain their way out of, or to outsource it. However, older women in France are now likely to be in employment in similar if not identical proportions to men. In the 55–59 age group,[9] whereas in 1975 only 41.3 per cent of women were in employment as compared with 80.4 per cent of men, by 2010 these figures had equalised to 56.9 and 64.3 per cent respectively. Between 2010 and 2017 employment rates in this age group had increased across the population following the rise in the pension age from 60 to 62 in 2010, and the gender gap had narrowed further with 74.8 per cent of men and 69.1 per cent of women being economically active (INSEE, 2019, Fig. 1). One result of this increase in activity rates among older workers is that a significant proportion of informal carers for the over 60s, whether partners or adult children, are in employment. The figure was 40 per cent in 2015 (Bruno, 2018, p. 89).

Daughters may be more available for intergenerational caring because on average they live closer to parents than do sons, a situation which in itself is an expression of the interiorisation of gender norms around obligation and care (Le Pape et al., 2018). Geographical proximity between care provider and care recipient is an important element in the provision of practical care. Seventy-five per cent of children caring for parents with whom they are not co-habiting live less than 30 km or 40 minutes travel time away (Diallo & Leroux, 2020, p. 74). All that said, even when individual characteristics such as labour market participation and geographical proximity to the care recipient are similar between siblings, parents are still more likely to receive care from daughters than from sons, giving credence to gender theories of domestic and care work (Haberkern et al., 2015). This is because their own and their parents' gender norms around informal caring lead daughters and sons to respond differently to the same resources.

[9] The average age of unpaid helpers for the elderly in 2008 was 59 (Soullier, 2012)

The contribution of professional carers for those with higher levels of dependency helps family members to reconcile employment and LTC to an extent. However, informal carers may still need to modify their employment to respond to care needs. Given that women still take on more informal LTC work than men despite their participation in the labour market, they will be more likely to have to modify their employment for this reason (Soullier, 2012). According to Labour Force Survey (LFS) data for France for 2016, 4.6 per cent of inactive women aged 50–64 declared they were inactive because of looking after children or incapacitated adults,[10] in contrast with 0.5 per cent of men. A further 6 per cent of women and 3.5 per cent men declared working part-time for the same reason. In this regard, France is again in an intermediate position in the EU. The average figures for the EU 28 were 5.5 per cent of women and 1.5 per cent of men being inactive and 10.1 per cent of women and 3.6 per cent of men working part-time due to caring responsibilities. The highest percentages of inactivity and part-time work due to caring responsibilities in this age group were recorded in the UK (12.5 per cent of women and 6.5 per cent of men being inactive and 20 per cent women and 7.7 per cent of men working part-time). The lowest percentages were recorded in the Nordic countries, for example Sweden (0.5 per cent of women and no men being inactive and 2.2 per cent of women and 3.3 per cent of men working part-time) (Spasova et al., 2018, p. 34).

In the absence of close kin to provide any or specific care tasks, other members of the family, including in-laws or non-kin such as friends or neighbours, may be called upon to help with activities such as shopping or transport. The *CARE* study found that of the over 60s requiring help with everyday activities, 3 per cent received care from their siblings, 4 per cent from their grandchildren and 7 per cent from a son or daughter-in-law. As concerns non-kin, 5 per cent received help from a friend and 3 per cent from others such as neighbours. Due to demographic factors, a smaller percentage of the over 75s received help from their siblings (2 per cent) and friends (4 per cent) and more from their grandchildren (5 per cent) or their son or daughter-in-law (9 per cent) (Brunel et al., 2019, p. 5 Table 2). Women were more likely to be engaged in providing support for the over 60s within these social relations (16.3 per cent) than men (11.9 per cent) whatever the relationship of informal caregiver to care recipient (Bruno, 2018, p. 90).

[10] There is no breakdown of these figures between childcare and LTC.

Comparative research suggests that France occupies an intermediate position in Europe as concerns the gendering of long-term caregiving. In a 13-country European comparison using the SHARE data, Da Roit et al. (2015) analyse the relationship between levels of state support for LTC and gender specialisation in caring for adults. On the one hand, Southern and Eastern European countries which have limited state support for LTC and require intensive levels of care from the family demonstrate high levels of gender specialisation in care. On the other hand, Nordic countries which have more extensive state support for LTC and require less input from the family demonstrate lower levels of gender specialisation in care. The study found that France and Germany have both relatively high levels of state support for LTC, but also relatively high levels of gender specialisation for care. A more recent comparison of the contribution of sons and daughters to caring for their parents in the EU comes to a similar conclusion as regards the relative position of France (Haberkern et al., 2015). In France, sons provided 35 per cent of the combined care hours dedicated to parents by children. This compared with 58 per cent in Denmark, the country with the highest contribution from sons, and 18 per cent in Italy, the lowest (Haberkern et al., 2015, p. 308 Table 1). The conclusion to be drawn from these comparisons is that it is both the level of state spending on LTC, but also the nature of the LTC support provided that account for gendering of informal care. State support for care at home, the complexity of care provision and direct support for informal carers all combine to increase the likelihood of women retaining a traditional caring role. French policy has all these characteristics (Haberkern et al., 2015). The Libault report recognises that the nature of policy towards LTC in France over the past 20 years has resulted in a fragmented and complex system with little standardisation which has not challenged the gendering of caring (Libault, 2019).

Policy to support informal carers treads a fine line between recognition of their status and importance of their work, on the one hand, and tacitly supporting traditional gender divisions of labour in society on the other. This is a similar problem to that discussed in Chap. 3 as concerns parental leave. Support by the state for employees to withdraw temporarily from the labour market to undertake informal caregiving can have the effect of solidifying traditional norms around gendered care responsibilities, particularly for the lower paid for whom such schemes are more financially attractive (Haberkern et al., 2015). The French state has implemented a range of tools to support informal carers in recent years. It has engaged in a process of creating a formal status of carer which can be used as a basis for granting rights to social security benefits (e.g., pension rights), the right to respite from caring, and employment rights (e.g., care leave or right to flexible working). In addition, cash-for-care benefits can be used under certain conditions to pay informal carers. This will be discussed in the section on "Professional Care" below.

Although there had been discussions about the role of family and informal care in addressing the problems accompanying an ageing population since the 1980s in France, no action was taken until the twenty-first century to recognise the status of informal carer. In part, this change came about due to a unified and more powerful lobby group for family carers coming into being—the *Association Française des Aidants (AFA)* (French Carers Association)—to promote the place and role of carers in society (Argoud, 2020). The *AFA* brought together bodies representing individuals and their carers experiencing a variety of health conditions or disabilities who had not before had a single voice. The *AFA* benefitted from the strength of the lobbying of researchers, professionals and carers for better treatment of and care for those with dementia, this being a health issue that had risen up the political agenda in the early 2000s, in order to promote the cause of informal carers more generally (Ngatcha-Ribert, 2012). In 2005 the law on the *Egalité des droits et des chances, la participation et la citoyenneté des personnes handicapées* (Equality of rights and opportunities, participation and citizenship of people with a disability) gave a legal status for the first time to family members who act as *aidants familiaux* (family carers) for those aged under 60. This law also created the *Caisse Nationale de Solidarité pour l'Autonomie* (*CNSA*) (National Solidarity Fund for Autonomy) as part of the Health Ministry. The status of *aidant familial* was extended to carers of the over 60s in 2007 (Argoud, 2020). According to Article 245-7 of the *Code de l'action sociale et des familles* (Social action and family code), an *aidant familial* is a spouse, civil or cohabiting partner or ascendant, descendant or collateral relative up to the fourth level of removal who gives human assistance other than in a professional or paid capacity to someone in need of ADLs or IADLs (Roy, 2019). A decade later, in 2016, Article 51 of the *ASV* law created the status of *proche aidant* (informal carer) in relation to the over 60s to include non-kin. The category of *proche aidant* includes family carers and others living with the care recipient or having close and stable relationships with them and who assist them regularly and frequently (Alberola &

Muller, 2020; Roy, 2019). The category of *proche aidant* does not feature in legislation regarding the under 60s.

As concerns the protection of informal carers' social security rights and working conditions, in 2019, Prime Minister Edouard Philippe launched a *Stratégie de mobilisation et de soutien en faveur des aidants* (Strategy to mobilise and support informal carers) which included measures securing the social rights of caregivers by standardising the way they are treated within different social security regimes alongside measures to protect their health and safety. The amount and challenge of the work involved in informal caring have also been addressed by policymakers. The 2016 *ASV* law confers the right to respite for carers for older people by providing temporary places in care homes and creating special centres to support them and their carers. As concerns work-care reconciliation, in 2007 family carers were granted the possibility of taking a *Congé de soutien familial* (Family support leave), now termed *Congé de solidarité familiale* (Family solidarity leave). The 2016 *ASV* law extended the right to this leave to all informal carers (*Congé de proches aidants*—Informal caregiver leave). Carers have the right to ask permission from their employer to interrupt their employment temporarily in order to care for someone who is unwell or someone with loss of autonomy. The carer can return to their employment and retain employment rights based on continuity of service. The leave is for three months but can be renewed for up to a year. At first, this right to leave was not accompanied by any allowance or benefit. However, in 2010, a special allowance for care of a terminally ill relative was introduced and in 2020, the *Allocation journalière du proche aidant* (*AJPA*) (Daily informal caregiver allowance), a daily benefit to accompany the caregivers' leave, was introduced. Additionally, legislation in 2019 imposed the obligation on social partners to negotiate measures aimed at facilitating the reconciliation of professional and personal life for their employees who are informal caregivers (Argoud, 2020).

During a review of care benefits for the under and over 60s in the late 1990s and early part of this century, there was no discussion of the impacts of measures on the gendering of care, even though this review took place under a Socialist government. The problem was framed uniquely from the perspective of the challenge of the ageing population and wellbeing of the care recipient with much less interest in the care provider, whether informal or professional. Containing the costs of care was also of major importance, necessitating reliance on informal care alongside formal provisions. In this period, feminist lobby groups were much more focused on childcare than LTC. Ledoux and Dussuet (2020) suggest that this is because disability and old age are difficult to relate to a social constructionist view of society. A further explanation of the lack of interest in gender equality issues as related to informal LTC among feminist groups and the Socialist government of the time is that responsibility for informal LTC has traditionally had less impact on women's employment than caring for children. As noted by the ILO (2018, p. 98), the "presence of older persons in the household is … a significant factor that negatively affects women's labour force participation, but to a lesser degree compared with the impact made by children under six years of age". This is essentially because the average age in France of informal caregivers is 59 as previously noted. In the late 1990s, the retirement age in France was 60 and inactivity rates in older age groups high. Indeed, part of the work sharing agenda of Socialist governments had been early retirement.

However, change started to occur in the second decade of the twenty-first century. In 2011, a delegation for equal rights between men and women from the National Assembly led by Mme Marianne Dubois was invited to participate in President Sarkozy's "great debate" on how to care for an ageing population. The delegation produced a report that considered all the inequalities confronting women in relation to LTC, both as consumers and as informal and professional care workers (Dubois, 2011). The National Assembly delegation was once more invited to submit a report on the bill for the 2016 *ASV* legislation. A recommendation that had appeared in 2011 and again in 2016 for respite care for informal carers was integrated into the 2016 *ASV* law. The debate on the *ASV* law was more attentive to questions of gender, and by 2018 one of the recommendations of the National Assembly delegation to introduce gender categories into national statistics pertaining to LTC had been implemented (Argoud, 2020). Furthermore, the 2019 Libault report has recommended increasing support to informal carers for older relatives and recognises gender concerns (European Commission, 2021).

This increased interest in the gendering of LTC came about for two reasons that are similar to those which explain the change of emphasis as regards childcare policy discussed in Chap. 3. On the one hand, the activation agenda in labour market policy of international bodies such as the EU and at national level under the Sarkozy administration included increasing the pension age and extending the working life of citizens as being central to confronting the challenges of the ageing population for welfare states. Improvements in the health particularly of the 60 to 75 age group facilitated this. Therefore, ensuring that older women could remain in the workforce gained traction in political considerations. Second, gender equality had become squarely part of the LTC agenda of international bodies. For example, gender equality is at the heart of the UN's Triple R framework for care, and gender equality issues are foregrounded in the latest EU report on the subject *Towards a common European action on care*, published in July 2022.

Professional Care

As discussed above, professional care constitutes a smaller percentage of the care landscape in France than informal care in terms of both the proportion of those in need of care and assistance using professional services and the time devoted to caring tasks of professional and informal carers. That said, given the fact of the ageing of the population over the next 30 years, professional carers are set to represent a growing group in the labour force. An OECD comparison of the number of LTC workers per 100 people aged 65 or over in 2019 found that with 4 workers per 100 people in this age category France had a below-average coverage rate (the average was 5.5 workers) and ranked 23rd out of 32 countries. The highest number of workers were to be found in Norway (12.5) and Sweden (12) (OECD, 2022).

Although home-based care remains the national priority in French policy (Libault, 2019), a significant number of individuals are looked after in institutional settings even if this is regarded as a solution of last resort. These institutions can be in the public, commercial or non-profit sectors. For example, in 2018, 22 per cent of places in *Etablissements d'hébergement pour personnes âgées dépendantes* (*EHPAD*) (nursing homes) were in private for-profit organisations, 28 per cent in private non-profit organisations and 50 per cent in the public sector (Libault, 2019, p. 28). In 2019, 53 per cent of those working in nursing homes were public-sector employees, 19 per cent employees in private for-profit organisations and 27 per cent employees in non-profit organisations. The workers in these institutions are mostly formal workers, both employees and agency staff. In 2019, 92,269 disabled adults under 60 were living in an institutional structure and 577,208 over 60s were in an *EHPAD*. Forty-eight per cent of residents in *EHPADs* were aged between 70 and 89, and a further 40 per cent were aged 90 plus. Between 2009 and 2019 the number of people cared for in *EHPADs* grew by 91,000. However, if the same proportion of the 60 plus population were in an *EHPAD* in 2019 as 2009, the number of residents would be approximately double what it in fact was (INSEE, 2022, p. 2).

The extent of functional limitations in conjunction with the presence or absence of a partner determines whether a person needing care stays at home or enters a care facility. The level of dependency at which individuals enter institutional care continues to rise, while having a partner, all other variables being equal, halves the likelihood of entering an institution (Renaut, 2021). Although restating the commitment to keeping older people in their own homes if they so wish, the Libault report acknowledges the limitations of home care, and therefore recommends improvements to residential care with renovations to buildings to make them more accessible to the community, improved carer–to–resident ratios and changing financing regimes to reduce the out-of-pocket cost to individuals. It also promises new care solutions such as temporary accommodation and collective (sheltered) housing (Libault, 2019). It should not be forgotten that those living in institutional settings may also continue to receive informal care and support from family or friends. The number of places and trends in residential care for the over 65 population in France are similar to that found in other Conservative welfare regimes, such as Germany, Luxembourg and the Netherlands. The situation in France contrasts to the Nordic countries where there have been substantial falls in numbers of residential home places, but from very high starting points. The coverage rates of places in institutions remain higher in the Social Democratic countries than elsewhere (Spasova et al., 2018, Fig. 3).

The majority of those in need of professional assistance with everyday life in France receive home care that is supported by the state through cash-for-care benefits in conjunction with schemes to encourage the use of PHS (see Chap. 5) rather than in-kind service provision by public sector or contracted private-sector workers. There are two principal social policy tools in France that provide cash-for-care benefits to adults in need of LTC, one for the under 60s and one for the over 60s. They can both also be used to contribute towards institutional care, but the majority are used for home-based care. As discussed in Chap. 2, policy for these two age groups was separated in 1997 as the existing benefit for those with a disability became unfit for purpose for the growing older and dependent population. For the under 60s, in 2006 the *Prestation de compensation du handicap* (*PCH*) replaced the *ACPT* putting more emphasis on the social integration of the working-age population with a disability or chronic health condition particularly via employment (Baradji et al., 2021). In 2016, 350,000 working-age adults (16–64-year-olds) were in receipt of the *PCH* or the *ACPT*,[11] 80 per cent of whom used it for human assistance either solely or in conjunction with other forms of support (technical, adaptation of living space, for pets, other expenditures) (*DREES*, 2020).

For the over 60s, the *Allocation personnalisée pour l'autonomie (APA)* was introduced in 2001 by Prime Minister Lionel Jospin's Socialist government, the reform of social care policy having been one of its policy pillars at election. It replaced the *PDS* but shared many features with its predecessor. It can be used for human assistance for ADLs or IADLs, or to pay for equipment. The differences between the *PDS* and the *APA* relate principally to eligibility criteria: in difference to the *PDS*, the *APA* is not means-tested, but the level of payment is reduced progressively for those above an income ceiling (Morel, 2007). It was also extended to people with lower levels of dependency. Furthermore, under the *APA*, the state could no longer reclaim care costs on the recipient's estate. The increased take-up of the benefit prompted the right-wing government of Prime Minister Jean-Pierre Raffarin to lower the income ceiling in 2003 in an attempt to rein in costs (Frinault, 2005). In 2016, the *APA* was claimed by 7.6 per cent of all French residents aged over 60. The Libault report has suggested replacing the *APA* to create a benefit with a third component—respite for informal carers (Libault, 2019, p. 48).

Both the *PCH* and the *APA* can be used to purchase services from any type of provider. Among those who purchase services from an organisation in France, in 2015 20 per cent were purchased from for-profit organisations, 70 per cent from non-profit organisations and only 10 per cent from the public sector. A major consequence of cash-for-care being the principal mode of support for home care services for the disabled and older people in conjunction with the promotion of PHS more generally in France has been the extension of the use of direct employment in LTC delivery (Le Bihan-Youinou et al., 2014). In 2020, there were one million direct employers among the over 60s in France, employing 549,000 PHS workers for 227.5 million hours of work, and representing half of all direct employers (Observatoire de l'Emploi à Domicile, 2022, p. 21). As discussed in Chap. 3 in relation to childminders and nannies, extending care services through encouraging direct employment is controversial because

[11] The ACPT is being phased out but is still drawn by some.

bipartite employment relations are regarded as less advantageous to employees than tripartite arrangements.

These benefits can also be used to pay family carers, thereby potentially acting as a wage-replacement benefit but only under certain conditions. The *PCH* can be used to employ a member of the family other than a partner, parent or child. However, where dependency is so severe that full-time care is required, any member of the family including partners and children can be employed. In those cases where the benefit cannot be used to employ a family member, these relatives can receive "compensation" for the hours they devote to caring duties, an assessment of which is made by social services. The family carer receives 50 per cent of the hourly minimum wage for each assessed hour of caring, or 75 per cent if the caring is extensive enough to warrant partial economic inactivity. In 2015, 70 per cent of *PCH* beneficiaries who used the benefit for human assistance paid family members, 29 per cent purchased services and 13 per cent employed a professional carer directly, with a further 1 per cent employing someone through an agency (Baradji et al., 2021, p. 4 Table 2).

The *APA* does not offer the possibility to compensate, rather than employ a close relative. Furthermore, partners cannot be employed under the scheme because they are bound under the Civil Code to provide care to their companion. However, it is possible to use the benefit to employ any other relative, including children and grandchildren. In their interview study of informal carers as part of the *CARE-Menages* research programme, de Bony et al. (2020, p. 22) found that only 8 per cent of *APA* beneficiaries employed a relative as their carer. This contrasts with comparable countries such as Austria, Germany and Luxembourg where the majority of older people receiving cash-for-care benefit use them to pay for family or informal carers (King-Dejardin, 2019).

In allowing the use of the *APA* or the *PCH* for family members, and particularly in the compensation mode within the *PCH*, the French state blurs the boundaries between professional and informal care. These payments may improve the financial situation of the carer in the immediate term but undertaking these roles may have medium- and long-term negative effects on their career and financial stability. For example, those receiving compensation rather than a salary do not accrue employment-related social security rights, such as to unemployment benefit. Directly employed carers, whether family members or not, have limited career opportunities (Giraud, 2019). This has negative consequences for women who are most likely to take up these roles, both due to gender norms and the gender wage gap. There is evidence from the *CARE-Ménage* study that salaried family carers found it difficult to view their caring activities as an occupation, either because they believed that money was not compatible with the moral and emotional obligations they owed to family members, or because the remuneration that they received was too low to be considered a salary. Some of those who were already retired or otherwise economically inactive prior to taking on caring duties used the benefit to subsidise the care of their relative rather than for themselves. In contrast, those taking care of relatives with the highest degree of dependency and receiving the highest salaries did view their activity as employment (de Bony et al., 2020).

Those with lower level needs who may not be eligible for *APA* or *PCH* payments are encouraged to use the incentives on offer for the use of PHS particularly for IADLs. Payments under the *APA* or *PCH* can also be used in conjunction with these schemes to pay for direct employment (Devetter et al., 2021). Households with individuals experiencing a loss of independence or aged over 70 with or without care needs are exempt from employer social security contributions for direct PHS employees (Ad-PHS, 2020). In 2020, 36 per cent of all those eligible for any degree of social security reduction on direct employee costs were in the over-70 age group. The *CESU* is also widely used by the over 60s who are one of the two principal categories of users alongside high-earning professional households (Devetter, 2016) (see Chap. 5). The Generation and Gender survey carried out by the *INED* in 2005 and again in 2008 asked the question, "Does your household regularly pay someone to do housework?" In 2005, 18 per cent of households of over 65s responded positively in comparison with 8.5 per cent of the under 65s. In 2008, three years after the introduction of the Borloo Plan, the percentage of the over 65s responding positively had risen to 22.5, but the increase was only to 9 per cent for the younger age group (Devetter, 2016, p. 372). In Devetter's (2016) analysis of the Generation and Gender study, he found that although the *APA* helped lower-income households afford PHS, income was still important in determining the likelihood of the over 65s paying someone to do housework: 18 per cent of households in the lowest income category (under 1000 Euros per month) purchased such services as compared with 51 per cent in the highest income category (above 5000 Euros). A more recent study in the Centre-Val de Loire region found that the over 65s represented 60 per cent of the 14.6 per cent of all households who used the provisions of the Borloo Plan to employ someone to carry out

PHS. The use of PHS increased with age with 19 per cent of households aged 65–79 and 44 per cent of households aged 80 plus using them (Goupil et al., 2019, p. 2).

Assessing the comparative position of France as concerns the percentage of the population receiving professional home-based care services is complex. This is because those with the lowest level of need who may not be eligible for cash-for-care benefits are still supported by the state through its PHS policies. However, they would not necessarily feature in all comparative studies depending on the data used (Devetter, 2016). A comparison of the percentage of the over 65 population receiving home-based care in 2014 undertaken by the OECD showed France in an intermediate position among high-income countries with 6.5 per cent of the population receiving such services, similar to Germany (9 per cent), but lower than countries with the highest rates such as Sweden (14.8 per cent) and the Netherlands (13 per cent) (Spasova et al., 2018, Fig. 1). However, a comparison of the self-reported use of home care services by age in 2014 by the European Union revealed that France alongside Norway, Sweden, the Netherlands and Belgium (another country with very highly developed PHS support) had the highest number of users of these services: 10.5 per cent of 65–74-year-olds and 33.5 per cent of the 75 plus age group as compared with the EU average of 4.5 per cent and 17 per cent respectively (Eurofound, 2020).

The low status and low pay associated with professional care work mean that it is those in the least advantageous position in the labour market who undertake it. First and foremost, it is a feminised sector. The overwhelming majority (around 95 per cent) of LTC employees are women (Ledoux & Dussuet, 2020). In similarity with childminders, they tend to be older and less well-qualified than average. Although slightly overrepresented in comparison with their numbers across the labour force, migrants, or those with a first- or second-generation migrant heritage, represent a minority of LTC workers in France at around 5 per cent (Condon et al., 2013, p. 6). This contrasts with countries such as Spain and Italy where migrants constitute the majority of care workers (between 65 and 90 per cent) (King-Dejardin, 2019). Such differences have two principal causes, one affecting documented migrant workers and the other undocumented workers. As concerns documented workers, countries such as Italy and Spain have sectoral agreements with countries outside the EU to recruit migrant workers for the care and PHS sectors. France has not had such agreements, for reasons that will be discussed in more depth in Chap. 5. Furthermore,

France has a relatively low proportion of undeclared care and PHS workers, including undocumented migrants, in comparison with other European countries in which cash-for-care benefits are used to fund direct employees. One reason for this is that the state retains control over the way these benefits are spent, reducing the possibility of employing workers on an undeclared basis, including undocumented migrant workers (King-Dejardin, 2019).

Professional care work is arduous both physically and emotionally. Personal care can involve bodily work that may also be considered dirty work as well as lifting which may pose health and safety issues. France has been identified as having the highest shares of LTC workers reporting accidents and work-related health problems in the EU (2021). Personalised relationships with the care recipient can also be a source of stress and leave workers open to abuse (Devetter et al., 2021). Migrant LTC workers and people of colour have been found to be exposed to racism (Avril, 2012). There are differences in the working conditions of LTC workers depending on their place and type of employment, reflecting a hierarchy that has already been discussed in relation to childcare: in comparison with home care workers, those working in institutions have more support from colleagues and managers; opportunities to engage in collective bargaining; and possibilities for career progression. They also work in spaces that are overseen by labour inspectors protecting their health and safety. Home workers have little control over the rhythm of their work and if working alone, little ongoing support throughout the day. They are more likely to work part-time than those working in institutions—42 per cent of home carers as compared with 26 per cent of those working in institutions (OECD, 2018). That said, residential institutions employ a high proportion of temporary agency workers (OECD, 2018). Home care workers who work for commercial, state, or non-profit organisations have more advantageous conditions than those who work as direct employees in that they are embedded in structures that provide support and opportunities for collaboration, career progression and collective bargaining. However, they may be expected to work at a very fast pace by their employers and have even less control of their work rhythms than direct employees. In home settings migrant workers have been found to experience worse employment conditions than their French counterparts as concerns the types of tasks they are expected to undertake, and the regularity of their work hours.

Concluding Summary

In similarity with the work required to care for children, the majority of LTC work in France is carried out on an unpaid basis within the household. However, there is a significant amount of care provided to older people by their adult children living in separate households. Informal care and professional care are often combined for those with higher levels of need, and even when the majority of care is provided by professionals, family members still need to contribute cognitive labour in the form of the management of care services. France has some of the highest percentages of older people reporting that they receive support from their families in Europe, comparable with countries with highly familialist welfare regimes such as Italy.

The French Civil Code stipulates that adult children bear a legal obligation to support their parents and other ascendants. Even though legal interventions concerning lack of care for ascendants are very rare, the existence of these obligations has the symbolic power to define norms around filial responsibilities and reinforces an ideological and institutional adherence to the family as social carers. There has been a political consensus in France that undermining the role of the family in LTC would be harmful to the cohesion of society, and in view of the aging population, it would be too costly for the state to assume a greater role. Whereas France was an early-bird in its development of childcare and work-family reconciliation policy, it was a late-comer country in terms of the development of LTC policy, particularly policy targeted at the over 60s which only dates back to the late 1990s. Spending on LTC is higher in France than the OECD average but lags significantly behind the highest spending countries such as the Netherlands and the Social Democratic states. The LTC policy framework in France is based on a mixed model favouring home care through cash-for-care benefits, rather than in-kind provision of services, embedded within informal care by the family. This orientation of policy is justified as responding to the wish of the majority of the population to remain in their own homes and integrated into society, and have a choice over what care they want, and how to source it. Furthermore, the concentration on cash-for-care benefits has been necessary in order to expand professional LTC as it is a less costly option than in-kind provision. The fragmented landscape of care to which this policy framework gives rise means that although spending on LTC in France is relatively generous, the levels of informal care required remain high. Assessing the comparative position of France as concerns accessibility to and use of professional services for those with LTC needs is complex. This is because those with the lowest level of need may not be eligible for benefits or access services through home help providers but may still be subsidised in their purchase of services by the state through its PHS policies. Depending on whether recourse to support for PHS is included or not in comparative studies, the position of France relative to other countries differs.

Women retain more responsibility for informal and professional LTC work than men in France. In different-sex couples, a higher percentage of men are cared for by their women partners than vice versa. Care for parents, all other things being equal, is more likely to be undertaken by daughters than sons, and having a sister significantly reduces the likelihood of having to take on such care work. The majority of professional care workers are women. That said, when in different-sex couples, men do take on caring roles for their partners, within the limits of the skill set that they have developed through their lives, and in relation to the degree to which they are prepared to outsource activities that were undertaken within the household prior to the incapacity of their spouse. Sons carry out personal care for fathers and stereotypically masculine domestic tasks for parents and other relatives.

France occupies an intermediate position in comparison with other high-income countries as concerns the degree of gendering of informal LTC work. This is because the policy framework in France combines state support for care at home, a wide range of sources of this care provision and support for informal carers, characteristics which combine to increase the likelihood of women retaining a traditional role in LTC. The Libault report recognises that the nature of policy towards LTC in France over the past 20 years has resulted in a fragmented and complex system which has not challenged the gendering of caring (Libault, 2019). The gendering of LTC was not prominent in political discourse in France until the 2010s at which time the problem was framed uniquely from the perspective of the challenge of the ageing population and wellbeing of the care recipient and of containing the costs of care of the ageing population. Feminist lobby groups and Socialist politicians were much more focused on childcare than LTC because responsibility for LTC has less impact on women's employment. However, by the 2010s more interest was directed towards the plight of informal caregivers, and the gendering of informal care. Not only did the issue of the rights of formal and informal carers rise up the agenda of supranational bodies, such as the UN and EU but the activation turn in labour market policy that led to the increase in the pension age from 60 to 62 in France meant that there was more interest in the keeping older men and women in the workforce.

The outcome of this increased interest in informal care providers and the gendering of informal care have been policies first to give a legal status to informal carers, and then on the basis of this status, to grant them social protection rights, employment and care leave rights and wage replacement benefits. In similarity to parental leave, policy to support informal carers in these ways treads a fine line between recognition of the importance of this unpaid work and those who carry it out, on the one hand, and the reinforcement of traditional gender divisions of labour in society on the other.

References

AD-PHS. (2020). *Country report – France*. Retrieved October 18, 2021, from www.ad-phs.eu/htag2/uploads/2021/01/cr_france.pdf

Alberola, E., & Muller, J. (2020). Aider un proche : une situation à risques. *Consommation et modes de vie, 314*, 1–4.

Argoud, D. (2020). La politique de soutien aux aidants en France : une articulation non aboutie avec le milieu associatif. *Enfances, Familles, Générations, 36*, 1–20. http://journals.openedition.org/efg/10779

Avril, C. (2012). Ressources et lignes de clivage parmi les aides à domicile. Spécifier une position sociale : quelles opérations de recherche ? *Actes de la recherche en sciences sociales, 191–192*(1), 86–105. https://doi.org/10.3917/arss.191.00869

Banens, M., Thomas, J., & Boukabza, C. (2019). Le genre et l'aide familiale aux seniors dépendants. *Revue française des affaires sociales, 1*, 115–131. https://doi.org/10.3917/rfas.191.0115

Baradji, E., Dauphin, L., & Eideliman, J.-S. (2021). Comment vivent les personnes handicapées Les conditions de vie des personnes déclarant de fortes restrictions d'activité. *Les dossiers de la DREES, 75*, 1–37. Retrieved September 7, 2022, from https://drees.solidarites-sante.gouv.fr/sites/default/files/2021-02/DD75.pdf

Brousse, C. (2015). Travail professionnel, tâches domestiques, temps « libre » : quelques déterminants sociaux de la vie quotidienne. *Economie et Statistique, 478-479-480*, 119–154.

Brunel, M., & Carrère, A. (2017). Les personnes âgées dépendantes à domicile en 2015. *Etudes et Résultats de la DRESS, 1029*, 1–6.

Brunel, M., Latourelle, J., & Zakri, M. (2019). Un senior à domicile sur cinq aidé régulièrement pour les taches du quotidien. *Etudes et résultats de la DRESS, 1103*, 1–6.

Bruno, C. (2018). Qu'est-ce qu'un·e aidant.e familial·e ? *Vie sociale et traitements, 139*(3), 85–90. https://doi.org/10.3917/vst.139.0085
Calasanti, T., & Bowen, M. E. (2006). Spousal caregiving and crossing gender boundaries: Maintaining gendered identities. *Journal of Aging Studies, 20*(3), 253–263. https://doi.org/10.1016/j.jaging.2005.08.001
Condon, S., Lada, E., Charruault, A., & Romanini, A. (2013). *Promoting integration of migrant domestic workers in France*. Retrieved September 4, 2018, from http://www.ilo.org/wcmsp5/groups/public/---ed_protect/---protrav/---migrant/documents/publication/wcms_232518.pdf
Da Roit, B., Hoogenboom, M., & Weicht, B. (2015). The gender informal care gap. A fuzzy-set analysis of cross-country variations. *European Societies, 17*(2), 199–218. https://doi.org/10.1080/14616696.2015.1007153
Daune-Richard, A.-M., Jönsson, I., Ring, M., & Odena, S. (2013). L'entrée en dépendance des personnes âgées : quelle prise en charge pour quelles différenciations sociales et sexuées ? *Revue française des affaires sociales, 2*, 148–168. https://doi.org/10.3917/rfas.122.0148
de Bony, J., Giraud, O., Petiau, A., Rist, R., Touahria-Gaillard, A., & Trenta, A. (2020). *Rémunération des aidants et relations familiales. Quelles incidences de la monétarisation de l'aide*. Retrieved March 26, 2022, from https://www.fepem.fr/wp-content/uploads/P190700971-Brochure-Re%CC%81mune%CC%81ration-des-Proches-Aidants_V4.pdf
Devetter, F.-X. (2016). Can public policies bring about the democratization of the outsourcing of household tasks? *The Review of Radical Political Economics, 48*(3), 365–393. https://doi.org/10.1177/0486613415594159
Devetter, F.-X., Dussuet, A., & Puissant, E. (2021). Aide à domicile: le développement du travail gratuit pour faire face aux objectifs inconciliables des politiques publiques. *Mouvements, 106*(2), 90–98. https://doi.org/10.3917/mouv.106.0090
Diallo, C. T., & Leroux, I. (Eds.). (2020). *L'aide et l'action sociales en France – édition 2020 Perte d'autonomie, handicap, protection de l'enfance et insertion.* Panoramas de la DRESS Social.
Direction de la recherche des études de l'évaluation et des statistiques (DREES). (2020). *L'aide et l'action sociale en France 2020.* Retrieved September 12, 2022, from https://drees.solidarites-sante.gouv.fr/sites/default/files/2021-06/L%E2%80%99aide%20et%20l%E2%80%99action%20sociales%20en%20France%20-%20Perte%20d%E2%80%99autonomie%2C%20handicap%2C%20protection%20de%20l%E2%80%99enfance%20et%20insertion%20-%20%C3%89dition%202020_1.pdf
Dubois, M. (2011). *Rapport d'information au nom de la Délégation aux Droits des Femmes et à l'égalité des chances entre les hommes et les femmes sur le genre et la dépendance*. Retrieved April 15, 2022, from https://www.vie-publique.fr/rapport/32171-genre-et-dependance

Eurofound. (2020). *Long-term care workforce: Employment and working conditions*. Publications Office of the European Union.

European Commission, Directorate-General for Employment, Social Affairs and Inclusion. (2021). *Long-term care report: Trends, challenges and opportunities in an ageing society. Volume II, country profiles*. Publications Office. https://data.europa.eu/doi/10.2767/183997

Fontaine, R., Gramain, A., & Wittwer, J. (2007). Les configurations d'aides familiales mobilisées autour des personnes âgées dépendants en Europe. *Economie et Statistique, 403–4*, 97–115.

Frinault, T. (2005). La dépendance ou la consécration française d'une approche ségrégative du handicap. *Politix, 72*, 11–31. https://doi.org/10.3917/pox.072.0011

Giraud, O. (2019). *Rémunérations et statuts des aidants et des aidantes, Fiche de résultats de recherche*. Retrieved May 21, 2022, from https://www.cnsa.fr/recherche-et-innovation/resultats-de-recherche/remunerations-et-statuts-des-aidants-et-des-aidantes#:~:text=La%20consolidation%20du%20statut%20de,mat%C3%A9rielles%2C%20mais%20aussi%20statutaires%20inextricables

Goupil, S., Hillau, M., & Taugourdeau, M.-A. (2019). 190000 ménages utilisateurs de services à la personne en 2030: un défi et une opportunité pour les secteur. *INSEE Analyses Centre-Val de Loire, 51*, 1–4.

Haberkern, K., Schmid, T., & Szydlik, M. (2015). Gender differences in intergenerational care in European welfare states. *Ageing and Society, 35*, 298–320. https://doi.org/10.1017/S0144686X13000639

Herlofson, K., & Brandt, M. (2020). Helping older parents in Europe: The importance of grandparenthood, gender and care regime. *European Societies, 22*(3), 390–410. https://doi.org/10.1080/14616696.2019.1694163

Igel, C., Brandt, M., Haberkern, K., & Szydlik, M. (2009). Specialization between family and state – Intergenerational time transfers in Western Europe. *Journal of Comparative Family Studies, 40*(2), 203–226. http://www.jstor.org/stable/41604275

ILO. (2018). *Care work and care jobs for the future of decent work*. Retrieved March 8, 2022, from https://www.ilo.org/wcmsp5/groups/public/---dgreports/---dcomm/---publ/documents/publication/wcms_633135.pdf

INED. (2022). *Population par sexe et âge au 1er janvier 2022*. Retrieved November 18, 2022, from https://www.ined.fr/fr/tout-savoir-population/chiffres/france/structure-population/population-sexe-ages/

INSEE. (2017). *Omphale – Projections de population 2013–2050 pour les départements et les régions*. Retrieved April 11, 2022, from https://www.insee.fr/fr/statiatiques/2859843

INSEE. (2018). Evolution de la structure de la société en 2015. *Recensement de la. Population*. Retrieved November 20, 2022, from https://www.insee.fr/fr/statistiques/3564100?sommaire=3561107

INSEE. (2019). Emploi par âge. *Tableaux de l'Economie Française* Edition 2019. Retrieved November 18, 2022, from https://www.insee.fr/fr/statistiques/3696937

INSEE. (2020). Esperance de vie – mortalité. *Tableaux de l'Economie Française Edition 2020.* Retrieved November 18, 2022, from https://www.insee.fr/fr/statistiques/4277640?sommaire=4318291#:~:text=En%20France%2C%20en%202019%2C%20l,7%20ans%20pour%20les%20hommes

INSEE. (2022). En 2019, 1.6 million de personnes vivent en communauté : Ehpad, internat, foyer de travailleurs. *INSEE Première, 1906*, 1–4.

Jany-Catrice, F. (2010). La construction sociale du « secteur » des services à la personne : une banalisation programmée ? *Sociologie du Travail, 52*(4), 521–537. https://doi.org/10.4000/sdt.15409

Jonsson, I., Daune-Richard, A.-M., Odena, S., & Ring, M. (2011). The implementation of elder care in France and Sweden: A macro and micro perspective. *Ageing and Society, 31*, 625–644. https://doi.org/10.1017/S0144686X10001327

King-Dejardin, A. (2019). *The social construction of migrant care work. At the intersection of care, migration and gender.* ILO. Retrieved September 12, 2022, from https://www.ilo.org/wcmsp5/groups/public/---ed_protect/---protrav/---migrant/documents/publication/wcms_674622.pdf.

Le Bihan-Youinou, B., Mallon, I., & Sopadzhiyan, A. (2014). Between Relief and Support: Differentiated Experiences of Respite for Carers of Dementia Patients. *Retraite et société, 69*, 77–98.

Le Pape, M.-C., Tenret, É., & Véron, B. (2018). Ce sont ceux qui en parlent le plus qui en font le moins. Pratiques et normes de solidarité familiale chez les femmes et les hommes dans la France contemporaine. *Nouvelles questions féministes, 37*(1), 31–51. https://doi.org/10.3917/nqf.371.0031

Ledoux, C., & Dussuet, A. (2020). Elder care allowances in action: Missed opportunities for gender transformation. *French Politics, 18*, 71–92. https://doi.org/10.1057/s41253-020-00114-w

Leitner, S. (2003). Varieties of familialism: The caring function of the family in comparative perspective. *European Societies, 5*, 353–375. https://doi.org/10.1080/1461669032000127642

Libault, D. (2019). *Grand âge, le temps d'agir, Concertation Grand âge et Autonomie. Ministère des solidarités et de la santé.* Retrieved September 14, 2022, from https://solidarites-sante.gouv.fr/IMG/pdf/rapport_grand_age_autonomie.pdf

Mestheneos, E., & Triantafillou, J. (2005). *Services for supporting family carers of elderly people in Europe. Characteristics, coverage and usage.* The EUROFAMCARE Consortium.

Morel, N. (2007). From subsidiarity to 'free choice': Child- and elder-care policy reforms in France, Belgium, Germany and The Netherlands. *Social Policy*

and Administration, 41(6), 618–637. https://doi.org/10.1111/j.1467-9515.2007.00575.x
Muller, M. (2017). 728000 résidents en établissements d'hébergement pour les personnes âgées en 2015. *Etudes et Résultats de la DRESS, 1015*, 1–4.
Ngatcha-Ribert, L. (2012). *Alzheimer : la construction sociale d'une maladie*. Dunod.
Observatoire de l'Emploi à Domicile. (2022). *Le secteur des particuliers employeurs et de l'emploi a domicile*. Retrieved September 12, 2022, from https://www.fepem.fr/wp-content/uploads/Web_fepem-rapportsectoriel2022.pdf
OECD. (2018). *Long-term care*. Retrieved April 16, 2022, from http://www.oecd.org/els/health-systems/long-term-care.htm
OECD. (2022). *Long-term care workforce: Caring for the ageing population with dignity*. Retrieved November 18, 2022, from https://www.oecd.org/health/health-systems/long-term-care-workforce.htm
Ogg, J., Renaut, S., & Trabut, L. (2015). La corésidence familiale entre générations adultes : un soutien réciproque. *Retraite et société, 70*(1), 105–125. https://doi.org/10.3917/rs.070.0105
Oliveira Hashiguchi, T., & Llena-Nozal, A. (2020). The effectiveness of social protection for long-term care in old age: Is social protection reducing the risk of poverty associated with care needs? *OECD Health Working Papers, 117*. https://doi.org/10.1787/2592f06e-en
Perron-Bailly, E. (2017). Handicap, dépendance et pauvreté : les Français solidaires des plus vulnérables. Études et Résultats, 990.
Picchi, S. (2016). The elderly care and domestic services sector during the recent economic crisis. The case of Italy, Spain and France. *Investigaciones Feministas, 7*(1), 169–190. https://doi.org/10.5209/rev_INFE.2016.v7.n1.52067
Renaut, S. (2021). Recours inégal aux professionnels pour les femmes et les hommes en couple après 60 ans. *Retraite et société, 87*(3), 73–93. https://doi.org/10.3917/rs1.087.0073
Roquebert, Q., Fontaine, R., & Gramain, A. (2018). Aider un parent âge dépendant. Configuration d'aide et interactions dans les fratries en France. *Population, 73*(2), 323–350. https://doi.org/10.3917/popu.1802.0323
Roy, D. (2019). Qui sont les proches aidants et la aides ? *Actualité et dossier en santé publique, 109*, 11–14. Retrieved September 7, 2022, from https://www.hcsp.fr/explore.cgi/Adsp?clef=171
Schmid, T., Brandt, M., & Haberkern, K. (2011). Gendered support to older parents: Do welfare states matter? *European Journal of Ageing, 9*(1), 39–50. https://doi.org/10.1007/s10433-011-0197-1
Soullier, N. (2012). Aider un proche âgé à domicile : la charge ressentie. *Direction de la recherche, des études, de l'évaluation et des statistiques (DREES) : Études et Résultats, 799*(March), 1–8.

Spasova, S., Baeten, R., Coster, S., Ghailani, D., Peña-Casas, R., & Vanhercke, B. (2018). *Challenges in long-term care in Europe. A study of national policies.* Directorate-General for Employment, Social Affairs and Inclusion.

Thomas, J., & Banens, M. (2020). Conjoint·e comme avant : genre et frontières des aides conjugale et filiale. *Gérontologie et société, 42*(161), 55–69. https://doi.org/10.3917/gs1.161.0055

Weber, F. (2006). Reconnaitre les aidants familiaux. *Connaissances de l'Emploi, 34*, 1–4.

Weber, F. (2010). Les rapports familiaux reconfigurés par la dépendance. *Regards croisés sur l'économie, 7*(1), 139–151. https://doi.org/10.3917/rce.007.0139

CHAPTER 5

Domestic Work in Contemporary France

The majority of domestic work[1] in France is conducted unpaid within the household, and the vast majority of adults have to undertake at least some unpaid domestic work for themselves or others on a regular basis. The interplay of a number of factors determines the volume of domestic work that there is for the household and the individual to do and the time it takes to do it. The type and size of housing in which one lives influence the amount of cleaning, tidying, DIY and gardening work required. Technological factors, such as the availability and affordability of domestic equipment and easy-care materials for clothes and household items, influence the productivity of domestic work and the amount of time required to produce a certain output. The type of household in which one lives is of significance. The amount of domestic work to be accomplished may be smaller overall in a single-person household but the work cannot be shared. The volume of domestic work rises with the number of people in

[1] Domestic work is defined for the purposes of this book as work required to produce the end-use goods and services necessary to ensure first the everyday maintenance of the health, wellbeing and social integration of individuals (cooking/washing up, laundry, associated shopping and administration) and second, the routine upkeep and maintenance of the material space of the home (cleaning, tidying, gardening, small maintenance/repairs/DIY/decoration and related shopping and administration). These activities can be undertaken in a variety of social relations. See Chap. 1 for a full discussion.

J. Windebank, *Domestic and Care Work in Modern France*, French Politics, Society and Culture,
https://doi.org/10.1007/978-3-031-33564-8_5

the household, particularly for activities such as food preparation or laundry, but there can be economies of scale in catering to the needs of multiple persons. However, catering to the needs of an adult or child who cannot or will not share domestic responsibilities increases the domestic workload of other household members. Particularly for those on lower incomes, unpaid domestic work can represent a vital form of subsistence work to bolster family living standards and replace the purchase of commodified goods and services (Collectif Rosa Bonheur, 2017; Weber, 2009).

Ideational factors, such as cultural housekeeping standards, expectations for the overall quality of domestic life and norms concerning personal presentation, influence the volume and type of domestic activities that need to be accomplished over and above those activities necessary for basic wellbeing (Craig & Baxter, 2014). Given its designation as dirty, invisible and routine work, and historical association with servitude, unpaid domestic work, particularly core domestic work,[2] is an activity from which many people gain little satisfaction. A sub-sample of 2600 participants in the 2010 *INSEE* time-use study were asked to rate the degree of (dis)satisfaction they gained from each daily activity they recorded on a scale of −3 to +3 (Brousse, 2015b, p. 126). Among the lowest ranked of 27 activities were washing up (26th), cleaning and tidying (25th) and laundry (23rd). Cooking scored more highly at 12th, as did the semi-leisure activities[3] of gardening/looking after pets in 6th place. However, even if domestic tasks are not experienced as fulfilling in themselves, undertaking unpaid domestic work does retain a moral value as a duty to be fulfilled, this being the view of 72 per cent of respondents in a 2018 survey in France (Barthelemy, 2018).

The need to undertake unpaid domestic work outside a care context does not usually prevent an individual from participating in the labour market but may limit opportunities as regards career progression, leisure activities or civic participation and create work-life conflicts with the potential to affect mental health. Individuals may therefore use outsourcing strategies such as the purchase of ready-to-consume goods or out-of-home or home-based services to liberate their time for other activities while continuing to enjoy a desired quality of domestic life. Their ability to do this depends on the availability and affordability of particular types

[2] Core domestic work is defined here as food preparation, washing up, laundry, cleaning/tidying and shopping (see Chap. 1).

[3] Gardening, DIY and pet care are included in this category (see Chap. 1).

of substitutes to unpaid domestic work. In addition, social norms influence beliefs about what individuals should do for themselves, and by extension, what it is acceptable to outsource and what types of outsourcing are appropriate. Work-family reconciliation policies, even though focused on parents and childcare, have an indirect impact on how domestic work gets done. This is because they not only determine the time availability, relative resources and gender norms surrounding domestic work for those with dependent children, but also express gendered assumptions about responsibility for care and domestic work and may impact the labour market engagement of women in the longer term. Furthermore, policies that include housekeeping work alongside care services under the PHS umbrella and subsidise the use of home-based services have both a material impact on individuals' and households' calculations of opportunity costs of carrying out domestic work themselves rather than buying services and an ideational impact in terms of normalising all types of outsourcing, including but not limited to the purchase of home-based services.

Unpaid Domestic Work

The importance of unpaid domestic work in France remains substantial in terms of the time it occupies in people's daily lives. However, the downward trajectory of the time-burden represented by this work begun in the latter part of the twentieth century has continued in the twenty-first century. Unpaid domestic and care work, termed in the *INSEE* time-use studies *activités domestiques*[4] (domestic activities), occupies similar amounts of time across French society as *activités professionelles*[5] (professional activities). In 2010, the French population aged over 18 spent on average

[4] In difference to the definition of domestic work used in this book which relies on the nature of the end-product of the activity, the *INSEE* term "domestic activities" refers to unpaid activities only and includes both domestic and care work. Unpaid domestic work as defined in this book equates to the core domestic activities (*INSEE* activities 4–8: food preparation; washing up; laundry/ironing; cleaning/tidying, shopping) and semi-leisure domestic activities (*INSEE* activities 10–13: knitting/sewing; DIY; gardening/pet care; other domestic work). Care for adults and children (*INSEE* activity 9) is defined as direct care work for the purposes of this book and discussed in Chaps. 3 and 4 (Brousse, 2015a, pp. 84–5).

[5] According to *INSEE* terminology, "professional activities" include commuting time, studying and training.

12 minutes per day[6] more on domestic activities than on professional activities. Across the French population, more time was spent on unpaid domestic work[7] (2 hours 58 minutes per day) than on unpaid direct care work for adults and children[8] (27 minutes per day), principally because care responsibilities are concentrated in particular groups of the population and direct care work is underpinned by indirect care (domestic) work. Furthermore, more time was spent on unpaid domestic work than on professional work[9] (2 hours 30 minutes). Although the relative amount of time devoted to unpaid domestic work as compared with professional activities has increased since 1974, this has come about in the context of a reduction in total paid and unpaid work time, and significant reduction in the time devoted to professional activities, particularly by men. The aggregate societal time spent on professional activities decreased by 20 per cent between 1974 and 2010, more than the 12 per cent reduction in the time devoted to unpaid domestic and care work (Brousse, 2015a, pp. 84–5 Table 1).

Time devoted to unpaid domestic work decreased by 15 per cent over this period with the decrease concentrated in core domestic work and the semi-leisure activities of knitting and sewing (Brousse, 2015a, pp. 84–5 Table 1). The time devoted to other semi-leisure activities increased as did time devoted to care for adults and children. These trends for the general population are the same as those that have been discussed in relation to parents in Chap. 3. The reduction in the time devoted to professional activities came about on the one hand from reductions in annual and weekly work time, including the increase in part-time work rates of the economically active, and on the other, from increases in the retired and unemployed populations, all offset by increases in the economic activity rates of women. The time devoted to professional activities only decreased by 5 per cent for women as compared with 28 per cent for men (Brousse, 2015a, pp. 84–5, Table 1). Therefore, women have reduced their time

[6] The figures are an average across the week including weekdays and weekends and are representative of the whole population aged over 18, including the economically inactive and unemployed.

[7] The definition of unpaid domestic work used in this book relates to *INSEE* time-use categories in the following: total of *INSEE* activities 4–8 (Core Domestic Work) and 10–13 (Semi-leisure Domestic Activities).

[8] *INSEE* activity 9 care for adults and children.

[9] *INSEE* activity 1 "Professional work" excludes commuting (activity 2) and studying (activity 3) in difference to "Professional activities" which include all of these.

availability for unpaid domestic work and increased their resources to bargain their way out of it. Evidence for the time availability theory of divisions of unpaid domestic work are borne out by the time-use studies in that economic activity suppresses unpaid work time for both men and women. However, the effect is stronger for men. In 2010, economically active men devoted 15 hours 20 minutes per week to domestic activities in contrast to men who were retired or unemployed who spent 23 hours 35 minutes on these activities, or 51 per cent more time. Economically active women spent 25 hours and 5 minutes on domestic activities while women who were retired, unemployed or otherwise inactive spent 32 hours and 50 minutes on them, or 31 per cent more time (Brousse, 2015b, p. 132).

The socio-economic context of twenty-first century France suggests the need for an increase in the volume of domestic outputs, if not unpaid domestic work. First, there has been an increase in the size of dwellings and the percentage of owner occupiers, both of which increase the amount of domestic work to be done. For example, the average size of primary residences in France grew from 82 m^2 in 1984 to 91 m^2 in 2006. In 1983, 51 per cent of households were owner occupiers in comparison with 58 per cent by 2013 (*INSEE*, 2014, p. 102). Second, there has been an increase in the number of single-person households, meaning that fewer people can benefit from the economies of scale for unpaid domestic work that can be achieved in multi-person households. In 1962 only 19.6 per cent of French households were single-person households. This had risen to 30.8 per cent by 1999 and 34.7 per cent by 2013 (Daguet, 2017, p. 1). Lastly, there has been an increase in the numbers of those needing direct and indirect care. As we have seen in Chaps. 3 and 4, the birth rate has been high in France since the beginning of the century, and the population is ageing rapidly.

Reductions in the time spent on unpaid domestic work is therefore the result of individuals and households leaving certain tasks undone, improving the productivity of their domestic work, or substituting unpaid labour with out-of-home or home-based domestic services. Trends in all these areas that had begun in the previously have continued into the twenty-first century. In a 2018 IPSOS survey in France, it was found that respondents often leave certain domestic tasks undone (Barthelemy, 2018). There was a clear gender divide in the reasons put forward for this: procrastination and putting the tasks off were mentioned equally by around half of all men and women, while men were more likely to cite lack of time, lack of expertise or seeing no point in doing the job as a justification and women cited tiredness, lack of stamina or the need to take turns with their partner. Furthermore, unpaid domestic work has continued to be subject to productivity increases facilitated by technological innovations that have improved domestic equipment and created easy-care materials for household goods and clothing (Plessz & Etilé, 2019). For example, it has been calculated that 25 per cent of the reduction on the time spent on laundry in France between 1974 and 2010 can be explained by a combination of the widespread use of automatic washing machines and easy-care fabrics, and 50 per cent of the decrease in time spent on washing up can be linked to the use of dishwashers (Brousse, 2015a, p. 97). By 2017 96.2 per cent of the population owned a washing machine (*INSEE*, 2019, Fig. 1), and the proportion of French households owning a dishwasher rose from 18 per cent in 1980 to 61.4 per cent in 2017 (*INSEE*, 2014, p. 101).

Furthermore, the availability and affordability of products and out-of-home services that reduce or eradicate the need for the input of unpaid domestic work to make them ready for consumption continued to be a major factor in the reduction of time spent on the activity. Food preparation is an interesting example in this regard. Time spent on food preparation in France decreased by 13 per cent between 1974 and 2010 (Brousse, 2015a, pp. 84–5 Table 1) even though France retains a traditional pattern of mealtimes. Riou et al. (2015, p. 12) in a study of the eating behaviours of Parisians found that 75 per cent followed a traditional pattern of three meals a day, often eaten at home, but the meals were not necessarily cooked from scratch. Rather, food deliveries or ready-prepared food in conjunction with microwaves was used to provide meals. There was a significant increase in the use of food delivery services in the early years of the twenty-first century in France: in 1998 12 per cent of households had purchased a food home delivery in the four weeks prior to being surveyed in comparison with 22 per cent in 2010 (Bittman, 2015, p. 325). A YouGov survey (2021) undertaken in 2020 found that 60 per cent of those purchasing food deliveries did so to save time and 47 per cent to simplify life. Spending on pre-prepared foods in France increased by 41 per cent between 1976 and 2006 (Besson, 2008, p. 2) while the percentage of households owning microwaves increased from 4 per cent in 1980 to 85 per cent in 2012 (*INSEE*, 2014, p. 101). Riou et al. (2015) also found that Parisians integrated eating out into their three-meal pattern, using out-of-home services such as restaurants, canteens and fast-food outlets particularly during the working day. Over the 1974 to 2010 period, the French practice of coming home to eat the main meal at lunchtime diminished: in 1974, 57 per cent of the French had lunch at home in comparison with only 33 per cent in 2010 (Brousse, 2015a, p. 97). Esping-Anderson (2009) argues that such outsourcing of domestic production can be explained by the broadening of purchasing power throughout the population, in part the result of the increase in dual-earner households. However, this increase in purchasing power does not translate on the whole to the purchase of home-based services. In contrast to the use of ready-to-consume goods or out-of-home services to substitute unpaid domestic work, the use of home-based paid domestic services, such as for housekeeping or gardening, by the working-age population with no care needs or responsibilities has remained a minority and socially exclusive practice, concentrated in high-earning households and SPC 3. These services will be discussed in detail in the next section "Personal and Household Services for Domestic Work".

Women in France continue to spend more time on unpaid domestic work than men, particularly on core domestic work. In 2010 women spent 2 hours 57 minutes per day on core domestic work (69 per cent of the total hours) in comparison with men who spent 1 hour 18 minutes on these activities (31 per cent of the total hours). There had been some equalisation of gender shares by the twenty-first century. Over the 1974 to 2010 period, women reduced the time they spent on core domestic work by 1 hour and 4 minutes per day, and men increased their core domestic work time by 16 minutes (Brousse, 2015a, pp. 84–5 Table 1). Brousse (2015a, p. 87) calculates that half the reduction in women's overall time spent on unpaid domestic and care work is explicable by sociodemographic changes (increased labour market participation; reduction in the number of housewives; reduction in number of children per person) and half by a change of practices, all other things being equal.

After an increase in men's core domestic work time in the 12 years between 1974 and 1986 of 11 minutes per day, in the 24 years from 1986 to 2010, there was only an additional 5-minute increase. This limited increase in men's aggregate contribution to core domestic activities is all the more disappointing in the context of demographic and economic changes that may have been expected to lead to more significant increases in their core domestic work time. For example, the diversification of households has increased the number of men who cannot depend on the unpaid domestic work of a woman and must therefore undertake these activities themselves. In 2010, men who lived alone devoted 3 hours and 10 minutes more per week to core domestic work than men who lived in a couple (Brousse, 2015b, p. 133). In addition, there has been a much higher level of decrease in time devoted to professional activities at the aggregate level for men than for women in the period to 2010, increasing their overall time availability for domestic activities. It has been calculated that the reduction in labour market activity as the result of higher levels of both unemployment and economic inactivity explains about 50 per cent of the increase in men's unpaid domestic and care work (Brousse, 2015b, p. 134).

In addition to the inequalities in time spent on unpaid domestic work by men and women, the gender specificity of particular domestic tasks as first defined in France by Zarca (1990) has remained stable over the last 30 years (*IFOP*, 2022; Papuchon, 2017). The most feminised of the core domestic work activities is laundry, with women spending four-and-a-half times more minutes per week on this activity than men in 2010, and since 1986 it has become more, not less feminised (Brousse, 2015a, p. 84–5 Table 1). Women have increased the time they devote to the traditionally male activities of DIY and gardening, while men now spend more time on the more gender-neutral activities of shopping and food preparation. Furthermore, it is necessary to consider the cognitive labour associated with unpaid domestic work and household management. Responsibility for the quality of domestic production, managing others' work (household members or employees), checking standards and planning all evade inclusion in time-use surveys (Wong, 2017). Qualitative studies have shown a wide gender gap in the cognitive labour and mental burden associated with unpaid domestic work (Bouffartigue, 2010; Daminger, 2019), while a 2019 survey in France reported that 78 per cent of women respondents agreed that it is still they who shoulder the mental burden of organising domestic life in their household (Opinion Way, 2019).

In different-sex couples, the higher their levels of qualification and salary and longer their working hours, the less time women devote to unpaid domestic work, particularly core domestic work, whereas higher educational levels are associated with more time devoted to these activities by men. Dual-earner couples in SPC 3 therefore demonstrate the highest levels of gender symmetry in unpaid domestic work (Brousse, 2015b, p. 125). There are demographic and employment differences between socio-professional groups which explain this situation to a great extent. Women in higher qualified occupations in SPC 3 and 4 tend to have fewer children and work part-time less often than women in SPC 5 and 6, and the women partners of men in SPC 5 and 6 are more often economically inactive than those whose partners have more highly qualified jobs (Clair, 2011). Furthermore, men in more highly qualified occupations have been found to have more gender-egalitarian attitudes and opportunities for flexibility in their jobs to allow them to participate more in the life of the household (Cartier et al., 2018). For more highly qualified and paid women, limiting time devoted to unpaid domestic work is achieved through leaving tasks undone and using a range of outsourcing strategies to reduce the overall domestic work burden for the household in addition to sharing tasks with their male partner. Only in couples where the woman has a significantly higher socio-professional status than the man is her decreased domestic work time offset entirely by an increase in the contribution of the male partner (Bittman, 2015; Sofer & Thibout, 2015).

The gender gap in time spent on unpaid domestic work is not limited to those living in different-sex couples. In 2010, women living in single-person households spent on average 5 hours and 11 minutes per week more on unpaid domestic and care work than men living alone. In addition to the possibility that women maintained higher levels of quality of domestic life than men, they used ready-to-consume goods, particularly food deliveries, less regularly than men living alone and received less unpaid help from individuals in other households for activities such as ironing and cleaning. There was no difference between men and women in recourse to home-based housekeeping services (Brousse, 2015b, p. 132). In similarity to findings concerning parenting work, research to date has concluded that in same-sex couples, there is more equality in unpaid domestic work between partners than in different-sex couples, with the work being shared in fluid, complex and deliberate ways. This is particularly the case in lesbian couples who are often strategic in their division of domestic work in order to counter in an explicit fashion the model of heterosexual divisions of unpaid labour (Stambolis-Ruhstorfer & Gross, 2021). Gay couples have been found to outsource more domestic work than lesbian couples (Stambolis-Ruhstorfer & Gross, 2021).

Unpaid domestic work may be undertaken for individuals living outside the household, sometimes as part of care responsibilities (see Chaps. 3 and 4) or on a mutual aid or exchange basis with friends or neighbours

(Doucet, 2000). The 2018 *Mon Quartier, Mes Voisins* (My Neighbourhood, My Neighbours) survey found that of the 68 per cent of respondents who reported doing favours in the neighbourhood, 33 per cent had undertaken DIY, gardening or repairs and 24 per cent had looked after pets. There were no reports of undertaking other kinds of domestic work (Authier & Cayouette-Remblière, 2021). Such exchange may have practical reasons, for example, the pooling of resources in economically deprived neighbourhoods (Collectif Rosa Bonheur, 2017) or social reasons, for example, maintaining kinship or community ties and developing social capital (Authier & Cayouette-Remblière, 2021). However, the volume of domestic work that is undertaken in these social relations is small. Ricroch (2012, p. 76) notes that in 1998 and 2010 according to the *INSEE* time-use surveys 10 per cent of households reported having received informal help with housework or meal preparation from relatives, friends or neighbours outside their household in the four weeks prior to the survey. However, the proportion of these instances that are associated with LTC work is not identified.

France shares with all other high-income countries a certain number of trends as regards the organisation and gender division of unpaid domestic work: the time women spend in unpaid domestic work has decreased. The time men spend on these activities has increased since the 1970s but not to an extent that can compensate the decrease in women's unpaid work time and for some activities has started to decrease again in France. The gender gap has attenuated but at a high level—nowhere is there equality in the gender division of unpaid domestic work (Sayer, 2010). However, the timing and degree of these changes show cross-national variation. In general, countries that have a narrow gender employment gap (high levels of full-time or long-hours part-time and continuous employment for women) supported by extensive state-provided or subsidised childcare, and in which public opinion supports gender egalitarianism have the lowest levels of gender inequality in unpaid domestic work (Aboim, 2010). France has not always conformed to this pattern, however. International comparisons of the gender division of unpaid domestic work in the early 2000s that used the 1998 *INSEE* time-use study or results from the 2002 International Social Survey Programme (ISSP) found that despite the integration of women into the labour market and progressive gender role attitudes in France, there was a persistence of a relatively traditional gender division of domestic and care work with high levels of work-life conflict for women with parenting responsibilities.

In a comparison of the ratio of the time spent on routine and non-routine unpaid domestic work[10] of 20–49-year-old men and women across a number of Social Democratic, Liberal and Conservative welfare regimes using the Multinational Time Use Study (1960s to early 2000s), it was found that on the basis of the 1998 time-use study that French women spent 2.1 times more minutes on domestic work than men. These results were very similar to those of the other Conservative regimes (Netherlands 2.1; Germany 2.25), but more unequal than in the Social Democratic countries (Sweden 1.4; Norway 1.6) or the North American Liberal countries (US 1.6; Canada 1.9) (Sayer, 2010, p. 23). A similar finding emerges from a comparison of the time devoted to unpaid domestic work by men and women living in different-sex couples aged 18–64 in France and Sweden.[11] In the study, French women undertook 29 hours and 36 minutes of unpaid domestic work per week, 2 hours and 26 minutes more than the Swedish women. French men undertook 14 hours and 8 minutes of domestic work per week, 2 hours and 8 minutes less than the Swedish men. The gender gap in domestic work hours was therefore 15 hours and 28 minutes in France as compared with 10 hours and 52 minutes in Sweden (Anxo et al., 2002, p. 128).

Furthermore, a comparison of work-life conflict for full-time employed women in France, the UK, Norway, Finland and Portugal using the 2002 ISSP data created a Division of domestic labour (DDL) index[12] for five tasks, four domestic work tasks (laundry, shopping for food, household cleaning and preparing meals) and one caring task (caring for sick relatives) (Crompton & Lyonette, 2006, p. 386 Table 3). With a mean DDL score of 19.23, France demonstrated a more traditional gendering of domestic work than the Social Democratic Nordic countries (Finland 18.23 and Norway 18.19) and also the Liberal country in the study, Britain (18.61) despite the French displaying similar attitudes to gender

[10] Routine domestic work included cooking, cleaning and laundry and non-routine included DIY, small repairs, gardening, care of adults, pet care and household administration.

[11] The data derives from the 1998 time-use study for France and a 1993 study in Sweden.

[12] A DDL is created on the basis of questions about whether a particular task is always or usually done by one person in a couple or shared. Five points are given if a woman always undertakes a task and one point if it is always a man. The higher the score, the greater is the woman's contribution to domestic work. An index can be compiled of scores for different tasks and then combined to create an overall score. The higher the score, the more traditional the DDL.

equality as the Finns, Norwegians and British. Portugal had the most traditional DDL at 20.49. In addition, Aassve et al. (2014), using data from the Generation and Gender Survey (GGS) collected between 2004 and 2010 from men and women living in different-sex couples under 60, created a DDL index for five household tasks (preparing daily meals; doing the dishes; shopping for food; vacuuming the house; small repairs) across a number of countries. The position of France was similar to that found in earlier research. The French score was less gender equal than that of Social Democratic Norway, despite having similar scores in terms of support for gender egalitarianism and women's employment rates. The French score was more gender equal than some of the Eastern European countries (Bulgaria, Hungary, Romania) but similar to that of Russia. As compared with other Conservative countries, France was similar to Austria, but its score was less equal than that of Germany and Belgium (Aassve et al., 2014, p. 1009, Table 1).

The question begs, therefore, of why France was in this anomalous position. The implicit woman-state contract in French work-family reconciliation policy with its lack of a strong gender-egalitarian frame or discussion of men's roles in unpaid work that pertained until the 2010s had both a direct and indirect influence on shares of unpaid domestic work between men and women more generally. Materially, the gendering of parenting and women's temporary full or partial withdrawal from the labour market using parental leave led to their availability for other kinds of domestic work in the immediate term and reduced the resources at their disposal beyond the child-rearing years to bargain their way out of these tasks (Anxo et al., 2002). Ideationally, the weakness of the gender-equality frame for work-family reconciliation policy reinforced an expectation that women could, and perhaps should, combine employment and unpaid domestic and care work with the help of the state rather than by sharing these responsibilities more equally with men. Cross-national comparisons of both domestic and care work suggest that for high levels of change in the gender division of unpaid labour to come about, there needs to be not only opportunities for women to reduce their unpaid work load by outsourcing it with state support, but also encouragement of men to change their behaviour and undertake more unpaid domestic work. Such encouragement can take the shape of public policies that explicitly endorse gender equality at the ideational level and prioritise gender equality in the design of policy at the material level as is seen in the Social Democratic countries, or the lack of state support for dual-earner parents and carers and the provision of market services by low-paid workers as is seen in the Liberal countries where families have to rely on their own resources to manage work-life conflicts (Crompton & Lyonette, 2006; Geist, 2005; Windebank, 2001).

All that said, there are indications that France's anomalous international position as regards the gender division of unpaid domestic work is changing. An 18-European country comparison of men and women aged 18–64 living in a couple with at least one child under 18 based on more recent data from the 2012 ISSP places France alongside Sweden, Denmark and Portugal in a cluster of countries with the lowest gender asymmetries in paid work, care work[13] and household work.[14] The data in this survey was generated through self-reporting of average hours spent on these activities. This cluster of countries had the highest overall allocation of time to paid work of men and women; the lowest allocation of time to care work by women; a significant allocation of time to care work by men; and a low allocation of time to household work by both women and men (Cunha & Atalaia, 2019, Fig. 2). Although these self-reported post-hoc estimations of work time cannot be equated with cross-national comparisons based on the results of time-use studies, the 2010 French time-use study showed trends that are compatible with the Cunha and Atalaia (2019) study with decreases in the time spent by women on domestic work and increases in the time spent by men on care work.

Furthermore, the ILO (2018, p. 44 Fig. 2.1) undertook a comparison of 67 countries based on time-use studies between 2009 and 2015, using the French 2010 study. In this comparison, France had the fourth lowest amount of time devoted by women to both domestic work[15] and all unpaid work in the EU, behind Finland, Belgium and Norway, and French men had the eighth highest amount of time devoted to domestic work and all unpaid work, behind Sweden, Denmark, Norway, Lithuania, Slovenia, Bulgaria, Germany and Poland. The ILO (2018, p. 55 Fig. 2.7) further found that[16], France was in eighth position among these countries in terms

[13] Evaluated on the basis of the question "On average how many hours do you spend looking after family members (e.g., children, elderly, ill or disabled members of the family)?"

[14] Evaluated on the basis of the question "On average how many hours do you personally spend on household work, not including childcare and leisure time activities?"

[15] ILO category: "housework", see Chap. 1

[16] ILO definition. The majority of this work is "housework", or unpaid domestic work for the household in the terminology used in this book.

of its "care gap" (11.3 per cent), that is the percentage increase in total unpaid care work that men would need to make in order for equality with women to be achieved. Three countries had substantially lower care gaps: Sweden (5.3 per cent), Norway (6.1 per cent) and Denmark (6.6 per cent). The care gap in France was similar to that in a range of countries with differing welfare regimes, for example, Canada (10.2 per cent), Finland (10.3 per cent), Estonia (10.3 per cent), the US (10.7 per cent), Belgium (11.8 per cent) and Germany (12.1 per cent). European countries with significantly higher gender care gaps were the Southern countries of Spain (17.6 per cent), Greece (22.1 per cent), Italy (23.8 per cent) and Portugal (29.7 per cent). The ILO (2018, p. 66) notes that for the population aged over 15 years from 1997–2001 and 2009–2015, there was a stagnation in changes to the gender care gap in the 23 countries for which they had data. Globally, women performed 63 per cent of all unpaid care work in the earlier period and 62.8 per cent in the later period. In some countries, men increased the time they devoted to this work, including countries with traditionally more equal shares (Sweden, Norway) and those with particularly unequal shares (e.g., Japan, Italy and Spain). However, in France both men and women reduced the time they devoted to these activities.

By the 2010s, a number of changes were coming about or taking effect in France that can help explain this shift. First, gender egalitarianism was beginning to influence work-family reconciliation, childcare and LTC policy to a greater extent than previously (see Chaps. 3 and 4). Second, there had been further equalisation of the time devoted to employment by men and women (Brousse, 2015a, pp. 84–5 Table 1). To a degree this was the result of the reduction in the statutory working week from 39 to 35 hours (see Chap. 3). One of the objectives of the 35-hour week was to reduce the difference in work patterns between full-time employed men and part-time employed women. Lastly, we need to consider the material and symbolic effects of policies to promote PHS, including home-based housekeeping services for the general population. France had the earliest and most extensive system of support for consumers of these services and has had one of the highest rates of their use in Europe. Although these paid services are only purchased by a socially exclusive minority, even for those who cannot afford home-based domestic services, the policies have the ideational effect of legitimising the outsourcing of domestic work.

Personal and Household Services for Domestic Work

Although using home-based domestic services is only one way that individuals and households can reduce their unpaid work burden, they have received the most attention from academics, given their place in evolving international divisions of labour and intersectional inequalities, and from policy makers, given their employment creation possibilities. By the second half of the twentieth century, full-time domestic servants had disappeared from the vast majority of homes. Today, only a few tens of thousands of French households can afford full-time domestic employees (Bozouls, 2021; Delpierre, 2021). Although middle-class higher income families continued to hire limited daily or weekly domestic help throughout the twentieth century, numbers of housekeeping staff declined until the 1990s when the use of home-based housekeeping services began to grow again, because of both increased demand from dual-earner professional households and a supportive policy framework. In 1974 7.6 per cent of the population over 18 declared employing an *aide-ménagère* (housekeeper), a figure that declined to 6.4 per cent in 1986 but increased to 9.1 per cent in 1998 and 10.8 per cent in 2010. This increase was more significant among the over 65 population, 9 per cent of whom employed a housekeeper in 1974 in contrast to 25 per cent in 2010 (Brousse, 2015b, p. 137).

A 2011 survey by the *DARES* found that 13 per cent of households purchased home-based domestic services, of which 77 per cent purchased housework, cooking, laundry and ironing services, and 14 per cent gardening services (Benoteau & Goin, 2015, p. 9). For women living in different-sex couples, buying housekeeping services can be a way of countering gender inequalities in unpaid work in their households (Ruppanner & Maune, 2016; Seierstad & Kirton, 2015). For parents, the purchase of such services can liberate time to devote to their children (Kilkey, 2010; Rezeanu, 2015). The effects of the purchase of housekeeping services on gender divisions of unpaid labour are debated. In the contemporary landscape, in difference to the early twentieth century, consumers only purchase on average two to four hours of domestic help a week (Bittman, 2015). When compared with hours spent on core domestic activities by men and women (see above), those households that do use such services are only relieved of a fraction of their domestic burden (Windebank, 2007). Although there has been little quantitative research in France, studies based on time-use in Australia (Craig & Baxter, 2014), the US (Killewald, 2011), the UK (Sullivan & Gershuny, 2013) and Spain (Gonalons-Pons, 2015) have all shown weak associations between recourse to housekeeping services and a more equal sharing of the remaining unpaid domestic-labour burden within different-sex couples. However, in France on the basis of a qualitative study, Puech and Devetter (2010) reach the conclusion that couples who use domestic services report more equal gender divisions of the remaining unpaid domestic work than couples who do not.

In 2005 the *Plan de cohésion sociale* (Social cohesion plan) or the Borloo Plan as it is termed, named after the centre-right Minister of Labour, Employment and Social Cohesion who introduced it, was launched. This plan represents a significant expansion in the ambition of PHS[17] policy in France which had been initiated in the 1990s (see Chap. 2). The Borloo Plan set about constructing a new category of economic activity and sector with its own regulations and modes of governance: *services à la personne* (services to the individual).[18] The category of services to the individual is a list of activities defined by law that are undertaken in the home of the consumer. They include activities formerly classified as *services domestiques* (domestic services) provided by *employés de maison/aides ménagères* (housekeepers) and *action sociale (social care)* provided by *aides à domicile* (home helps/care workers)[19] (Jany-Catrice, 2010; Laville, 2008). Currently there are 21 activities[20] listed but house cleaning, childcare and LTC services represent over 90 per cent of the total hours of work supported, the remainder being divided between gardening services, tutoring and home IT support services (Devetter, 2016). The objective of the Borloo Plan was to normalise the use of PHS throughout the general

[17] Although PHS policy is used to support childcare and LTC as discussed in Chaps. 3 and 4, it is discussed in detail in this chapter because it is the only policy that supports domestic work outside that related to care needs (see Chap. 1).

[18] The term *services à la personne* poses a problem for academic and public statisticians as it does not map on to existing professional categories in France. Many consider it to be more a political than a scientific categorisation.

[19] Beginning in 2005 the French Working Conditions survey assigned each PHS occupation its own socio-professional category: "home-based childcare provider" (code 563a), "home aides for the elderly" (563b) and "house cleaners for private individuals" (563c). These are all included in SPC 5 (Avril, 2012, p.103).

[20] For the up-to-date list of activities covered see: *Ministere de l'Economie et des Finances, Services à la personne*, see https://www.entreprises.gouv.fr/files/files/directions_services/services-a-la-personne/publications/le-cesu-prefinance.pdf

population beyond care needs. Commercialising previously non-market activities in this way would create jobs. As discussed in Chap. 2, the French state had a long-standing interest in commodifying unpaid work to increase employment and GPD. The Borloo Plan suggested that 500,000 jobs could be created between 2006 and 2008. Through advertising campaigns organised by the *Agence Nationale des Services à la Personne* (*ANSP*) (National Agency for Services to Individuals), the government called on households to purchase three hours of services per week to create two million jobs and lower unemployment (Dussuet, 2017). The Plan also aimed to reduce undeclared work in home-based services.

There are three pillars to the Borloo Plan. The first pillar simplifies the procedures for an individual to become a direct employer of a worker providing services to the individual as defined in the legislation. This is done through the *CESU* which replaced the *CES* and *TES* in 2005 (see Chap. 2). The second pillar subsidises the cost of services to the individual, even for those without care needs. Direct employers can benefit from advantageous arrangements for employer social security contributions. Meanwhile, all users, including those buying services from service providers (non-profit associations, for-profit companies or other registered organisations) can benefit from tax breaks on the cost of services. Users benefit from a tax reduction or tax credit equivalent to 50 per cent of expenditure on these services subject to an annual ceiling which is higher for those requiring care services for children and for older people or those with disabilities who require services (Ad-PHS, 2020). The third pillar allows services to the individual to be offered as rewards or benefits. Similar to the *TES*, an employer can award a *CESU prefinancé* (pre-paid *CESU*) to their staff as part of a reward package and claim a 25 per cent tax deduction on this expenditure. Benefit-awarding agencies (mutual insurance organisations, works committees, welfare and pensions institutions, local authorities) can also award a *CESU prefinancé* as a social voucher to their clients (*Ministère de l'Economie et des Finances*, 2019).

By the early 2000s, although right-wing governments had been promising reforms to make the French labour market more flexible and reduce the cost of labour for some years, change had been slow due to a high number of strong veto points to such change and hostile public opinion (Palier, 2000). Low-skilled work and low-qualified workers in France remained too expensive and the wage gap too small to allow PHS to develop without intervention (Carbonnier & Morel, 2015). The Cahuc-Debonneuil report (Cahuc & Debonneuil, 2004), co-authored by Michele Debonneuil as head of the *CGP*, set about addressing this issue (Jany-Catrice, 2010). As discussed in Chap. 2, the *CGP* had been interested in the economic potential of monetising unpaid work in the home since the 1980s. The Cahuc-Debonneuil report repeated arguments that had been put forward by business stakeholders in the 1990s that the regulation of the labour-market and of care services undermined job creation in this sector meaning that the commodification and commercialisation of these services would not come about spontaneously (Jany-Catrice, 2010). Rather, state intervention was required that would facilitate their development as well as a new regulatory regime that would reduce the cost of low-qualified employment in the sector by limiting employment protection and promoting the development of part-time jobs (Cahuc & Debonneuil, 2004). There was then significant lobbying by professional associations to have their activities included in the Borloo Plan because the tax advantages thereby gained would make them affordable to more people and increase demand.

The schemes of the 1990s and the Borloo Plan have been successful in increasing the number of consumers and declared workers in services to individuals. The policies enacted in the 1990s (see Chap. 2) had brought about a doubling of the numbers working formally in the sector[21] in France between 1990 and 2005 (Benoteau & Goin, 2015, p. 10). The Borloo Plan led to a further significant rise in the use of services to individuals, accounted for both by an absolute increase in the number of users and a movement of activity from undeclared to declared work. In 2006 alone, the number of users of the *CESU* grew by 11.4 per cent in relation to users of the *CES* and *TES* combined in 2005 and the numbers of all direct employers in services to individuals (childcare excluded) whether using the *CESU* or not grew by 6.2 per cent. These increases were followed by a 10.5 per cent rise in *CESU* users, and a 4.3 per cent rise in all direct employers for services to individuals except childcare in 2007 (Collin et al., 2010, p. 1 Table 1). The schemes were also successful in reducing undeclared work in the sector. According to *DARES*, Ministry of Labour and *Caisse d'Epargne* figures, rates of undeclared work in this sector reduced from 50 to 45 per cent through the 1990s (*Caisse d'Epargne*, 2006). Subsequent to the introduction of the Borloo Plan this

[21] Official statistics on direct employment differentiate between services for childcare and non-childcare services. However, they do not produce annual figures broken down by the age of the employer. Therefore, they do not reflect the balance between users of services within an LTC context and for housekeeping services for the general population.

figure reduced further to 25 per cent by 2011 (*Ministère du Travail, de l'Emploi et de l'Insertion*, 2019).

However, the increase in formal direct employment within the services to individuals sector was dampened by the fallout from the financial crisis in 2008. By 2011, the number of direct employers other than for childcare started to decline (-1.1 per cent), gathering pace by 2013 (-3.2 per cent) (Maj & Zamfir, 2015, p. 6 Table A). This decline has persisted (Maj et al., 2018). It was the use of services by the working-age population rather than older age groups that proved particularly sensitive to economic conditions. Between 2006 and 2011, growth was concentrated in the under-60 age group and from 2013 onwards, the decline in use was concentrated in this same age group (Maj & Zamfir, 2015, p. 6 Table A). That said, it must be remembered that these figures relate to direct employment only. Some of the decreases in the use of direct employment are in fact due to consumers turning to service-provider organisations to access services. There is evidence that France is moving slowly away from a bipartite direct employment structure for services to individuals and towards a tripartite service-provider structure (Kulanthaivelu, 2020, p. 1 Fig. 1). Between 2016 and 2018, employing organisations saw a 2.5 per cent increase in the percentage of hours of all services to the individual that they provided. Most employing organisations are non-profit associations, but growth in private companies has been more rapid with the commercial service-provider market share rising from 38.8 per cent in 2017 to 41.4 per cent in 2018 (Maj et al., 2022, p. 5 Fig. 1).

With financial pressures on households following the banking crisis, it could be possible that declines in declared direct employment are explained in part by the return of some housekeeping services to the undeclared sector. However, no data substantiate this supposition. Indeed, in a recent survey of direct employers for services to the individual in April–May 2021 (*FEPEM*, 2021), it was found that in the previous two years, only 5 per cent of respondents had declared none of the hours and 29 per cent had declared only some of the hours of services purchased over the previous two years. The rest had declared all hours. Seventy-eight per cent of respondents cited the incentives on offer such as tax credits as underpinning their decision to employ someone on a declared basis, with 82 per cent of those who declare all work benefitting from tax credits. Undeclared work was found to be concentrated among younger employees working on an occasional and irregular basis undertaking PHS tasks such as babysitting or tutoring.

Despite the attempts to normalise the use of services to the individual by the Borloo Plan, users of paid services for non-care-related domestic work have remained concentrated in upper income groups and dual-earner professional and managerial households (Bittman, 2015; Devetter, 2016). In 2010, around a fifth of those in SPC 2 and 3 employed a housekeeper in contrast to around a tenth of workers in SPC 4 and fewer than one in twenty in SPC 5 and 6 (Brousse, 2015b, p. 18). In 2011 workers in SPC 3 constituted half of all households in employment that used housekeeping services (Benoteau & Goin, 2015, p. 18). As concerns income levels, controlling for age, the rate of recourse to housekeeping services starts to grow from the seventh highest income decile onwards (Devetter, 2016, p. 374), culminating in 33.5 per cent of those in the top income decile purchasing such services in comparison with 10 per cent in the 2nd to 6th deciles (Benoteau & Goin, 2015, p. 18). The 2010 *INSEE* time-use study had similar findings: the highest earning 10 per cent of households represented 28 per cent of those employing a housekeeper (Brousse, 2015b, p. 136 Table 7).

The social exclusivity of the use of housekeeping services is explained by the fact that they are highly price sensitive as they have to compete with self-provisioning. In difference to childcare and LTC services which are necessary to allow parents to go to work or for the wellbeing of adults with LTC needs, domestic services are not viewed as essential, but rather luxury purchases (Devetter & Rousseau, 2005). In qualitative research, it has been found that the under 65s who purchase housekeeping services justify doing so by referring to the difference in cost of buying the services and the value of their own time, in other words, their opportunity cost of carrying out the work unpaid themselves. Professional choices and status (involving high incomes and long working hours) legitimised outsourcing rather than absolute need due to work-family conflict issues (Devetter, 2016). In addition to cost, there are other barriers to the use of housekeeping services that help explain their limited use. Social norms such as fearing the intrusion of a third party into the private sphere of the household or avoidance of taking on the role of employer are important influences on decisions about whether to hire a housekeeper. In social groups in which using paid domestic services has been a more normalised practice, such concerns are lesser. Furthermore, in a circular cause-effect relationship, access to services is concentrated in large urban areas with high numbers of well-paid professional residents, and there is a paucity of supply in less affluent and particularly more rural areas (Windebank, 2010).

The support offered by the Borloo Plan through tax and social security exonerations has been modified over the years in response to the lack of democratisation of the use of housekeeping services. Initially, the tax breaks for the use of services to the individual came in the form of tax deductions. The structure of the taxation system in France means that only around half the employed population pays income tax (53 per cent in 2020). Consequently, the principal financial incentive of the Borloo Plan did not apply to many potential consumers. Therefore, in 2007 the tax deduction was transformed into a tax credit for the economically active, but not for the retired. In 2017 the tax credit was extended to the retired. However, this change had little impact on democratising the use of these services within the working population, one reason being that the full price of the service had to be paid at the point of purchase, and the tax credit claimed at the end of the tax year when annual declarations are made, with credits paid up to 18 months after the initial expenditure (Favaque, 2015). Further modifications have now been made and from January 2022 service users have been able to claim an advance on their tax credit ahead of their tax declaration.[22]

The arrangements for social security contributions for direct employers of PHS staff have also been modified to make them less advantageous for the employer and more advantageous for the employee. Until 2013 direct employers of employees providing services to individuals could make a flat-rate declaration in regard to their employer social security contributions and were charged at the minimum-wage rate for their employee, even if the salary paid was in fact higher. The flat-rate declaration lowered the cost for employers but to the detriment of employees in terms of their level of social protection. In 2013, under the Socialist administration of President Hollande, the flat-rate declaration was replaced by a standard hourly deduction of social contributions for direct employers (Ad-PHS, 2020). The current rate is a reduction of 2 Euros per hour worked up to a ceiling.[23] However, these changes have not been sufficient to counter the essential price sensitivity of housekeeping services.

Critics of the Borloo Plan and similar schemes argue that subsidising housekeeping services despite their socially exclusive clientele is an

[22] For details see: https://www.service-public.fr/particuliers/actualites/A15750#:~:text=Lorsque%20vous%20faites%20appel%20%C3%A0,%E2%82%AC%20maximum%20dans%20certains%20cas)

[23] For details, see https://www.service-public.fr/particuliers/vosdroits/F12384

example of client politics (Wilson, 1980), that is, policies whose costs are diffused through the population, but whose benefits are concentrated on a particular, and in this case, advantaged group. Furthermore, these policies subsidise demand for rather than the supply of services, thereby encouraging bipartite direct employment relations which structure power relations to the detriment of the employee (Glenn, 2010; Gorz, 1988). In this way, the French state has deregulated the domestic-services labour market, but only for specific target groups, reinforcing the dualisation of the labour market, albeit with higher rates of employment for the lower qualified (Morel, 2015).

For the most commonly used service of housekeeping,[24] the vast majority of employees (96 per cent) are women (Marbot, 2008a, p. 28). Housekeeping is a profession that shares many characteristics with childminders and home-based LTC workers but has an even lowlier status. Housekeeping does not require any qualifications or provide the opportunity to gain accreditations or qualifications in difference to childcare and LTC work (Sohler & Levy, 2013). Housekeepers are the least well qualified of all PHS workers: in 2005, 47 per cent of workers providing services to individuals had no qualifications, but this percentage rose to 65.5 per cent for domestic helpers and cleaners (Marbot, 2008a, p. 28 Table 2). The average age of entering into this type of work was 38 in 2017 (Queval et al., 2019, p. 10). In 2015, the average age of direct employees providing services to the individual was 46 as compared with 41 for the overall active population (unemployed or employed) (Ad-PHS, 2020). This is because housekeeping is not chosen as a first entry into employment but represents an option for those having to change careers. In similarity to childminding or LTC, workers often become housekeepers having occupied other insecure jobs, jobs in declining sectors (e.g., in the textile industry) or posts which are now obsolete (e.g., shorthand typist, sewing machine operator). Some who have worked in commercial cleaning transfer to domestic cleaning when they can no longer keep up with the demands in the commercial sector where workers are often paid according to productivity and have constraints such as undesirable shifts patterns and non-standard work times imposed on them (Favaque, 2013).

Housekeepers tend to live in poor households, defined as those with an income that is 60 per cent or less of the median household income (Marbot, 2008b). This is because their work is characterised by instability

[24] ISCO 9111 domestic helpers and cleaners.

and underemployment. In 2016, 46 per cent of domestic cleaners and helpers worked short part-time hours, which is often combined with pay at minimum wage. In 2020, direct PHS (other than childcare) employees paid through the *CESU* undertook on average 46 hours of work per month and had an average of 2.8 employers (Maj et al., 2022, p. 4). Furthermore, there is little to no pay or career progression in this field. In 2009 for those working under the *CESU* scheme, the net hourly salaries of those entering housekeeping work were very similar to those of experienced workers, all being paid only slightly above the level of the minimum wage (Collin et al., 2010, p. 5). That said, housekeepers in private homes working as direct employees on a declared basis in France have protections similar to those in other home-based professions under a set of regulations in the Labour Code (see Chap. 3). However, the fact that this work takes place in private homes limits the applicability of labour law (Avril, 2012) as has been discussed in the cases of childcare and LTC workers (see Chaps. 3 and 4) and isolates workers from the support of colleagues and managers, and from opportunities for collective action.

In similarity with discussions on childcare and LTC employment, there is a good degree of consensus among academics that work conditions are better for housekeepers when they are employed in a tripartite arrangement with a service-providing organisation rather than in a bipartite arrangement with a direct employer not least because workers are not as isolated and can benefit from support from co-workers or managers, and potentially have opportunities for career progression. Research has found that working conditions are particularly favourable for those working for associations or local authorities, rather than private companies (Manoudi, 2018). A recent OECD report (2021) compares policies to formalise housekeeping work in five countries investigating whether they encourage a bipartite or tripartite employment relationship. As discussed here, French policy, alongside that of Germany and Belgium, encourages a bipartite employment structure for housekeeping services for those both with and without care needs. This contrasts with Sweden and Finland where the majority of housekeeping services are provided for those with care needs within a tripartite relationship between consumer, employee and local authorities with little development of housekeeping services outside the care context. The report concludes that a tripartite structure better protects workers from precarious work and provides better training opportunities. However, some studies in France and elsewhere have found the lack of control suffered by housekeepers working for organisations over work time and productivity can make their conditions worse than for direct employees. Whereas in childcare and LTC, the immediate needs of the person being cared for dictate work rhythms and patterns, housekeepers working for direct employers have more opportunity to set their own pace. Furthermore, they may be able to choose employers who offer the least arduous working conditions particularly in areas where demand for services outstrips supply (Avril, 2012).

Despite its client politics and the social and economic inequalities on which the development of PHS for those without care needs rest, the Borloo Plan has remained popular among the French population because of the success of the framing of PHS policies in public narratives as necessary and important for French society. In 2011 a poll revealed that 82 per cent of the French agreed that services to the individual could create a significant number of jobs; 74 per cent agreed it was essential for future economic growth; and 65 per cent agreed that the sector contributed to fighting undeclared employment. Discourses that are often created by employer lobbying groups such as the *FEPEM* and *SEPS* and used by government officials, political parties, trades unions and the press downplay the costs of the policy measures for non-users and promote the benefits for the population, all the more so since the measures cover care and non-care-related services. These narratives can be modified to appeal to different publics on left and right: supporting work-family reconciliation can appeal to feminist or family interest groups while solidaristic and left-leaning organisations (political parties and trades unions) value the fight against undeclared work. Those with more right-wing values or business interests appreciate that the measures encourage an entrepreneurial spirit and the creation of service companies (Guiraudon & Ledoux, 2015). Critics are mostly academics and intellectuals and have little access to the government and the media.

Furthermore, there has been a positive feedback loop between the EU and France in developing support for PHS. The approach of the EU has mirrored that of France in that those domestic services responding to social care needs (childcare, eldercare, care for the disabled) and domestic services geared towards households with no care needs (consumer services) have been conceptualised or redefined as services responding to a similar logic, and which can therefore be similarly supported and structured through public policies. This interest in the development of domestic services on the part of the European Commission and its link to French policy can be traced back to the 1993 White paper *Growth, competitiveness, employment* overseen by the former French socialist minister Jacques Delors (see Chap. 2). In the Lisbon strategy in 2000, reinforced by the Barcelona summit of 2002, PHS came into focus with an employment rationale of activation, particularly of women, rather than a social or welfare rationale. The issue became one of both providing women with the necessary services to support their gainful employment and of creating new job opportunities for lower qualified women. The Lisbon strategy's aim to turn Europe into a dynamic and competitive knowledge-based economy also led to a focus on enabling the more highly skilled to invest more time into paid work by freeing themselves from caring and household tasks. This interest in promoting PHS was re-affirmed in the *Europe 2020* strategy published in 2010.[25]

As a pioneer country in terms of policy to support the development of PHS outside the care arena, it is unsurprising that both the use of these services is more extensive and they are more likely to be undertaken on a declared basis in France than in other European countries (Guiraudon & Ledoux, 2015). In 2011 according to Eurostat figures for NACE 97 and NACE 88, three EU countries were far above the others in terms of numbers of PHS workers, with around 600,000 or more. These countries were France, Italy and Spain. 2.3 per cent of total employment in France was in the NACE 97 and 88 categories, in comparison with 0.1 per cent of total employment in the UK for the same year (Favaque, 2013). The OECD (2021, p. 12 Fig. 2.1) shows that France continued to have one of the highest shares of registered domestic cleaners and helpers[26] among total registered employment in OECD countries in 2018, in joint second place with Portugal with a 2.6 per cent share, and behind Spain with 2.9 per cent. The OECD average was 1.3 per cent. France is also found to have relatively low levels of undeclared work in comparison with countries that have high levels of PHS work. For housekeeping (non-care) work, the OECD (2021) compared data from household expenditure surveys in category 05.6.2 (Domestic services and household services) and data from the ISCO on total employment levels. Its findings suggest that on average across European countries, about 57 per cent of these services are provided on an undeclared basis. For some countries such as Belgium (13 per

[25] https://ec.europa.eu/regional_policy/en/policy/what/glossary/e/europe-2020-strategy#:~:text=Europe%202020%20is%20the%20EU's,against%20poverty%20and%20social%20exclusion

[26] ISCO 9111.

cent) along with France (35 per cent), the extent of undeclared work in the non-care household service sector is comparatively low, while in Germany and Finland more than 75 per cent of work in this sector is undeclared.

Migrants are over-represented among domestic cleaners and helpers in France in comparison with their presence in the general population, and more so than among childcare and LTC workers. However, migrants constitute a lower proportion of domestic cleaners and helpers (ISCO definition) than in other countries with high levels of paid domestic service employment (Ad-PHS, 2020; Galotti & Mertens, 2013). In 2011, 25 per cent of domestic cleaners and helpers were migrants composed of 17 per cent EU nationals and 8 per cent TCNs (Condon et al., 2013, pp. 7–8). In 2016, according to the *Ministère du Travail* (2019, Supplementary Table E), a third of cleaners working in private homes were migrants. Migrant workers are concentrated in the Ile de France (region around Paris) representing 68 per cent of all declared housekeepers compared with 25 per cent in the rest of the country (Sohler & Levy, 2013, p. 44). In contrast, in Spain and Italy, the substantial growth in PHS workers seen in the early years of the new century was attributable in very large part to migrant workers: in Spain, 60 per cent of PHS workers were migrants in 2012, up from only 5 per cent in 2000. The proportion of migrants in PHS work in Italy grew from 50 per cent to 80 per cent over the same period (Galotti & Mertens, 2013, p. 14).

These cross-national variations are due to differences in the interaction of PHS policy which incentivises declared work and immigration policy for TCNs (Condon et al., 2013). For more than four decades, immigration policies in France have been increasingly restrictive, introducing complex conditions for living and working in the country, and longer timescales for regularising one's migration status. The influence of far-right political actors, reflecting and shaping the attitudes of the public to migration, has been important in this process. Laws in 2006 and 2011 privileged the movement of skilled or highly skilled people while introducing measures to restrict the free movement of those identified as low-skilled other than for individuals coming to work in defined occupational sectors or seasonal labour. These sectors and occupations appear in shortage lists. In difference to Italy and Spain where PHS workers have been actively recruited through such agreements, PHS have scarcely featured on such occupational lists in France with the exception of bilateral agreements drawn up with Senegal and Mauritius shortly before the banking crisis in 2008, when employment in PHS was increasing significantly. However, when the lists were updated several years later, these occupations disappeared from the agreements.

The absence of PHS from shortage lists is explained because the development of PHS has been viewed primarily as a remedy for domestic unemployment and reducing joblessness among the young and less qualified, including EU and TCN migrants already in France rather than in order to provide services to the population by recruiting from other countries (Scrinzi, 2010). Migrants arriving in France with other types of authorisations have been directed towards the *ANSP* in order to be trained as PHS workers following an agreement between the Ministry of Immigration and the Ministry of the Economy (Scrinzi, 2010). Furthermore, the personalised programmes designed to help the unemployed find jobs have similarly been found to direct women, and particularly migrant women and women of colour, into PHS work, the result of gender and racial stereotyping (Talbot, 2017).

The lack of regular migration routes to France based on PHS work for TCNs may lead to undeclared work as undocumented migrants have no choice but to work on this basis. Undocumented migrants in France are subject to a dual informality, exposing them to exploitation (Moujoud, 2018). This status limits such workers to more dependent employer-employee relationships. Particularly newly arrived migrants may be obliged to accept live-in arrangements which subjects them to what Condon et al. (2013, p. 10) term a "logic of domesticity". Live-in arrangements make women even more vulnerable to having to accept poor conditions of pay and work hours, and in some cases bullying and violence. Personal recommendations are an important recruitment tool in these informal networks meaning that workers have to acquiesce to the demands of their employers in the hope of finding a better position. Once established in France, workers may be able to move to either live-out domestic work or to another type of employment. However, the vulnerabilities linked to their undocumented status remain. The French state undertook several large-scale regularisation programmes of undocumented workers in 1986, 1997 and 2008. Subsequently, in a circular of November 2012, Prime Minister Emmanuel Valls set out procedures and criteria for ongoing regularisation of undocumented workers by local Prefects.[27] Among conditions for regularisation is included 10 years' residence in France. However, undocu-

[27] For further details, see: https://www.legifrance.gouv.fr/download/pdf/circ?id=44486

mented migrant workers in the PHS sector working as direct employees in private homes find it more difficult to prove this residency than other categories of workers (Sohler & Levy, 2013). This is because of the reluctance or refusal of employers to give support to domestic workers in their attempts to regularise their status (Devetter, 2016).

Concluding Summary

In contrast to parenting and LTC work, the vast majority of adults have to undertake at least some unpaid domestic work for themselves or others on a regular and ongoing basis. On a societal level, more time is devoted to domestic work in France than to professional activities. However, domestic equipment and easy-care materials, the purchase of ready-to-consume goods and out-of-home services, particularly for food, alongside changes to housekeeping norms have served to reduce the amount of time individuals and households have to spend undertaking unpaid domestic work. Unlike childcare and LTC, very little domestic work is carried out by those outside the household, whether this be in the form of unpaid favours by kin or non-kin, or home-based domestic services.

Unpaid domestic work remains gendered with women spending around twice the amount of time on these activities as men. Within different-sex couples, women take on the majority of the domestic work of the household while women living alone spend more time on these activities than men in a similar situation. The gap between men and women has lessened, but although between the 1970s and 1980s, this reduction came about by women reducing their domestic work time and men increasing theirs, in the early years of the twenty-first century, both men and women in France reduced the time they spent in domestic work, particularly core domestic work activities, but women did so at a faster rate than men. France shares with all other high-income countries the trends of an attenuation rather than an eradication of gender inequality in domestic work. However, the timing and degree of these changes show significant cross-national variation. Based on data from the late 1990s and early 2000s, France had an unusually traditional gender division of unpaid domestic work given its relatively small gender employment gap, high spending on work-family reconciliation policy and gender-egalitarian attitudes among the population. Comparisons using later data have found a change in France's relative position. Gender divisions of unpaid domestic work are now more in keeping with the progressive gender-equality attitudes, integration of

French women into the labour force and work-family policies to be found in the country. This has been brought about by the decrease in time spent on unpaid domestic work by women, rather than on an increase by men.

Cross-national comparisons of both domestic and care work suggest that for high levels of change in the gender division of unpaid labour to come about, there needs to be not only opportunities for women to reduce their unpaid workload by outsourcing it with state support, but also the encouragement of men to change their behaviour and increase their contribution to domestic work. In France, the lack of a strong gender-egalitarian frame for work-family reconciliation policy and the implicit mother-state contract for childcare with little discussion of men's roles that pertained into this century have had both a direct and indirect influence on shares of unpaid domestic work between men and women more generally. Materially, the gendering of parenting and full or partial withdrawal from the labour market of women for parenting duties led to their availability for other kinds of domestic work and reduced the resources at their disposal over the longer term beyond the child-rearing years to bargain their way out of these tasks. Ideationally, the weakness of the gender-equality frame for work-family reconciliation policy reinforced an expectation that women could, and perhaps should, combine employment and unpaid domestic and care work with the help of the state without needing a significant reallocation of responsibilities with men. However, by the 2010s, gender egalitarianism had begun to influence work-family reconciliation, childcare and LTC policy to a greater extent in France and there had been further equalisation of the time devoted to employment by men and women.

Furthermore, as discussed in Chap. 2, France was a forerunner in the development of policies to support the use of paid housekeeping services outside the care context. This strategy accelerated in 2005 with the introduction of the Borloo Plan, which sought to create a new sector of services to the individual with the aim of normalising the use of housekeeping services in the general population by merging care and non-care policy. The primary objective in the construction of this policy was to increase employment opportunities for the low skilled in France's highly regulated labour market. Following the introduction of the Borloo Plan, there was a significant increase in the use of home-based services for housekeeping among two groups in French society: first, older people, mainly in the context of LTC as discussed in detail in Chap. 4, and second, those in SPC 3 and the 30 per cent of highest income earners. France has some the highest numbers of domestic cleaners and helpers in Europe. However, the Borloo Plan did not manage to normalise or democratise the use of housekeeping services outside the care context, and their use remains socially exclusive. There is a very significant gap in terms of wealth and socio-professional status between consumers and providers of these services, as domestic cleaners and helpers have some of the worst pay and conditions of all home-based PHS providers and consumers are from high-income and high-status groups. Furthermore, following the economic difficulties caused by the 2008 banking crisis, the use of services to the individual declined in the under 60 population, evidence of their high degree of price sensitivity. Despite its client politics and the social and economic inequalities on which the development of PHS for those without care needs rests, the Borloo Plan has remained popular among the French population because the narratives created around it have had the ideational effect of legitimising the outsourcing of domestic work, a set of tasks that the majority of the population do not find satisfying.

References

Aassve, A., Fuochi, G., & Mencarini, L. (2014). Desperate housework. *Journal of Family Issues, 35*(8), 1000–1022. https://doi.org/10.1177/0192513X14522248

Aboim, S. (2010). Gender cultures and the division of labour in contemporary Europe: A cross-national perspective. *The Sociological Review, 58*(2), 171–196. https://doi.org/10.1111/j.1467-954X.2010.01899.x

AD-PHS. (2020). *Country report – France*. Retrieved October 18, 2021, from www.ad-phs.eu/htag2/uploads/2021/01/cr_france.pdf

Anxo, D., Flood, L., & Kocoglu, Y. (2002). Offre de travail et répartition des activités domestiques et parentales au sein du couple : une comparaison entre la France et la Suède. *Economie et Statistique, 352*(2), 127–150.

Authier, J.-Y., & Cayouette-Remblière, J. (2021). *Les formes contemporaines du voisinage. Espaces résidentiels et intégration social.* Retrieved October 4, 2022, from https://mon-quartier-mes-voisins.site.ined.fr/fichier/s_rubrique/31550/les.formes.contemporaines.du.voisinage_authier_cayouette_vf.fr.pdf

Avril, C. (2012). Ressources et lignes de clivage parmi les aides à domicile. Spécifier une position sociale : quelles opérations de recherche? *Actes de la recherche en sciences sociales, 191–192*(1), 86–105. https://doi.org/10.3917/arss.191.0086

Barthelemy, L. (2018). *Les Français et le partage des tâches : à quand la révolution ménagère?* Retrieved October 14, 2021, from ipsos.com/fr-fr/les-francais-et-le-partage-des-taches-quand-la-revolution-menagere

Benoteau, I., & Goin, A. (2015). Services à la personne : aides publiques et cout pour l'utilisateur. *Document d'Etudes de la DARES, 194*, 1–55. Retrieved April 9, 2022, from https://dares.travail-emploi.gouv.fr/sites/default/files/pdf/de_194_services_a_la_p.pdf

Besson, D. (2008). Le repas depuis 45 ans : moins de produits frais, plus de plats préparés. *Insee Première, 1208*, 1–4.

Bittman, S. (2015). Ressources économiques des femmes et travail domestique des conjoints : quels effets pour quelles tâches ? *Economie et Statistique, 478-479-480*, 305–338.

Bouffartigue, P. (2010). The gender division of paid and domestic work. Some remarks in favour of a temporal perspective. *Time and Society, 19*(2), 220–238. https://doi.org/10.1177/0961463X09337855

Bozouls, L. (2021). Travail domestique et production d'un style de vie : Les femmes au foyer de classes supérieures. *Travail, genre et sociétés, 46*, 97. https://doi.org/10.3917/tgs.046.0097

Brousse, C. (2015a). La vie quotidienne en France depuis 1974. Les enseignements de l'enquête Emploi du temps. *Economie et Statistique, 478-479-480*, 79–117.

Brousse, C. (2015b). Travail professionnel, tâches domestiques, temps « libre » : quelques déterminants sociaux de la vie quotidienne. *Economie et Statistique, 478-479-480*, 119–154.

Cahuc, P. and Debonneuil, M. (Eds). (2004) Productivité et emploi dans le tertiaire. La Documentation française.

Caisse d'Epargne. (2006). *Services à la personne : modes de vie, modes d'emploi*. Retrieved March 23, 2022, from https://www.extranet.caisse-epargne.fr/portailmedia/Pdf-CE/obs_2006_doc.pdf

Carbonnier, C., & Morel, N. (Eds.). (2015). *The political economy of household services in Europe*. Palgrave Macmillan.

Cartier, M., Letrait, M., & Sorin, M. (2018). Travail domestique : des classes populaires conservatrices ? *Travail, genre et sociétés, 39*, 63–81. https://doi.org/10.3917/tgs.039.0063

Clair, I. (2011). La découverte de l'ennui conjugal. Les manifestations contrariées de l'idéal conjugal et de l'ethos égalitaire dans la vie quotidienne de jeunes de milieux populaires. *Sociétés contemporaines, 83*, 59–81. https://doi.org/10.3917/soco.083.0059

Collectif Rosa Bonheur. (2017). Des 'inactives' très productives. Le travail de subsistance des femmes de classes populaires. *Tracés. Revue de sciences humaines, 32*, 1–15.

Collin, B., et al. (2010). Les particuliers employeurs en 2009 : un secteur en croissance malgré la crise. *ACOSSTAT Bilan, 116*, 1–8.

Condon, S., Lada, E., Charruault, A., & Romanini, A. (2013). *Promoting integration of migrant domestic workers in France*. Retrieved September 4, 2018, from http://www.ilo.org/wcmsp5/groups/public/%2D%2D-ed_protect/%2D%2D-protrav/%2D%2D-migrant/documents/publication/wcms_232518.pdf

Craig, L., & Baxter, J. (2014). Domestic outsourcing, housework shares and subjective time pressure: Gender differences in the correlates of hiring help. *Social Indicators Research, 125*(1), 271–288. https://doi.org/10.1007/s11205-014-0833-1

Crompton, R., & Lyonette, C. (2006). Work-life balance in Europe. *Acta Sociologica, 49*(4), 379–393. https://doi.org/10.1177/0001699306071680

Cunha, V., & Atalaia, S. (2019). The gender(ed) division of labour in Europe: Patterns of practices in 18 EU countries. *Sociologia, 90*, 113–137. https://doi.org/10.7458/SPP20199015526

Daguet, F. (2017). Des ménages toujours plus nombreux, toujours plus petits. *INSEE Première, 1663*, 1–4.

Daminger, A. (2019). The cognitive dimension of household labor. *American Sociological Review, 84*(4), 609–633. https://doi.org/10.1177/0003122419859007

Delpierre, A. (2021). Des femmes si privilégiées? La fatigue d'être servi.e par des domestiques. *Travail, genre et société, 46*(2), 115–131. https://doi.org/10.3917/tgs.046.0115

Devetter, F.-X. (2016). Can public policies bring about the democratization of the outsourcing of household tasks? *The Review of Radical Political Economics, 48*(3), 365–393. https://doi.org/10.1177/0486613415594159

Devetter, F. X., & Rousseau, S. (2005). L'incitation à la création d'emplois de femmes de ménage est-elle socialement juste ? *Revue de Philosophie Economique, 12*(2), 73–95.

Doucet, A. (2000). "There's a huge difference between me as a male carer and women": Gender, domestic responsibility, and the community as an institutional arena. *Community Work and Family, 3*(2), 163–184. https://doi.org/10.1080/713658907

Dussuet, A. (2017). Le « travail domestique » : une construction théorique féministe interrompue. *Recherches Féministes, 30*(2), 101–117. https://doi.org/10.7202/1043924ar

Esping-Anderson, G. (2009). *The incomplete revolution: Adapting to women's new roles.* Polity Press.

Favaque, N. (2013). *Developing personal and household services in the EU. A focus on housework activities.* Report for the DG Employment, Social Affairs and Social Inclusion. Retrieved March 8, 2022, from https://www.employment-studies.co.uk/resource/developing-personal-and-household-services-eu-focus-housework-activities

Favaque, N. (2015). *European Employment Policy Observatory Ad Hoc Request Personal and household services France.* Directorate-General for Employment, Social Affairs and Inclusion, European Employment Policy Observatory.

FEPEM. (2021). *Le recours et les pratiques de travail non déclaré à domicile.* Retrieved August 29, 2022, from https://www.securite-sociale.fr/files/live/sites/SSFR/files/medias/HCFIPS/2021/IPSOS%20enque%CC%82te%20particuliers%20employeurs.pdf

Galotti, M., & Mertens, J. (2013). Promoting integration for migrant domestic workers in Europe: A synthesis of Belgium, France, Italy and Spain. *ILO International Migration Papers, 118.*

Geist, C. (2005). The welfare state and the home: Regime differences in the domestic division of labour. *European Sociological Review, 21*(1), 23–41. https://doi.org/10.1093/esr/jci002

Glenn, E. (2010). *Forced to care: Coercion and caregiving in America.* Harvard University Press.

Gonalons-Pons, P. (2015). Gender and class housework inequalities in the era of outsourcing hiring domestic work in Spain. *Social Science Research, 52,* 208–218.

Gorz, A. (1988). *Métamorphoses du Travail – Quête du sens.* Galilée.

Guiraudon, V., & Ledoux, C. (2015). The politics of tax exemption for household services in France. In C. Carbonnier & N. Morel (Eds.), *The political economy of household services in Europe* (1st ed., pp. 39–59). Palgrave Macmillan.

IFOP. (2022). Observatoire de la répartition des tâches ménagères Volet 3 : la question du délit de non-partage des tâches domestiques. Retrieved April 12, 2022, from https://consolab.fr/etude-une-francaise-sur-deux-favorable-au-delit-de-non-partage-des-taches-menageres/

ILO. (2018). *Care work and care jobs for the future of decent work.* Retrieved March 8, 2022, from https://www.ilo.org/wcmsp5/groups/public/%2D%2D-dgreports/%2D%2D-dcomm/%2D%2D-publ/documents/publication/wcms_633135.pdf

INSEE. (2014). Fiches thématiques Conditions de Vie et société. *Trente ans de vie économique et sociale Edition, 2014,* 100–115. Retrieved September 18, 2022, from https://www.insee.fr/fr/statistiques/1374373?sommaire=1374377

INSEE. (2019). Equipements des ménages. *Tableaux de l'Economie Française.* Retrieved September 18, 2022, from https://www.insee.fr/fr/statistiques/3676680?sommaire=3696937

Jany-Catrice, F. (2010). La construction sociale du « secteur » des services à la personne : une banalisation programmée ? *Sociologie Du Travail, 52*(4), 521–537. https://doi.org/10.4000/sdt.15409

Kilkey, M. (2010). Men and domestic labor: A missing link in the global care chain. *Men and Masculinities, 13*(1), 126–149. https://doi.org/10.1177/1097184X10382884

Killewald, A. (2011). Opting out and buying in: Wives' earnings and housework time. *Journal of Marriage and the Family, 73,* 459–471. https://doi.org/10.1111/j.1741-3737.2010.00818.x

Kulanthaivelu, E. (2020). Les services à la personne en 2018 : Légère baisse de l'activité, hausse du recours aux organismes prestataires. *DARES Résultats.* Retrieved October 14, 2020, from https://dares.travail-emploi.gouv.fr/IMG/pdf/dares_resultats__services_a_la_personne_2018.pdf

Laville, J.-L. (2008). Services aux personnes et sociologie économique pluraliste. *Revue Française de Socio-Économie, 2*(2), 43–58. https://doi.org/10.3917/rfse.002.0043

Maj, S., & Zamfir, V. (2015). Les particuliers employeurs au premier trimestre 2015. *ACOSS Conjoncture, 212*, 1–8. Retrieved November 27, 2022, from https://www.servicesalapersonne.gouv.fr/particuliers-employeurs-au-premier-trimestre-2015

Maj, S., Bargoin, N., Kesler, G., Le Cosquer, C., & Soleilhac, N. (2018). L'activité des particuliers employeurs reste en baisse en 2017 malgré le dynamisme de la garde d'enfants à domicile. *ACOSS Bilan, 279*, 1–8. Retrieved November 27, 2022, from https://www.urssaf.org/en/accueil/statistiques/nos-etudes-et-analyses/particuliers-employeurs/nationale/particuliers-employeurs-1/l'activite-des-particuliers-empl.html

Maj, S., Bargoin, N., Kesler, G., Soleihac, N., & Venzac, M. (2022). En 2020, la crise sanitaire accentue le recul de l'emploi direct des particuliers employeurs. *Stat'ur Bilan, 336*, 1–8. Retrieved March 3, 2022, from https://www.urssaf.org/files/Publications/Stat_ur/Stat_ur_336.pdf

Manoudi, A. (2018). *An analysis of PHS to support work-life balance for working parents and carers, synthesis report ECE thematic review.*

Marbot, C. (2008a). Travailler pour des particuliers : souvent une activité d'appoint. *Les Salaires en France* Edition 2008.

Marbot, C. (2008b). En France, qui recourt aux services à domicile ? In *France : Portrait Social* (pp. 143–162). La Documentation Française.

Ministère de l'Economie et des Finances. (2019). *Les services à la personne : pour tout savoir.* Retrieved October 14, 2020, from https://www.servicesalapersonne.gouv.fr/files_sap/files/publications/les-sap-pour-tout-savoir.pdf

Ministère du Travail. (2019). Les métiers du nettoyage : quels types d'emploi, quelles conditions de travail ? *Dares Analyses, 043*, 1–13. Retrieved March 23, 2022, from https://dares.travail-emploi.gouv.fr/publications/les-metiers-du-nettoyage-quels-types-d-emploi-quelles-conditions-de-travail

Morel, N. (2015). Servants for the knowledge-based economy? The political economy of domestic services in Europe. *Social Politics, 22*(2), 170–192. https://doi.org/10.1093/sp/jxv006

Moujoud, N. (2018). Les sans-papiers et le service domestique en France : femmes et non-droit dans le travail. *Recherches féministes, 31*(1), 275–291. https://doi.org/10.7202/1050665ar

OECD. (2021). Bringing Household Services Out of the Shadows: Formalising Non-Care Work in and Around the House. OECD Publishing. Retrieved April 15, 2022, from https://doi.org/10.1787/fbea8f6e-en

Opinion Way. (2019). *Les Français et la charge mentale liée à la gestion du linge*. Retrieved September 24, 2021, from https://www.opinion-way.com/fr/component/edocman/opinionway-pour-lg-les-francais-et-la-charge-mentaleliee-a-la-gestion-du-linge-juin-2019/viewdocument.html?Itemid=0

Palier, B. (2000). Defrosting' the French welfare state. *West European Politics, 23*(2), 113–136. https://doi.org/10.1080/01402380008425369

Papuchon, A. (2017). Rôles sociaux des femmes et des hommes : l'idée persistante d'une vocation maternelle de femmes malgré le déclin de l'adhésion aux stéréotypes de genre. Insee Références, édition 2017 - Dossier - Rôles sociaux des femmes et des hommes, 81–96.

Plessz, M., & Etilé, F. (2019). Is cooking still a part of our eating practices? Analysing the decline of a practice with time-use surveys. *Cultural Sociology, 13*(1), 93–118. https://doi.org/10.1177/1749975518791431

Puech, I., & Devetter, F.-X. (2010). *L'externalisation des tâches domestiques : quels liens avec l'égalité entre hommes et femmes?* Working paper.

Queval, S., Lagandre, V., & Puech, I. (2019). Qui sont les salarié(e)s des particuliers employeurs et dans quelles conditions travaillent-ils(elles)? *Les Cahiers de l'Observatoire des emplois de la famille*. Retrieved May 24, 2022, from https://www.fepem.fr/wp-content/uploads/Qui-sont-les-salari%C3%A9s-PE_VF.pdf

Rezeanu, C.-I. (2015). The relationship between domestic space and gender identity: Some signs of emergence of alternative domestic femininity and masculinity. *Journal of Comparative Research in Anthropology and Sociology, 6*(2), 10–29.

Ricroch, L. (2012). En 25 ans, moins de tâches domestiques pour les femmes, l'écart de situation avec les hommes se réduit. In *INSEE Femmes et hommes – regards sur la parité* (2012th ed.). Retrieved March 16, 2019, from https://www.insee.fr/fr/statistiques/1372773?sommaire=1372781

Riou, J., Lefèvre, T., Parizot, I., L'Huissier, A., & Chauvin, P. (2015). Is there still a French eating model? A taxonomy of eating behaviors in adults living in the Paris metropolitan area in 2010. *PLoS One, 10*(3). https://doi.org/10.1371/journal.pone.0119161

Ruppanner, L., & Maune, D. J. (2016). The state of domestic affairs: Housework, gender and state-level institutional logics. *Social Science Research, 60*, 15–28. https://doi.org/10.1016/j.ssresearch.2016.04.006

Sayer, L. (2010). Trends in housework. In J. Treas & S. Drobnič (Eds.), *Dividing the domestic: Men, women and household work in cross-national perspective* (pp. 19–34). Stanford University Press.

Scrinzi, F. (2010). Masculinities and the international division of care: Migrant male domestic workers in Italy and France. *Men and Masculinities, 13*(1), 44–64. https://doi.org/10.1177/1097184X10382880

Seierstad, C., & Kirton, G. (2015). Having it all? Women in high commitment careers and work-life balance in Norway. *Gender, Work and Organization, 22*(4), 390–404. https://doi.org/10.1111/gwao.12099

Sofer, C., & Thibout, C. (2015). La division du travail selon le genre est-elle efficiente ? Une analyse à partir de deux enquêtes Emploi du temps. *Economie et statistique, 478-479-480*, 273–304.

Sohler, K., & Levy, F. (2013). Migration careers and professional trajectories of irregular domestic workers. In A. Triandaifyllidou (Ed.), *Irregular migration and domestic work in Europe: Who cares?* (pp. 43–70). Routledge.

Stambolis-Ruhstorfer, M., & Gross, M. (2021). Qui lave le linge sale de la famille? *Travail, genre et sociétés, 2*, 75–95. https://doi.org/10.3917/tgs.046.0075

Sullivan, O., & Gershuny, J. (2013). Domestic outsourcing and multitasking: How much do they really contribute? *Social Science Research, 42*(5), 1311–1324. https://doi.org/10.1016/j.ssresearch.2013.05.004

Talbot, C. (2017). Les politiques d'insertion comme processus d'assignation au travail domestique : l'exemple des plans locaux pour l'insertion et l'emploi français. *Recherches féministes, 30*(2), 139–156. https://doi.org/10.7202/1043926ar

Weber, F. (2009). *Le travail à-côté. Une ethnographie des perceptions.* Editions de l'EHESS.

Wilson, J. (1980). *The politics of regulation.* Basic Books.

Windebank, J. (2001). Dual-earner couples in Britain and France: Gender divisions of domestic labour and parenting work in different welfare states. *Work, Employment and Society, 15*(2), 269–290. https://doi.org/10.1177/09500170122118959

Windebank, J. (2007). Outsourcing women's domestic labour: the Chèque Emploi-Service Universel in France. *Journal of European Social Policy, 17*(3), 257–270. https://doi.org/10.1177/0958928707078368

Windebank, J. (2010). Barriers to outsourcing domestic chores in dual-earner households. *International Journal of Sociology and Social Policy, 30*(7/8), 387–398. https://doi.org/10.1108/01443331011060733

Wong, J. S. (2017). Competing desires: How young adult couples negotiate moving for career opportunities. *Gender and Society, 31*(2), 171–196. https://doi.org/10.1177/0891243217695520

Yougov. (2021). *Les Français et la livraison à domicile.* Retrieved November 19, 2022, from https://fr.yougov.com/news/2021/11/29/les-francais-et-la-livraison-domicile/

Zarca, B. (1990). La division du travail domestique : poids du passé et tensions au sein du couple. *Economie et statistique, 228*, 29–40.

CHAPTER 6

Domestic and Care Work in France in COVID Times

In the wake of the announcement by the World Health Organization (WHO) of the COVID-19 global pandemic on 11 March 2020, the French parliament passed a law on 23 March giving powers to the prime minister and cabinet to declare a state of health emergency to combat the spread of the virus (Legifrance, 2020). During the ensuing states of health emergency, and the transition periods out of them,[1] measures were implemented that restricted and altered everyday life in France to an extent that had not been witnessed before in peacetime. Different types and levels of restrictions were imposed on the country that were legally enforceable. Infected persons and their contacts had to self-isolate. Full lockdowns were imposed, with French residents being legally obliged to stay at home other than for sanctioned essential purposes (e.g., employment for key workers, medical treatment, essential shopping or restricted exercise).

[1] The first state of health emergency was in place between 23 March and 10 July 2020. This was followed by a period of transition out of these measures from 11 July to 31 October. However, on 17 October 2020, it was necessary to re-introduce a state of health emergency that lasted until June 2021, after which time the country entered a second phase of transition. The law allowing the prime minister to declare a state of health emergency ended on 1 August 2022. https://www.vie-publique.fr/fiches/273947-quest-ce-que-letat-durgence-sanitaire#:~:text=Pour%20r%C3%A9pondre%20%C3%A0%20la%20crise,n'est%20plus%20en%20vigueur

J. Windebank, *Domestic and Care Work in Modern France*, French Politics, Society and Culture,
https://doi.org/10.1007/978-3-031-33564-8_6

Outside periods of lockdown, more limited measures such as restrictions on entering the homes of others, public gatherings and the use of commercial spaces or curfews were implemented. There were closures of businesses and workplaces and educational and childcare establishments. School and university classes moved online. Work-from-home (WFH) orders for all those who could do so were in place for extended periods. A range of other sanitary measures such as social distancing, mask wearing and national/international health passes had impacts on the ability of some businesses to trade at pre-pandemic levels, and therefore had repercussions for employment.

In order to support those who could not work due to the pandemic, the government made changes to the *activité partielle* (partial economic activity) scheme.[2] This scheme was already in place prior to the pandemic and was designed to support businesses experiencing economic difficulties that resulted in the need to lay off staff partially or fully for a defined period. Eligible employers continued to pay a percentage of the salary of the lost work hours to their employees and were compensated by the government. The scheme was extended to respond to the problems posed by the pandemic in a number of ways. The difference between the level of government compensation and the level of salary was reduced; the scheme was extended to include part-time workers; procedures for employers to access the scheme were simplified; and article 7 of the ordinance extended the scheme exceptionally and temporarily for home-based directly employed PHS workers and childminders. Furthermore, under the provisions of the *activité partielle garde d'enfant COVID*[3] (partial economic activity for COVID childcare), one parent of a child under 16 whose school or class was closed, who was in isolation during term time or whose childminder was in isolation could benefit from the scheme. More than a third of those employed prior to the pandemic drew these benefits during the first lockdown (Givord & Silhol, 2020; Maj et al., 2022).

These measures directly and indirectly affected the conditions for undertaking unpaid domestic and care work, the work-life arrangements

[2] For further details, see: https://travail-emploi.gouv.fr/emploi-et-insertion/accompagnement-des-mutations-economiques/activite-partielle-chomage-partiel/article/activite-partielle-chomage-partiel

https://www.legifrance.gouv.fr/jorf/id/JORFTEXT000041762501?init=true&page=1&query=l%27activite+partielle&searchField=ALL&tab_selection=all

[3] For further details, see: https://www.juritravail.com/Actualite/activite-partielle-pour-garde-d-enfants-ou-arret-de-travail-des-changements-en-2022/Id/326294

of individuals and households and the work conditions of domestic and care employees in France. The pandemic saw temporary shifts in the location of domestic and care work away from the public sphere and employment relations with the closure of workplaces, schools and businesses offering out-of-home services and towards the private sphere of the home and the social relations of unpaid work in the household. The legal restrictions and impact of the pandemic on certain businesses or occupations determined whether individuals could continue in their jobs and if so, under what conditions (such as working from home). Any resulting changes in employment affected the time individuals had available to perform domestic and care work and their resources to outsource it, or bargain with other household members over its execution. Furthermore, these health-emergency measures increased the volume of unpaid domestic and care work that individuals were required to do. This was because they and anyone they lived with or who were dependent on them were obliged to spend more time at home due to not being able to work, working from home, school and childcare closures and lockdown and curfew restrictions. Additionally, the measures limited the availability of services that individuals and households previously relied on to help with the domestic and care workload, such as schools and crèches, canteens and restaurants or housekeepers. Lastly, these measures affected the work conditions and opportunities of domestic and care employees.

The most severe measures of full lockdown[4] were in place from 17 March to 11 May 2020, and much of the research on the effects of the pandemic on domestic and care work took place during that period.[5]

[4] For full details, see: https://www.vie-publique.fr/en-bref/273932-coronavirus-les-mesures-de-confinement

[5] A number of national studies have been undertaken in France on the social and economic impacts of the pandemic: The *Coronovirus et Confinement: enquête longtitudinale* (*CoConEL)* (Coronovirus and Lockdown Longitudinal Survey) was conducted using a random sample of the national population that simultaneously took into account working arrangements, living conditions and wellbeing, and allowed for an intersectional analysis of social inequalities by gender and socio-economic status https://www.ined.fr/fichier/rte/General/ACTUALIT%C3%89S/Covid19/COCONEL-note-synthese-vague-11_Ined.pdf); a survey by Harris Interactive (2021) on the gender equality impacts of the pandemic was undertaken on behalf of the *Secrétariat d'Etat chargé de l'Egalité entre les femmes et les hommes et de la lutte contre les discriminations*; the *EpiCoV* survey on health and living conditions was undertaken by the *Institut national de la santé et de la recherche médicale* (*Inserm*); and the Drees with support from the *INSEE* undertook a survey on living conditions under COVID https://www.epicov.fr/

There was a further extensive lockdown between 30 October and 15 December 2020 but during this time, schools and crèches remained open and more occupations (e.g., construction) were allowed to continue operations.

Impacts of COVID19 Restrictions on Employment and Availability for Unpaid Domestic and Care Work

As we have seen in previous chapters, the employment status, work time and pay of an individual are all closely related to their time availability for domestic and care work and the resources they have to free themselves of these responsibilities. In the first lockdown, according to the *EpiCov* survey, hours worked in employment reduced by 34 per cent in comparison with the same period in 2019 (Barhoumi et al., 2020, p. 18). However, the impacts on different types of employment and employees were very varied. Those in essential occupations[6] continued to work on site often under great pressure and in some instances conditions that put them at severe risk of contracting the virus throughout the pandemic. Their availability for domestic and care work was at best the same as before the lockdown, and potentially far less. Those who could worked from home. By May 2020, 29 per cent of the population in employment before lockdown was working from home. Those in administrative and clerical occupations in the service industry, and professionals and managers were most likely to be able to do so. This possibility disproportionately benefitted those in higher level occupations. For example, 86 per cent of those working in SPC 3 worked from home in the first lockdown (Lambert et al., 2021, p. 6). Working from home was viewed by the public as an advantage for well-qualified workers (Leclerc, 2020). Women were as likely to work from home as men (Lambert et al., 2021).

Working from home as practised during the pandemic was an extreme example of the encroachment of employment into the private space of the home and therefore potentially the free time of the worker that had been developing prior to the pandemic (Chung et al., 2021; Glass & Noonan, 2016). This had been the result of flexible working practices and the increased ease of using information technology and communications tools

[6] https://dares.travail-emploi.gouv.fr/sites/default/files/c278f247774c7b8cf9e4a5d9b48c7b20/Document%20d%27%C3%A9tudes_m%C3%A9tiers%20deuxi%C3%A8me%20ligne.pdf

outside the workplace. It has long been established that these new ways of working affect men and women differently (Chung et al., 2021). On the one hand, social norms continue to dictate that women should use flexible employment options such as flexible hours in the workplace, part-time work or working from home to meet demands for unpaid domestic and care work. On the other hand, this blurring of boundaries between personal and work life leads men to invest more in their employment, as they experience and are able to respond to an expectation to work overtime off site and during non-standard hours (Glass & Noonan, 2016). Due to the work stress that such practices entail, as well as the gender inequalities, the administration of President Macron had introduced into the Labour Code in January 2017 the "right to disconnect" from work emails, messages and telephone calls outside normal work hours, obliging companies with over 50 staff to negotiate the modalities of this right in their annual consultation on gender equality.[7]

These existing gender disparities were reflected in the conditions in which men and women worked when they were at home during the pandemic and influenced the degree of work-life interference from which they suffered. Access to workspace is important for employees working from home. For those in multi-person households, and particularly those with care responsibilities, having a dedicated and private workspace allows them to distance themselves physically and therefore psychologically from the domestic and care needs of other members of the household. The *CoConEL* survey found that 39 per cent of women working from home shared their workspace with at least one other household member, compared with only 24 per cent of men (Lambert et al., 2021, p. 6). This gender gap widened when children were present, with 47 per cent of women working from home sharing their workspace compared with 20 per cent of men. Lack of private workspace for women made them more available to respond to the needs of household members as they arose (Avril & Ramos Vacca, 2020). In contrast, 45 per cent of men living with children worked from a room specifically designated as their workspace, compared with only 27 per cent of women. This result reflects structural inequalities in employment and pay, with men tending to have higher level occupations than their women partners when they live in different-sex couples giving them reason to occupy undisturbed space to carry out their

[7] https://travail-emploi.gouv.fr/archives/archives-courantes/loi-travail-2016/les-principales-mesures-de-la-loi-travail/article/droit-a-la-deconnexion

employment (Georges-Kot, 2020). Furthermore, Baudot et al. (2021) found that when space was limited, children were given priority for private workspace for homework or online study over women who were working from home.

Those in non-essential occupations who could not work from home were paid through the partial activity scheme. If this was not possible, for example, because the business for which they worked closed, they had to find alternative work or draw unemployment benefit. This was principally a problem for manual workers and service-sector workers in customer facing posts in non-essential hospitality, tourism, retail or welfare activities that were disproportionately affected by social distancing and lockdown measures (Blasko et al., 2020; Fana et al., 2020). In the first lockdown, 54 per cent of those in SPC 6 and 36 per cent in SPC 5 were not working (including those being paid under the partial activity scheme) (Barhoumi et al., 2020, p. 19). Women in France, in similarity with most high-income countries, are overrepresented in public-facing service sector jobs, especially those that require fewer qualifications. French women were therefore more likely than men to stop working during the lockdown periods. In the first lockdown in France, one in three women in employment had stopped working by May 2020, compared to one in four men (Lambert et al., 2020a, p. 5).

It was not only restrictions on their employment that led people to reduce their work hours or stop working. It was also necessary for some in order to look after their children, particularly when they could not work from home. Around twice the proportion of women stopped work or took a special leave to look after children in France than men. Albouy and Legleye (2020) found that 21 per cent of women with parenting responsibilities in comparison with 12 per cent of men stopped work for this reason in the first lockdown while Berhuet et al. (2021, p. 2) report that in April 2020 15 per cent of women in contrast to 8 per cent of men had stopped work to look after children because of the closure of schools and childcare placements. In addition to the social norms that assign care responsibilities to women, this gender imbalance can also be attributed to the way in which the partial activity for COVID childcare scheme operated. Only one parent could claim this status. Although the scheme was generous, providing 84 per cent of previous net salary up to a ceiling of 4.5 times the minimum wage, for the majority of different-sex coupled parents, it would have been economically rational for the woman to stop working due to the gender wage gap.

This gendered pattern of employment during the pandemic was similar internationally. The OECD (2021a) in their 2020 *Risks that Matter* survey presented evidence that when schools and childcare facilities shut down, women across OECD countries took on the majority of additional unpaid parenting work and, correspondingly, they experienced labour market penalties and stress. Mothers of children under 12 were the group most likely to move from employed to not employed status between Q4 2019 and Q3 2020 (OECD, 2021b). There were cross-national differences in the medium-term impacts of this gender inequality, however. Due to the generosity and design of the partial activity scheme in France, there was a 0.7 per cent increase in women's and no change in men's labour force participation rates between Q4 2019 and Q1 2021. This compares with an OECD average fall of 1 per cent in participation rates for both men and women. In the EU27 there was an average drop of 0.3 per cent for men and 0.7 per cent for women in participation rates across this time period (OECD, 2021a, Fig. 1).

Impacts of COVID 19 Restrictions on Increasing Unpaid Domestic and Care Work in the Home

Working from home, school, university and childcare closures alongside stay-at-home orders meant that during some periods in the pandemic, people were spending much greater lengths of time at home than under normal circumstances. This resulted in an increased volume of unpaid work to be carried out, particularly but not exclusively for those with parenting and caring responsibilities. All survey data show that women took on a greater proportion of this extra domestic and care work, whether at a societal level, or in terms of the micro-level division of labour within different-sex couples. During the first lockdown, 19 per cent of women and 9 per cent of men spent at least four hours per day on core domestic work (cooking, shopping, washing up, housework and laundry), whereas 40 per cent of men but only 17 per cent of women declared spending less than 30 minutes per day on these activities (Barhoumi et al., 2020). The Harris Interactive (2021) survey found that respondents reported spending on average 2 hours 22 minutes each day on domestic work with women spending 22 minutes more on the activities (2 hours 34 minutes) per day than men (2 hours 10 minutes). Within different-sex couples, women took on a greater share of domestic tasks than their spouse irrespective of their employment status during lockdown (Pailhé et al., 2020, p. 26). Indeed, Barhoumi et al. (2020) show that working outside the home lessened men's contribution to domestic and care work in comparison with men working at home, but for women this was not the case.

A significant change affecting many individuals and households was that people were more often at home to eat, increasing the need for food shopping, cooking and washing up. In a study of cooking habits, Sarda et al. (2022, p. 4) found that before the pandemic, there had been a steady reduction in domestic food preparation in France due to a lack of time, the wide availability of low-cost ultra-processed food products and decline in cooking and food skills. However, the first lockdown led to a significant rise in home cooking with 42 per cent of all participants in their study reporting having cooked more frequently (with only 7.0 per cent cooking less). Barriers such as time constraints were reduced which allowed people not only to undertake food preparation but importantly to gain the necessary knowledge and skills to cook from scratch as well. This was particularly the case in more affluent households where affordability of ingredients was not an obstacle. This increase in cooking frequency remained stable for six out of ten respondents after the lifting of the first lockdown measures in 2020. Sarda et al. (2022) also showed that families with at least one child tended to cook more frequently than those without children, suggesting the important role played by children in structuring eating patterns during the lockdown. This finding is echoed by Philippe et al. (2021, p. 9) whose study reported that 66 per cent of parents declared cooking more during the first lockdown and that 71 per cent declared spending more time cooking alongside their children. Sarda et al. (2022) also found that women increased their cooking frequency significantly more than men, as did the Harris Interactive (2021) survey in which 63 per cent of women said they did the cooking most often in their household.

For those with children, the increase in parenting work due to the COVID-19 measures was very substantial, with the World Bank recognising this burden as one of the major social impacts of the pandemic (World Bank, 2021). Parents working from home had to combine looking after their children with employment because they were not eligible for the partial activity for COVID childcare scheme. In comparison with 2019, in 2020 there was a decrease in the volume of formal childcare[8] accessed by

[8] Nursery school is not included here as a form of childcare as it is part of the national education system.

children under six in France of 317.3 million hours (*Observatoire National de la Petite Enfance* [ONaPE], 2021, p. 2). Collective forms of care saw the largest decrease in hours of 28.4 per cent, followed by nannies working in employers' homes of 16 per cent and childminders of 8.2 per cent. France closed schools fully or partially for 12 weeks from March to June 2020, less time than in 90 per cent of 193 countries in a UNESCO (2021) comparison, and less than all European countries other than Switzerland and Croatia. During this period, each school region organised provision for the children of frontline key workers who had no other sources of childcare. Learning was provided online, particularly for older children. Support with online learning created an additional layer of responsibility for parents. Barhoumi et al. (2020, Fig. 5.2) report that during the first lockdown 60 per cent of parents with children at *collèges* (11–15 years old) and 29 per cent of those at *lycées* (15–18 years old) spent one or more hours per day helping children with their schoolwork, and all spent at least some time doing so during the week. Schools remained open in the second lockdown. Difficulties continued for parents, however, as due to infections childcare facilities and schools sometimes had to ask groups or classes of children to stay at home, childminders could not work or children themselves had to isolate.

The ways in which parents navigated this increased parenting work reflect the trends in the gender distribution of domestic and care work discussed in Chaps. 3 and 5 and the impacts of the pandemic on the employment of men and women. In all surveys, women were found to undertake more of this extra parenting work than men, whether or not they remained in employment, or worked from home. According to the *EpiCoV* survey, 43 per cent of women with parenting responsibilities as opposed to 30 per cent of men spent more than six hours daily looking after children during the first lockdown (Pailhé et al., 2020, p. 27). These figures were higher for parents of young children: 74 per cent of women and 40 per cent of men whose youngest child was three or younger and 65 per cent of mothers and 45 per cent of fathers whose youngest child was six or younger. Furthermore, 45 per cent of women who continued to work during this time whether at home or outside the home undertook a double day accumulating more than four hours of employment and more than four hours of looking after children. This was the case for only 29 per cent of men (Hoibian et al., 2021, p. 3).

Similar results were produced by an IPSOS (2020) survey of the time spent on activities with children during the first lockdown and by the

OECD *Risks That Matter* survey in which 53.4 per cent of mothers in comparison with 20.9 per cent of fathers said that they took on the majority or all of the additional unpaid childcare work caused by school and childcare closures (OECD, 2021b Fig. 4). Berhuet et al. (2021, p. 2) found that in 55 per cent of households with at least one child under 20, parental activities during the first lockdown were the preserve of one of the parents only, mostly the mother (39 per cent) rather than the father (16 per cent). In a qualitative study, Lambert et al. (2021) discovered that women living in different-sex couples with children felt overwhelmed by the situation they were in, very often because they were working from home and their partners, particularly those working outside the home, contributed insufficiently to housework and online schooling.

Although not to the same extent as women with parenting responsibilities, men did increase the time they spent responding to the parenting demands and related domestic work presented by the pandemic. The gender gap in time devoted to domestic and care work was found in one survey to be significantly lower in couples with two children (19 minutes per day) than couples with no children (42 minutes per day) during the first lockdown (Harris Interactive, 2021), suggesting that the intensity of the work for parents caused by the closure of school and childcare facilities obliged men to participate. Nevertheless, this participation was dependent on their employment. The main driver of the shift towards more paternal care and domestic work was their women partners working outside the home (Boll et al., 2021), providing more evidence for the fact that men's involvement in domestic and care work is often borne of necessity rather than opportunity (Boll et al., 2021; Sevilla & Smith, 2020; Zamarro & Prados, 2021). Gender gaps in a household's unpaid care in different-sex couples were largest, on average, when the man continued to be employed while the mother was not. This relationship was not reciprocated to the same degree in households where the man was out of paid work and the woman was in paid work (OECD, 2021b).

It appears that with relatively short school closures and generous support based on previous earnings for those who could not continue to work, gender inequality in parenting work at this time was lesser in France than in some other countries. In an OECD comparison of parents with at least one child under 12 France had the fourth lowest percentage of mothers (50.5 per cent) and seventh highest percentage of fathers (25 per cent) who reported that they took on all or the majority of the additional care work caused by school or childcare facility closures in 2020 (OECD,

2021b, p. 9). The OECD found that historically higher levels of spending on family supports, as in the case of France, were associated with smaller gender gaps in the distribution of additional care of children during COVID-19 (OECD, 2021b).

Impact of COVID 19 Restrictions on Informal Support and Paid Services for Domestic and Care Work

During the pandemic, the need for favours for domestic and care activities such as shopping, fetching prescriptions or walking pets grew as individuals who were more at risk from the virus because of age or medical conditions had to take particular precautions in going out, or shield in their homes. Furthermore, anyone who had been infected with COVID or been in contact with someone who was, was obliged to self-isolate. Consequently, a certain mythology about the rebirth of community spirit and helping one another out developed in the media with publications giving advice on how to be a good neighbour.[9] However, concerns about the virus and the need to respect the measures to prevent its spread complicated and limited what unpaid domestic and care work people could exchange between households. The *CoCoNel* study looked at the intensity and frequency of exchanges of favours between households during the first lockdown (although they did not isolate activities that could be described as domestic and care work) (Lambert et al., 2020b, p. 9). It found that the intensity of these exchanges and favours was the same during the first lockdown as in the month before it. Forty per cent of the sample did a favour for someone in their neighbourhood at least once in the first lockdown and 29 per cent received at least one favour. Families with children received a little less help than before (26 per cent declared having received at least one favour in contrast to 35 per cent in the month before) whereas those aged 75 plus received more help (46 per cent received help during the first lockdown as opposed to 31 per cent in the month before). People in the older age group also helped less (85 per cent

[9] See for example the article in the *Le Nouvel Observateur* "Comment venir en aide à ses voisins âgés pendant le confinement (sans contaminer)? (How to help your elderly neighbours (without infecting them)? March 20th 2020. https://www.nouvelobs.com/coronavirus-de-wuhan/20200320.OBS26321/comment-venir-en-aide-a-ses-voisins-ages-pendant-le-confinement-sans-les-contaminer.html

had done a favour before lockdown as opposed to 60 per cent during). Seventy-one per cent who did favours during the lockdown had done so prior to the pandemic. Before the lockdown, there was a certain symmetry in the giving and receiving of favours: 66 per cent of those doing favours had received them and 83 per cent of those reporting having received a favour had done them as well. The lockdown created more asymmetry in these exchanges in favour of those who were older, understandable in the light of the differential risks of the virus depending on age. Lockdown highlighted the relational vulnerability of older people and dependence on informal networks.

Within the restrictions of the first lockdown, leaving home was permitted for serious family reasons such as caring for a vulnerable adult or providing childcare. Indeed, two qualitative studies undertaken during the first lockdown with family carers of older people requiring intensive caregiving found that their workload increased during the pandemic because of the heightened sanitary measures required to avoid infection for the care recipient, the reduction in availability of paid help or the active avoidance of using paid help because of infection concerns (Giraud et al., 2020; Touhahria-Gaillard, 2021). Those directly employing a single carer with whom they had a long-term relationship were more likely to continue to use paid care than those using agency services as they had more trust in the care provider not to introduce the virus into the home.

The anti-COVID measures also had effects on the availability of out-of-home services that substitute unpaid domestic and care work. For example, during the first and second lockdowns, restaurants, cafes and bars were not allowed to open to the public and at other times had extensive restrictions on their modes of operation. Take-away services were allowed to continue. However, demand for on-the-go consumption of take-away foods declined because of the restrictions. Therefore, both traditional restaurants and existing take-away establishments turned to home delivery services to sustain their business and respond to increasing demand. Home delivery of prepared meals had already been a strongly growing sector of activity before the pandemic: in 2019 there had been a 25 per cent increase in the number of such home delivery businesses but this increased to 46 per cent in 2020 (Gourdon, 2022, Fig. 1). A YouGov (2021) survey in October 2021 in France found that 33 per cent of their nationally representative sample had used a home delivery of prepared meals in the prior six months, of whom 47 per cent reported having increased this practice due to the circumstances of the pandemic and 64 per cent said that they would continue to use these services after the COVID measures were lifted. The age group in which there was the highest proportion of users was 18- to 34-year-olds (41 per cent) followed by the over 55s (24 per cent).

Home-based PHS services were allowed to continue during the lockdown periods in France because the structuring of essential care work and non-essential housekeeping and other services into the single sector of services to the individual made it difficult to differentiate them in legal terms. The proliferation of direct employment in this sector also meant that decisions on whether services would continue or not were being taken at an individual level. That said, in the personal attestations that they had to take with them on leaving the house during the lockdowns, individuals had to declare that the work they were leaving home to do could not be postponed. Furthermore, infection concerns reduced demand for services, and if suitable sanitary measures were not provided by employers, employees had the right to withdraw their labour.[10] During the first lockdown, there were very marked differences between categories of direct employer as regards maintenance of consumption of services according to how essential these services were: 33 per cent of those employing nannies, 48 per cent of those employing childminders, 36 per cent of those employing housekeepers (outside LTC) in contrast to 83 per cent of those employing home helps (for LTC) continued to purchase services. In the second lockdown, there was less difference between these categories. Of those who had purchased services in February 2020, 96 per cent of those employing nannies, 98 per cent employing childminders, 96 per cent employing housekeepers (outside LTC) and 95 per cent employing home helps (for LTC) were doing so in October 2020 (Lagandre et al., 2021, p. 2). The higher use of childcare and housekeeping services in the second lockdown in comparison with the first is due to the fact that schools and crèches were open and more occupations were allowed to work outside the home (Lagandre et al., 2021, p. 2).

Lagandre et al. (2021) note that despite a 6.1 per cent drop in declared hours of direct employment in the home in the first quarter of 2020, followed by a 13.7 per cent drop in the second quarter, there was a strong

[10] For details, see: https://travail-emploi.gouv.fr/le-ministere-en-action/coronavirus-covid-19/questions-reponses-par-theme/article/responsabilite-de-l-employeur-droit-de-retrait#:~:text=Dans%20quelles%20conditions%20un%20salari%C3%A9,sa%20vie%20ou%20sa%20sant%C3%A9

rebound in the third quarter with an increase of 22.4 per cent. This increase was due to several factors: first 98 per cent of direct employees had either continued with their employment during the first lockdown or returned to it afterwards. Second, certain activities that could not be undertaken during the lockdown were deferred until the third quarter. And finally, the over 70s did not go on holiday as much in summer 2020 as normal because of COVID and therefore maintained their consumption of services over the third quarter whereas this normally reduces in comparison with the rest of the year.

Those who provide home-based domestic and care services have a vulnerable position in the labour market and difficult work conditions under normal circumstances, particularly those who work as direct employees. The pandemic exposed them to additional difficulties notably as regards danger of infection or infecting their clients, lack of monitoring of the sanitary conditions in which they had to work and loss of income due to their customers no longer wanting their services or they themselves needing to avoid the risk of infection (Delpierre, 2020). Forty-seven per cent of PHS direct employees continued to work during the first lockdown, either at the same or reduced number of hours. The percentage was much higher (83 per cent) for those working with dependent adults (IPSOS, 2020). Direct employees were for the first time entitled to cover from the partial activity scheme for the duration of the pandemic. Ninety-two per cent of direct employers who suspended the employment of their PHS worker continued to pay them, with 30 per cent paying the salary themselves and 62 per cent using the partial activity scheme of whom 57 per cent paid a supplement to the support given by the scheme. Only seven per cent did not pay for non-worked hours (IPSOS, 2020). Maj et al. (2022, p. 6 Table 1) show that between March and December 2020, 789,000 direct employers in private homes of providers of non-childcare services and 346,000 direct employers of childcare providers, including childminders, used the partial activity scheme, on behalf of 366,000 and 214,000 employees respectively. Those working for service-providing companies or associations could also be supported through the partial activity scheme. However, undeclared workers, including undocumented migrants, were dependent on the willingness of their employer to continue with their employment or compensate them for lost working hours.

Concluding Summary

The COVID pandemic has served to show that progression towards more gender equality in unpaid domestic and care work remains fragile in France. It has also highlighted that progress to date has been based on the reduction of unpaid domestic and care work through lowered output and increased outsourcing and the willingness of men to increase the time they spend in parental work than on the redistribution of unpaid work more generally between men and women. Critical junctures such as the COVID-19 pandemic can produce reactions that result in a fallback to traditional divisions of labour. During the pandemic, the gender pay gap and gendered social norms around women's responsibility towards the family resulted in women working in less advantageous conditions when working from home, withdrawing from the labour market for childcare reasons if they could not work from home, and undertaking a greater share of the extra unpaid work and care burden than men. However, necessity can also bring about changes in behaviour on the part of men that opportunity will not (Delhomme & Petillon, 2022; Lambert et al., 2021). For example, in response to the substantial increase in unpaid parenting and related domestic work caused by school closures, men did respond with increased participation in this work. Furthermore, the pandemic measures had less of an impact on women's employment in France than in many other high-income countries. The gender division of unpaid work was also found to be more equal. This is in keeping with trends discussed in Chap. 5 concerning the change in the comparative position of the country on this measure over the last decade or so. Long-standing support for work-family reconciliation, short school closures, the generous partial activity scheme and continued access to PHS of the general population all contributed to this situation.

It is not yet clear what, if any, long-term effects the pandemic has had on the organisation and divisions of labour of domestic and care work. The pandemic served to highlight at a societal and individual level the importance of both informal exchanges of support and the contribution of workers providing PHS to the functioning of households and to societal wellbeing. However, as we move on from the pandemic, it is questionable whether a long-term re-evaluation of the importance of this work has taken place. The area in which the pandemic may have had the most significant impact is in hastening the development of working from home. Given that other measures to give workers more flexibility in their employment, such as part-time work, resulted in the entrenchment of stereotypical gendered work-family arrangements, the danger is that increased working from home will have similar effects, and not produce a positive outcome for gender equality in domestic and care work.

References

Albouy, V., & Legleye, S. (2020). *Conditions de vie pendant le confinement : des écarts selon le niveau de vie et la catégorie socioprofessionnelle.* Retrieved March 28, 2022, from http://www.epsilon.insee.fr:80/jspui/handle/1/130545

Avril, C., & Ramos Vacca, I. (2020). Se salir les mains pour les autres. Métiers de femme et division morale du travail. *Travail, genre et sociétés, 43*(1), 85–102. https://doi.org/10.3917/tgs.043.0085

Barhoumi, M., et al. (2020). Les inégalités sociales à l'épreuve de la crise sanitaire : un bilan du premier confinement. *Insee Références.* Retrieved April 2, 2022, from http://insee.fr/fr/statistiques/4797670

Baudot, P., Martin, A., Lebrun, A., Clerc, M., Carrier, A., Guellier, M., Taillefer, C., & Clavier, L. (2021). Le confinement de l'intérieur : Appropriations genrées de l'espace domestique. *Revue des politiques sociales et familiales, 141*, 107–117. https://doi.org/10.3917/rpsf.141.0107

Berhuet, S., Coulange, M., Croutte, P., & Hoiban, S. (2021). Les opinions en matière de politiques familiales et sociales en 2020 et sur le partage des tâches familiales pendant le premier confinement. *L'e-ssentiel, 205*, 1–4.

Blasko, Z., Papadimitriou, E., & Manca, A. R. (2020). *How will the COVID-19 crisis affect existing gender divides in Europe.* Publications Office of the European Union. https://doi.org/10.2760/37511

Boll, C., Müller, D., & Schüller, S. (2021). *Neither backlash nor convergence: Dynamics of intracouple childcare division after the first COVID-19 lockdown and subsequent reopening in Germany.* IZA discussion paper. Retrieved March 17, 2022, from https://covid19.iza.org/publications/dp1

Chung, H., Birkett, H., Forbes, S., & Seo, H. (2021). Covid-19, flexible working, and implications for gender equality in the United Kingdom. *Gender and Society, 35*(2), 218–232. https://doi.org/10.1177/08912432211001304

Delhomme, I., & Petillon, X. (2022). Une articulation des temps de vie plus difficile pour les femmes. *Insee Analyses Pays de la Loire, 103*, 1–4.

Delpierre, A. (2020, March 31). Travailleur.e.s a domicile : envisager une vraie protection au-delà de la crise. *The Conversation.* Retrieved October 4, 2022, from https://theconversation.com/travailleur-e-s-a-domicile-envisager-une-vraie-protection-au-dela-de-la-crise-134833

Fana, M., Tolan, S., Torrejon Perez, S., Urzi Brancati, M. C., & Fernandez Macias, E. (2020). *The COVID confinement measures and EU labour markets.* Publications Office of the European Union. https://doi.org/10.2760/079230

Georges-Kot, S. (2020). Écarts de rémunération femmes-hommes : surtout l'effet du temps de travail et de l'emploi occupé. *Insee Première, 1803*, 1–4.

Giraud, O., Petiau, A., Rist, B., Touahria-Gaillard, A., & Trenta, A. (2020). 'Ça fait des années qu'on est confinés'. La crise sanitaire du Covid-19 révélatrice de la condition des proches aidant·e·s de personnes en situation de dépendance. *Revue française des affaires sociales, 4*. https://doi.org/10.3917/rfas.204.0243

Givord, P., & Silhol, J. (2020). Confinement : des conséquences économiques inégales selon les ménages. *Insee Première, 1822*, 1–4.

Glass, J. L., & Noonan, M. (2016). Telecommuting and earnings trajectories among American women and men 1989–2008. *Social Forces, 95*(1), 217–250. https://doi.org/10.1093/sf/sow034

Gourdon, H. Essor des créations d'entreprises de vente à distance et livraison à domicile pendant la crise sanitaire. *INSEE Focus*, 247. Retrieved November 19, 2022., from https://www.insee.fr/fr/statistiques/5417312#consulter

Harris Interactive. (2021). *Le regard des Français sur les services à la personne*. Retrieved March 8, 2022, from https://www.ess-et-societe.net/Le-regard-des-Francais-sur-les

Hoibian, S., Berhuet, S., Coutte, P., Coulange, M., & Brice, L. (2021). La crise sanitaire provoque un retour à des rôles genrés traditionnels. *Consommation et modes de vie, 316*, 1–4.

IPSOS. (2020). *COVID-19 : quel impact sur le secteur des particuliers employeurs et de l'emploi à domicile*. Retrieved April 9, 2022, from https://www.ipsos.com/fr-fr/covid-19-quel-impact-sur-le-secteur-des-particuliers-employeurs-et-de-lemploi-domicile

Lagandre, V., Petit, F., & Puech, I. (2021). L'emploi à domicile résiste à la crise sanitaire au second semestre 2020. *Le Baromètre des Emplois de la Famille, 35*, 1–4.

Lambert, A., Cayouette-Remblière, J., Guéraut, É., Le Roux, G., Bonvalet, C., Girard, V., & Langlois, L. (2020a). Le travail et ses aménagements : ce que la pandémie de covid-19 a changé pour les Français. *Population and Sociétés, 579*, 1–4. https://doi.org/10.3917/popsoc.579.0001

Lambert, A., Cayouette-Remblière, J., Guéraut, E., Le Roux, G., Bonvalet, C., Girard, V., & Langlois, L. (2020b). Comment voisine-t-on dans la France confinée ? *Population et Sociétés, 578*, 1–4. https://doi.org/10.3917/popsoc.578.0001

Lambert, A., Girard, V., & Gueraut, E. (2021). Socio-economic impacts of COVID 19 on working mothers in France. *Frontiers in Sociology, 6*, 1–9. https://doi.org/10.3389/fsoc.2021.732580

Leclerc, A. (2020). *Privilège pour les uns, exclusions pour les autres : le travail à distance crée une nouvelle scission entre travailleurs*. Retrieved April 9, 2022, from https://www.lemonde.fr/economie/article/2020/12/28/privilege pour-les-uns-exclusion-pour-les-autres-le-travail-a-distance-cree-une-nouvellescission-entre-travailleurs_6064653_3234.htm

Legifrance. (2020). *Décret n° 2020–293 du 23 mars 2020 prescrivant les mesures générales nécessaires pour faire face à l'épidémie de covid-19 dans le cadre de l'état d'urgence sanitaire.* Retrieved April 2, 2022, from https://legifrance.gouv.fr/jorf/id/JORFTEXT000041746694

Maj, S., Bargoin, N., Kesler, G., Soleihac, N., & Venzac, M. (2022). En 2020, la crise sanitaire accentue le recul de l'emploi direct des particuliers employeurs. *Stat'ur Bilan, 336*, 1–8. Retrieved March 3, 2022, from https://www.urssaf.org/files/Publications/Stat_ur/Stat_ur_336.pdf

Observatoire national de la petite enfance (ONaPE). (2021). *La Lettre de l'Observatoire national de la petite enfance, 6*, 1–10. Retrieved May 4, 2022, from https://www.caf.fr/sites/default/files/medias/cnaf/Nous_connaitre/Recherche_et_statistiques/Onape/Lettre_ONAPE_6.pdf

OECD. (2021a). *Main findings from the 2020 risks that matter survey.* OECD Publishing. Retrieved March 19, 2022, from https://doi.org/10.1787/b9e85cf5-en

OECD. (2021b). *Caregiving in crisis: Gender inequality in paid and unpaid work during COVID 19.* Retrieved March 19, 2022, from https://read.oecd-ilibrary.org/view/?ref=1122_1122019-pxf57r6v6k&title=Caregiving-in-crisis-Gender-inequality-in-paid-and-unpaid-work-during-COVID-19

Pailhé, A., Raynaud, E., & Solaz, A. (2020). *Même quand elles travaillaient à l'extérieur, les femmes ont consacré plus de temps que les hommes aux tâches domestiques et à s'occuper des enfants.* Retrieved March 10, 2021, https://www.insee.fr/fr/statistiques/4797670

Philippe, K., Chabanet, C., Issanchou, S., & Monnery-Patris, S. (2021). Child eating behaviors, parental feeding practices and food shopping motivations during the COVID-19 lockdown in France: (How) did they change? *Appetite, 161*, 105–132. https://doi.org/10.1016/j.appet.2021.105132

Sarda, B., Delamaire, C., Serry, A.-J., & Ducrot, P. (2022). Changes in home cooking and culinary practices among the French population during the COVID-19 lockdown. *Appetite, 168.* https://doi.org/10.1016/j.appet.2021.105743

Sevilla, A., & Smith, S. (2020). Baby steps: The gender division of childcare during the COVID-19 pandemic. *Oxford Review of Economic Policy, 36.* https://doi.org/10.1093/oxrep/graa027

Touhahria-Gaillard, A. (2021). *L'accompagnement des particuliers employeurs fragiles en temps de COVID-19* (pp. 1–12). L'Observatoire de FEPEM.

UNESCO. (2021). *Education: From school closures to recovery. COVID-19 recovery.* Retrieved November 19, 2022, from https://www.unesco.org/en/covid-19/education-response#durationschoolclosures

World Bank. (2021). *Face aux conséquences de la COVID-19 sur l'éducation, il faut agir vite et efficacement.* Retrieved November 19, 2022, from https://www.banquemondiale.org/fr/news/immersive-story/2021/01/22/urgent-effective-action-required-to-quell-the-impact-of-covid-19-on-education-worldwide

Yougov. (2021). *Les Français et la livraison à domicile.* Retrieved November 19, 2022, from https://fr.yougov.com/news/2021/11/29/les-francais-et-la-livraison-domicile/

Zamarro, G., & Prados, M. (2021). Gender differences in couples' division of childcare, work and mental health during COVID-19. *Review of Economics of the Household, 19*(1), 11–40. https://doi.org/10.1007/s11150-020-09534-7

CHAPTER 7

Domestic and Care Work in France: Gender, Family and the State

This book has had twin aims: to explain how a nationally specific organisation of domestic and care work is constructed using the case study of France and to understand social and economic change in the country in the twentieth and twenty-first centuries through an examination of these most routine of activities. The book has first demonstrated how domestic and care work is organised in France, exploring the social relations in which parenting and childcare, long-term care (LTC) for adults and domestic work are performed. It has discussed the relative importance of unpaid work in the family and household, the kinship group and the community, on the one hand, and paid work in the public sector, for non-profit or commercial organisations or in direct-employment relationships on a declared or undeclared basis on the other. Furthermore, the book has examined the divisions of labour that underpin this organisation, focusing primarily on gender, class and citizenship status. The organisation and divisions of labour of domestic and care work in France have been compared with those in other high-income countries and the ways in which international trends that affect domestic and care work pass through the prism of national policy frameworks and cultural norms in the country have been explored.

Second, the book has explained why domestic and care work is organised in these ways in France. In order to do this, the book has drawn on

J. Windebank, *Domestic and Care Work in Modern France*, French Politics, Society and Culture,
https://doi.org/10.1007/978-3-031-33564-8_7

resource-based and gender-based theories of individual behaviours and related these to the social welfare, family and care, labour market and worktime, and migration regimes in the country. These policies exert both material and ideational influences on individuals' constraints, opportunities, behaviours and decision-making concerning domestic and care work directly and indirectly. Materially, policy is a major factor in allocating economic resources and affects the relative power of different actors in the family and the labour market to determine divisions and conditions of labour and the costs and benefits of undertaking unpaid work or engaging in domestic and care outsourcing. Furthermore, policy structures the employment opportunities, pay and working conditions of domestic and care employees, and influences the supply and affordability of paid domestic and care labour. Ideationally, policy contributes to defining social and cultural norms and structuring world views concerning who should undertake or be responsible for particular types of domestic and care work based on attitudes towards gender, the family and the role of the state. In a democracy policy is in a symbiotic relationship with cultural norms. On the one hand, political parties must put forward manifestos to the electorate that respond to these norms while individual practices may challenge institutions to change. In turn, if policies are in place for sufficient time, they shape citizens' attitudes through policy feedback mechanisms and insert influential keywords and narratives that introduce social and economic problems and their solutions into the national conversation. The third and final stage of the analysis in this book has been to investigate how the material and ideational historical legacies of the twentieth century and beyond have created path dependencies in policies and institutions and influenced the social norms that structure domestic and care work in France.

Significant changes in the organisation and divisions of labour of domestic and care work have taken place in France over the course of the twentieth and twenty-first centuries. The amount of time necessary to undertake core domestic work activities has greatly reduced. Women have become integrated into the labour force, limiting the time they have available for unpaid domestic and care work. A significant proportion of care work for children and adults with LTC needs has been professionalised, and there has been a re-emergence of the use of housekeeping and domestic services, but only among a socially elite group outside the care context. However, two characteristics of the organisation and divisions of labour of domestic and care work have remained constant since the mid-twentieth century. First, the unpaid work of members of the household and the family remains the primary way in which domestic and care work gets done and second, women still undertake the majority of domestic and care work, whether unpaid in the household, kinship group or community or as paid employees. French women are still far more likely than men to modify their employment to fit childcare responsibilities, and to a lesser extent LTC responsibilities. Furthermore, they spend more than twice the time on unpaid domestic and care work as men, even though men have increased their contribution to parenting and to some aspects of LTC work.

The time devoted to domestic work, and particularly core domestic tasks, has decreased since the mid-twentieth century in France as in other high-income countries in large part due to increases in productivity. This has been facilitated by technological advances in domestic equipment for cleaning, laundry and cooking, and easy-care materials for clothing and home decor. Furthermore, there has been an increase in the availability and affordability of ready-made products, particularly food and clothing, and out-of-home services to replace unpaid domestic work. In the contemporary period, the time required to accomplish domestic work outside caring responsibilities is no longer considered a full-time occupation and thus an obstacle to employment. That said, most adults still have to perform unpaid domestic work for themselves or others regularly. Care work for children or adults with LTC needs is more resistant to productivity gains than domestic work. Caring responsibilities continue to represent a major obstacle to labour-market participation almost exclusively for women who are still expected to fulfil these caring duties in society. Caring is expensive to outsource, and without state intervention would be unaffordable for many in the population. Furthermore, care needs are increasing in all high-income countries and France is no exception. An ageing population is increasing demand for paid and unpaid care. Furthermore, the time spent on parental work has increased because parents are expected actively to develop their children's human, social and cultural capital to prepare them for an increasingly competitive global labour market. In France, these increased parental demands have been coupled with relatively high birth rates over the past 30 years. Those with caring responsibilities who use paid services still spend significant amounts of their time whether they are employed or not undertaking practical unpaid care activities and the cognitive labour of the management of care provision by paid or unpaid others. The oversight of care services for dependents remains within the family. On a societal level, more time is still devoted to domestic and care work in France than to professional activities.

There are very significant cross-national variations in women's employment rates and work patterns, in gender divisions of unpaid labour and the extent and structure of paid domestic and care work across Europe and other high-income countries. These variations are in large part explained by the social welfare and work-family reconciliation policy frameworks in operation in particular countries and the extent and the modalities of state support for caring work, and where they exist, for domestic work, that these policies provide. By influencing the possibilities and obligations of different categories of citizens to engage in the labour market, these policies indirectly affect their availability for unpaid domestic and care work. State support may include wage replacement benefits and employment rights for carers, and in-kind provision or cash benefits for domestic and care services. Policy frameworks can be categorised along two axes. The first is their degree of de-familialisation, that is, the extent to which the state supports the outsourcing of domestic and care work traditionally carried out on an unpaid basis. The second is their degree of de-gendering, that is, the extent to which the state encourages the more equal sharing of the remaining unpaid work between men and women. There is a consensus on the basis of cross-national research to date that policies that remove external constraints on men so as to give them opportunity to participate in unpaid work will only bring about limited change in their behaviours. There also needs to be pressure on men to contribute more to these activities. This can be through policies such as incentives for men to take care leaves, or through campaigns to change attitudes and encourage men to develop internal identities that recognise their responsibility for these activities (Himmelweit & Sigala, 2004). The absence of de-familialising policies can also have the effect of obliging men to contribute to care work so that their partners can earn a wage. If the state de-familialises enough unpaid domestic and care work so as to allow women to participate in the labour market without significant change on the part of men and does not engage in de-gendering strategies, it is possible for a situation to develop in which women are integrated into the labour market but change in the gender division of unpaid labour is not far-reaching.

In France, both work-family reconciliation and LTC policy can be described as having been more de-familialising than de-gendering. Defamilialising policies for childcare in France were in place by the early 70s, with a cash-for-care childcare benefit for employed parents, a limited number of low-cost local-authority creche places for the under threes, and free nursery schools providing care for three- to six-year-old pre-schoolers. In consequence, by the 1980s parenting responsibilities were less of an impediment to employment for French women than in many other countries and by the 1990s their participation in the labour market over the life course, including through the early years of parenthood, had become normalised. Other factors that had contributed to the development of women's employment in France at the time had been the demise of the patriarchal family, brought about by the granting of full civil rights to married women and legalisation of the contraception in the 1960s, and by the second-wave feminist campaigns in the post-68 period. Post-Fordist changes in the economy also contributed to drawing women into employment as the family wage declined and demand for flexible labour in the service sector increased. France has had high proportions of dual-earner coupled parents and high employment rates among single parents. The age of their children has had a relatively limited effect on women's employment rates, although having three or more children has been more of an obstacle. Rates of part-time employment for French women were relatively low in the 1980s at around 20 per cent but increased in the 1990s to the EU average of approximately 30 per cent. Attitudinal surveys demonstrate a high degree of approval of women's and mothers' employment and gender-egalitarian attitudes.

France occupied an intermediary position as regards rates of women's employment, higher than in other Conservative countries, but lower than in the Social Democratic Nordic countries. This is because work-family reconciliation and LTC policies were more optionally familialist than entirely de-familialist. Policy for the under threes prioritised giving choice to families. This choice had two aspects. First, policy gave equal support to those who wanted to stay at home with their very young children through long parental leaves accompanied by wage-replacement benefits, and to those who were employed and needed to access childcare through cash-for-care benefits and in-kind provision. As concerns LTC, policymakers have been at pains to retain the role of the family in its role as social carers. Indeed, the French Civil Code still stipulates that adult children bear a legal obligation to support their parents, and other ascendants. This emphasis on the role of the family and wage replacement benefits for care, long established for childcare and more recently introduced for LTC, has the effect of embedding stereotypical gender roles around caring when not accompanied by explicitly de-gendering policies. Second, the state supported the use of a wide variety of childcare options, ranging from collective care in local authority creches to home-based care by childminders and nannies. LTC policy has also emphasised the importance of choice of provision for the care recipient. The majority of LTC support is provided through cash-for-care benefits, the justification for which is that the care recipient can choose the care best suited to them. In similarity to parental leave, the state also supports informal carers to provide care with carer benefits and employment rights.

The overall positive picture of women's employment in France hides a bifurcation of the labour market with low-qualified, low-skilled younger women, particularly those with parenting responsibilities, much less likely than average to be employed. Similar effects are seen as regards LTC with those in lower income households and in SPC 5 and 6 more likely to take on informal caring duties and for this to create an impediment to economic activity. The policy model described above based on support both for informal and professional care, and for a wide range of professional care options has created difficulties of access for lower income individuals and households. This is for two reasons. First, carer benefits in France are paid at a low flat rate rather than being indexed on previous earnings as in some other countries. These benefits are therefore more financially attractive to those with less earning potential. Particularly for those with an already fragile position on the labour market, any withdrawal from employment can affect future employment prospects and standards of living. Second, the complexity and comparatively higher cost to the consumer of using cash-for-care benefits to fund individualised childcare or LTC through direct employment fosters social inequalities of access whereas universal and easily accessible in-kind provision of care services, such as represented by nursery schools in France, leads to fewer social inequalities in their use.

Gender disparities in unpaid domestic and care work have at best only been attenuated and not eradicated even in the most gender-equal, de-familialising and de-gendering of countries. Women in all countries still undertake the majority of unpaid domestic and care work, whatever their degree of integration into the labour market, both in relation to their partners in different-sex couples and at an aggregate societal level. However, the degree of gender equality in this regard varies cross-nationally. In the late 1990s and early 2000s France had an unusually traditional gender division of unpaid domestic and care work in comparison with countries with similar gender employment gaps and positive attitudes towards gender equality. This situation has been termed the French paradox (Morgan, 2006). It was not until the late 2000s and 2010s that gender divisions of unpaid domestic and care work in France progressed to become more equal and in cross-national comparisons, more in keeping with the other characteristics of the country. This change has come about by both men and women decreasing the time they spend on unpaid labour, but the decrease having been more pronounced for women.

The question arises of why France developed work-family reconciliation and childcare policy earlier than some comparable states within an optionally de-familialising frame but was late to develop LTC policy and later still to introduce de-gendering elements to any of these policies. The answers lie in the historical legacies of French Republicanism and Republican Universalism, and the power of pronatalism as a frame of reference in social welfare policies. France shares with other Conservative countries an emphasis on the importance of and the responsibility of the state to support the family. This is not only because of the historical power and continued presence of the Catholic Church in the country, but also a legacy of French Republicanism which is at the root of state familialism. As first conceived in the Revolution in 1789, Republicanism attributed human rights to individuals (men) as natural rights. This had the consequence of undermining the social body of the time based on feudal orders and corporations, causing social instability. When a more conservative Republican faction, the Thermidorians, took power in 1794, they selected the family as the best mechanism to restore social cohesion. Subsequently, in 1804 the Napoleonic Civil Code established the patriarchal family as a social institution by withholding civic rights to married women. As a consequence, French Republicanism developed into a political model that promoted the equality and freedom of the individual in the public sphere and the patriarchal family as the institutional model for the private sphere. Although support for the patriarchal family was abandoned in the 1960s, support for the family per se, and more recently the family in its modern diverse forms has remained an important aspect of social welfare in France and there has been a political consensus that undermining the role of the family would be harmful to the cohesion of society. Work-family reconciliation and LTC policies have therefore been careful to preserve the role of the family and give choices to families as to how to organise themselves.

Pronatalism has also played a significant role in shaping policy towards work-family reconciliation and women's employment. The practice of limiting births within marriage began in the nineteenth century in France, much earlier than in comparable countries. This was due to the social and political instability caused by the Revolution, the abolition of primogeniture by the Napoleonic Code, Republican refusal of the teachings of the Catholic Church and the influence of Malthusianism. By the end of the century, panic about the birth rate and size of the French population had given rise to pronatalist movements among both Republicans and Catholics, putting further emphasis on the need of the state to support the interests of the family, and particularly families with three or more children. Pronatalism has been used as a justification to limit women's participation in the public sphere. At times when there was less need for women in the labour force, and particularly when more conservative political forces gained influence, the state gave financial encouragement to French women to stay in the home and take responsibility for unpaid domestic and care work in the hope that in this way they would produce more children. This was the case from the 1920s until the 1960s when family benefits, particularly for larger families and single-earner families, became increasingly generous. Furthermore, from its inception in 1986 until its first reform in 1994, parental leave benefit was only offered for the third child or subsequent children in the family. Even today, the benefit is more generous for the second or subsequent children than it is for the first child.

However, pronatalism and demographic concerns have also served to inform policies to support women's employment. This is because women have been required to fulfil two roles: as employees, to compensate the lack of male workers, and as parents to raise the next generation of French citizens. Dating back to the beginning of the twentieth century, in times and circumstances when the labour market required women as workers, the French state supported women's employment either tacitly or actively so as to avoid making them choose between parenting and employment. This happened at the beginning of the twentieth century, with the introduction of paid maternity leave in 2013. The pursuit of pronatalist family policies through the first half of the twentieth century placed the family centre stage of the burgeoning welfare state, and in 1944 the national social security system was constructed around a state familialist model that focused on horizontal distribution of resources towards families with children, rather than between rich and poor. This state familialist model gave rise to the creation of a powerful state bureaucracy around the family in which family lobby groups such as the *UNAF* and demography experts such as those working for the *INED* exerted significant influence. Such formal institutional structures are very important in France due to the strength and centralisation of the state which controls the access of stakeholders to decision-making. In the 1970s, the early introduction of childcare benefits in France were facilitated by state familialism being co-opted to support optionally de-familialising work-family reconciliation policies. As long as these policies did not challenge the central role of the family in national life, they could garner cross-party support.

Furthermore, the struggles between the Third Republic and the Catholic Church for the hearts and minds of young children and their families through the provision of social welfare and education led to the early development of collective childcare in the form of creches and nursery schools in France. Throughout the nineteenth century, the Catholic church had provided welfare services in the form of crèches and *salles d'asiles*, that would become nursery schools, part of its strategy directly to influence the attitudes of the population during periods when it was politically marginalised. During the Third Republic, the state sought to remove the Church from this position of influence by co-opting these institutions. Creches were brought under local authority control and nursery schools were integrated into the national education system, and therefore provided free of charge. Although not originally created to facilitate women's employment, these institutions would undergo institutional conversion towards the end of the twentieth century, professionalising aspects of childcare work and facilitating women's participation in employment earlier than in comparable Conservative countries.

Although the state familialism and early childhood institutions to which Republicanism gave rise facilitated women's early integration into the labour market in France, Republicanism created obstacles to France developing policies to de-gender unpaid labour in the private sphere due to its espousal of universalism. Republican Universalism promotes the individual citizen in their direct relationship to the state without intermediary affiliations. Universal equality under this model is associated with the rejection of claims to difference, viewed negatively as communitarianism. Special treatment for particular groups is seen as unequal. However, this apparent universalism serves as a cloak for traditional stereotyped assumptions, particularly concerning gender, to go unchallenged. Scholars have identified this phenomenon as gender-biased universalism where identifying gender differences in policy is ruled out based on Republican equality while established gender norms still place women in inferior positions to men (Onasch, 2020). Furthermore, the institutional structures created around the family in the construction of the welfare state excluded feminist policy actors, such as women's policy agencies and feminist groups, from influence over work-family reconciliation and childcare policies which come under their jurisdiction. Unable to influence the family bureaucracy, feminists turned away from work-family reconciliation policy and directed their attention rather to equal opportunities in the workplace, an area of policy that was more amenable to their influence. Lastly, the late development at the end of the 1990s of LTC policies directed towards the over 60s in France is also attributed to the difficulties posed by Republican Universalism in categorising the population in terms of age.

This lack of a state feminist frame for work-family reconciliation and care policy also meant that through the last decades of the twentieth century and indeed into the twenty-first century, these policies could fall prey to be shaped by other priorities with the potential to reinforce the gendering of domestic and care work. As we have seen, pronatalism had re-emerged as a frame of reference in the 1980s and influenced the construction of parental leave benefit. However, more important for work-family reconciliation and LTC policy during this period has been the impact of persistently high unemployment and the measures introduced to combat it.

Unemployment, alongside the ageing population, has meant that the welfare system in France has been financially constrained and the expansion of childcare and LTC provision has had to be brought about using cost-effective methods. This meant that cash-for-care benefits, being less costly to develop, were prioritised over in-kind service provision in both areas. The use of cash-for-care benefits has impacts on both consumers and workers. As concerns consumers of services, the impacts on low-income families and for gender equality have been discussed above. For workers, the provision of domestic and care services through the state supporting demand with cash-for-care benefits has led to the dominance of direct employment with the majority of employees in this sector working in bipartite arrangements. This bipartite employment structure has negative consequences for work conditions. However, in comparison with other countries with high rates of direct employment, rates of undeclared work are low in France. The tax and social security reductions offered to direct employers and the oversight of the use of LTC cash benefits by the authorities have lessened the use of undeclared work in these sectors.

In the 1980s under the Socialist governments of President Mitterrand, France adopted a strategy of labour-shedding to address the high incidence of unemployment through such measures as early retirement and increasing the uptake of post-16 education. It is argued that the creation of parental leave benefits in the mid-1980s was informed by this labour-shedding strategy. Furthermore, influenced by the self-management movement of the 1970s, the Socialists had adopted a strategy of work sharing as an answer to unemployment and jobless growth. Work sharing entailed reducing work time and making work hours more flexible for the benefit of existing workers, and by redistributing the work hours thus liberated, creating jobs for the unemployed. The implementation of this work-sharing strategy had a number of elements: the reduction of the working week, initially from 40 to 39 hours, then in 2002 to 35 hours; the addition of a fifth week of paid annual leave; and more controversially from a gender perspective, the encouragement of part-time work. The reduction of the work week was an aspect of this policy that had the potential to improve work-family reconciliation and increase men's contribution to unpaid labour. However, the absence of any de-gendering policies and the annualisation of these reduced hours meant that such positive impacts were limited. The encouragement of part-time work although superficially gender neutral, had negative impacts on the employment rates of women with parenting responsibilities and thereby increased their availability for unpaid labour. The right-wing governments of the late 1980s and 1990s continued with policies to encourage part-time work but with the objective of rendering the labour market more flexible for the benefit of employers rather than to bring about a *revolution du temps choisi*.

However, when informed by ALMP objectives, the power of labour-market policy to shape work-family reconciliation and care policy has also had the result of supporting feminist calls for the de-gendering of policy. This is because the ALMP approach seeks to integrate as high a percentage of those of working age as possible into the labour market by activating sectors of the population who may have previously remained marginal to the labour market. By the 2000s, the call of the feminist lobby to put more emphasis on the de-gendering of parenting responsibilities in work-family reconciliation policy began to gain ground within the bureaucratic institutions surrounding the family because it chimed with the social investment approach to welfare and the activation paradigm within labour-market policy promoted by the right-wing governments of the time. Additionally, during this same period, the gendering of care rose up the agenda of supranational bodies, for example, the EU with the Lisbon and Barcelona agreements of the early 2000s as concerns work-family reconciliation and the 2022 EU Strategy for caregivers and care recipients, the ILO with its "high-road to care" and the UN's Triple R framework to Recognise, Reduce and Redistribute care work.

A major step towards de-gendering work-family reconciliation policy and thereby parenting work has been the changes to paternity leave and parental leave policy to include measures to oblige men to contribute more to parenting. Having been introduced in 2002, paternity leave was extended in 2021, but importantly, one week of leave was made compulsory. Furthermore, in 2014, a major change was made to parental leave benefit. The *PreParE* shortened the period of leave that one parent in a couple can take obliging parents to share the leave if they want their child to be looked after at home until they start nursery school in the case of the second or subsequent children, or until they are one year old in the case of the first child. The change to this policy had two objectives, only one of which has been successful to date. The first was to reduce the amount of time women remain absent from the labour market by shortening the leave period. This was important because the take up of long parental leaves was much more prevalent among young and low-qualified women than average, leading to their medium- to long-term marginalisation or indeed exclusion from the labour market. In this respect, the policy has had some success. The second objective was to increase men's take-up of parental leave. Indeed, this policy represents the first attempt in France to curtail the choice of parents over how to look after very young children in the name of gender equality, even if the pronatalist aspect of the policy remains intact in that parents of one child have less advantageous conditions. In this regard, the policy has so far failed with only marginal increases in men's take-up of the leave having been achieved. An important reason for the lack of impact on men's behaviours lies with the fact that the benefit is still paid at a low flat rate, rather than indexed on previous salary, and therefore in most different-sex couples it remains too financially disadvantageous for the man to take the leave.

There has also been some move away from individualised bipartite employment arrangements for childcare workers, if not for LTC workers in more recent years. The French state has attempted to change the balance between provision of childcare places in creches and provision of childcare places by childminders for the under threes. The need for more creche places arose from two sources. The first was demand from parents, who viewed creches as providing more educational and developmental opportunities for their children than childminders, in keeping with the social investments approach to welfare. The second was the need to provide cheaper childcare options for low-income parents to overcome the problem of the bifurcation of the labour market between more and less well-qualified women. However, a number of plans to increase childcare places, particularly in creches in deprived areas, have failed to meet their targets, mainly because of the effects of the 2008 financial crisis. These failures to expand childcare places also help explain why the more far-reaching changes to parental leave policy including shortening the leave period to one year and indexing the benefit on previous salary that had been discussed during the 2010s were not implemented in 2014.

In LTC, it is clear from the Libault report that no change in policy away from support for direct employment for home-based professional LTC care is envisaged (Libault, 2019). However, there has been increased interest in gender issues in LTC policy in the last decade, a facet of a developing interest in the experiences of informal carers who are predominantly women. This interest is also attributable in part to the activation turn in labour-market policy, one aspect of which is to retain older people in the workforce for longer. For example, the pensionable age rose from 60 to 62 in France in 2010. Previously, given that the average age of informal carers was 59 and pensionable age 60, responsibility for informal LTC was not viewed as a labour-market issue. However, now it is increasingly seen as an obstacle to activating this age group. This increased focus on informal carers has resulted first in policies giving them a legal status and on the basis of this status, granting them social protection rights, employment rights to care leave, and wage replacement benefits. However, as has been seen in the case of parental leave, policy to support informal carers in these ways treads a fine line between recognition of the importance of their work and providing them with support, on the one hand, and the reinforcement of traditional gender divisions of care labour in society on the other.

Persistently high unemployment also led to the French state to look at ways of creating service sector jobs for the low skilled. In Liberal Market Economies, the wide wage gaps that exist between lower and higher skilled workers create a situation in which the higher skilled can purchase services, including domestic and care services, provided by the lower skilled, thereby creating employment. In Coordinated Market Economies such as France, labour-market protections reduce the wage gap making such services less affordable without state intervention. France was one of the first countries to introduce policies to subside the costs of the use of housekeeping and other home-based services by the general population and merge these subsidies with those available for individuals with childcare or LTC needs in order to create jobs in the 1990s. However, it was the 2005 Borloo Plan that cemented this strategy by creating a new sector of services to the individual, more commonly termed PHS in English, with the aim of normalising the use of these services outside the care context. However, the Borloo Plan did not succeed in this regard, and the use of non-care-related services to the individual has remained socially exclusive. Furthermore, even though the Borloo Plan was successful in increasing the use of services to the individual among these socially elite groups of the general public initially, following the recession caused by the 2008 banking crisis, their use in the under-60 population declined even though demand has remained strong in older age groups. Indeed, France has some of the highest numbers of domestic cleaners and helpers in Europe. In some high-income countries migrants constitute a significant group among PHS workers as part of global care chains. This has been less the case in France than elsewhere because the French state designated PHS as a means of providing employment for those with fewest qualifications or experience in the labour market already residing in France, in other words, within an employment logic rather than a social logic of recruiting labour to provide services to those with care needs.

The COVID pandemic has demonstrated that gender equality in unpaid domestic and care work is far from being achieved in France. During the pandemic, the gender pay gap and social norms concerning women's family responsibilities had the consequence of women working in less advantageous conditions when working from home, withdrawing from the labour market for childcare reasons more often if they could not work from home, and undertaking a greater share of the extra unpaid work and care caused by the pandemic than men. However, necessity can also bring about changes in behaviour on the part of men who did increase their participation in the unpaid parenting and related domestic work caused by school closures, even if their contribution was not equal to that of women. Furthermore, in cross-national comparisons of the impacts of anti-COVID measures, France performed well both as regards women's employment and the gender division of unpaid work. This is in keeping with long-standing trends in women's employment and more recent trends concerning gender divisions of unpaid work in the country. Well-established support for work-family reconciliation, short school closures, the generous partial activity scheme, continued access to PHS and the adaptation of out-of-home services such as meal delivery to the constraints of the sanitary measures meant that French households retained more ability to outsource domestic and care work for longer periods than in other countries.

It is not yet clear what, if any, long-term effects the pandemic has had on the organisation and divisions of labour of domestic and care work. The pandemic served to highlight at a societal and individual level the importance of both informal exchanges of support and the contribution of workers providing PHS to the functioning of households and to societal wellbeing. However, it is not certain that a long-term re-evaluation of the importance of this work has taken place. The area in which the pandemic may have had the most significant impact is in hastening the development of working from home. Given that other measures to give workers more flexibility in their employment, such as part-time work, resulted in the entrenchment of stereotypical gendered work-family arrangements, increased working from home may similarly pose dangers for the further development of gender equality in domestic and care work in France and internationally.

References

Himmelweit, S., & Sigala, M. (2004). Choice and the relationship between identities and behaviour for mothers with pre-school children. *Journal of Social Policy, 33*, 455–478. https://doi.org/10.1017/S0047279404007779

Libault, D. (2019). *Grand âge, le temps d'agir, Concertation Grand âge et Autonomie*. Ministère des solidarités et de la santé. Retrieved September 14, 2022, from https://solidarites-sante.gouv.fr/IMG/pdf/rapport_grand_age_autonomie.pdf on September 14 2022

Morgan, K. (2006). *Working mothers and the welfare state: Religion and the politics of work: Family policies in Western Europe and the United States*. Stanford University Press.

Onasch, E. (2020). Framing and claiming "gender equality": A multi-level analysis of the French civic integration program. *Gender and Society, 34*(3), 496–518. https://doi.org/10.1177/0891243220916453

Index[1]

[1] Note: Page numbers followed by 'n' refer to notes.

J. Windebank, *Domestic and Care Work in Modern France*, French Politics, Society and Culture,
https://doi.org/10.1007/978-3-031-33564-8

Kolibri 360 GmbH
Ferdinand-Jühlke-Straße 7
99095 Erfurt, Deutschland
produktsicherheit@kolibri360.de